THE TREE IN THE MIDDLE OF MY GARDEN

THE TREE IN THE MIDDLE OF MY GARDEN

Georgia,
Blessings as
you wait
on
Jesus,

02-29-08

Gal. 2:20

MOSES CAESAR

Content-Meant Publishers and others are praying for God's opportunity to impact your life through this book. We would love to hear from you. Please send comments and stories to the address below or email to: mystory@mosesbook.com

Published by

Content-Meant
Publishers
McKinney, TX 75070 USA

The Tree in the Middle of My Garden
©2004 by Dr. Moses Caesar
All rights reserved
Printed in the United States of America

ISBN # 0-9762485-0-6

Subject Heading: CHRISTIAN LIVING/SPIRITUAL GROWTH

Mail all inquiries to: mosesbook 175 E. Graycrest Ave., Collierville, TN 38017
This title is available as an Audiobook. Please visit www.mosesbook.com

Library of Congress Cataloging-in-Publication Data has been ordered and is available upon request.

DEDICATION

This book is dedicated to my Lighthouse Friends:

Sabina Brady

Scott Burks

Randall & Arinée Glass

Patrick and Christy Lafferty

Carol Mc Doniel

Lt. Steve Moses

Charlie Reavis

Robert Walker

I call them "Lighthouse Friends" because they are a very special group of people who selflessly provided care for me during a difficult season. Like a lighthouse, they served two purposes. Imagine a lighthouse within a sailor's sight. In one way, a lighthouse brings an end to the anticipation of land. Every sailor finds joy with this realization. In another way, the placement of the lighthouse indicates the presence of treacherous waters capable of destroying the ship. Here, sailors are compelled to exercise caution and thoughtfully navigate along a safe passage to the shore. My "Lighthouse Friends" blessed me in both of these ways. Their care and support enabled me to affirm God's sovereignty and yield to His guidance. I love every memory of their service for my benefit. I praise God for them. I thank God for using them in my life to bring about His good purposes.

I also dedicate this book to:

my parents,

Beulah Margret Jerrie and P.B. Caesar

Thank you for unconditional love.
Thank you for your sincerity.
Thank you for teaching me to reverently fear God.

my siblings and their spouses,

Joshua and Dr. Renuka Caesar
Hans and Dr. Rajani Ruth de Jong

Thank you for the strong bond of family love.
Thank you for the level of care that is uniquely
captured within this bond.
Thank you for believing in me.

ACKNOWLEDGEMENTS

Dr. James Bryant, thank you for seeing and affirming God's creativity in my life. **Dr. Thomas Jones**, thank you for modeling Godly professionalism. **Donna Schnyder** and **Martha Jones**, thank you for being my readers and my fans. Thank you for blessing me in this process.

Dr. Sam Shaw (Sr. Pastor, Germantown Baptist Church), **Doug Metzger** (former Pastor, Magnolia Avenue Baptist Church), **Dr. Ron Ellis** (President, California Baptist University), and **Dr. Mark Foley** (President, University of Mobile), thank you for allowing me an opportunity to participate in God's mission under your leadership. You have all afforded me the great privilege of working with you to secure glory for God. Dr. Foley, I say a special thanks.

GBC Staff, I am honored to serve by your side. **GBC College/Singles staff and volunteers**, thank you for tangibly blessing the body of Christ with your wonderful service and thoughtful time. **College students and Singles at Germantown Baptist Church**, thank you. You are a very, very, very, very special group of people to me. You cannot know how much you have blessed me. Each person and each class has a special place in my heart. **The Bottom Line Business Lunch & Metro Bible Study**, thank you for affirming God's communication of truth through my teaching.

Timothy, Preston, Mark, Fabiola, Gary, Vic, Peter, and other members of my coffee shop family, thank you for checking my progress and cheering each step.

Moises (MIO) and Lori-Lynn Navarro, thank you for blowing me away with your kind generosity. Your heart for God is not only known in your music but also in your actions. **Geron Craig**, thank you for responding to my tech needs as if we were brothers. **Michelle Hicks**, thank you for proofing this project. Thank you for your skillful appreciation of God's voice in this book. **Bettye Jenkins**, **Mark Parry**, and **Timothy Kukkala**, thank you for your part, encouragement, and support. **Bill Arnold**, thank you for doing the final reading. You are a great man of God with a sincere and humble spirit. Thanks for being available.

Finally, I love my memory of **Frances Poynor** (decd. July 31, 2004). She asked to hear finished chapters from this book during her extensive hospital stays. I will never forget her voice praising God as I concluded each reading. Wow! "Yes, Frances, God is good. He is very, very good. Thank you for always reminding me how faithful He is."

CONTENTS

FOREWORD

Moses Caesar is one of the most creative persons I have ever known. Both intellect and heart converge in him personally, and both are reflected in this book. In one sense, this book begins as an allegory. Yet, it has a ring of historical reality. There are angels, righteous and fallen, fresh from the time of Lucifer's rebellion. They are "watchers" of the human drama played out in the Garden of Eden. But that is not the only garden they watch. They watch the human drama in the middle of Charlie's garden, which seems to be everyone's garden. While all of us are affected by the Fall of Adam and Eve, somehow each of us seems to reenact that fall in our own garden. This writing approach acts like a hook to catch us up personally in the story from the beginning to the last word.

The Tree in the Middle of My Garden brings us face to face with the cosmic battle between good and evil. That battle is as old as Lucifer's fall from heaven and as new as today. Moses Caesar seems to be able to weave a story between freedom and inevitability that is seldom seen today. Most writers come down on one side or the other, the freewill of man or the sovereignty of God. The author has captured twin biblical truths and applies both to angels and humanity. Yet he never loses sight of a sovereign, loving, merciful, yet just and holy God. There is no doubt about Who won, Who is winning, and Who will win in the end.

Be prepared to read the first section of this book in one sitting, even if it takes you well after your usual bedtime. The first section is just the beginning. The rest of the book is a journey that equips you to be successful in your own garden. It is that kind of book.

Dr. James W. Bryant, Senior Professor of Pastoral Theology
The Criswell College, Dallas, Texas

THE TREE

CHRIS PLENIO TOOK THIS TREE PICTURE *in Namibia, Africa
in 1997. He fondly recalls the events surrounding his opportunity
to capture this image. Etosha National Park requires all safari goers
to return before sunset to various camp compounds located within the
park for their own safety. Chris found this tree just before his return.
After taking its picture, he remembers the rain falling so hard that
visibility became impossible. He and the members of his party
breathed a great sigh of relief after entering to their compound.
He tells the story with color and drama. His story is compelling.
His picture is also compelling. I am captivated. Over time, my
affection for this tree has grown because it seems to symbolize
life for me in the material world. Look at the picture.*

*Do you notice the tree stands alone? The tree provides the perfect
picture of life. No matter how many people surround you in the
material world, ultimately you stand alone before your Creator.*

Do you notice there is no garden? I define a garden as any type of aesthetic cultivation. So, a rock garden and a rose garden are similar to me. Both are a product of control being exercised over a piece of land. With no real control over life, how possible or sustainable is a garden in life?

Do you notice the storm clouds? No matter how grand life looks, something is always brewing. The storm clouds in this picture symbolize how life looks in the valley. A dash of light pressing through the clouds conveys that hope is always present.

Finally, do you notice the branch stretching from the tree? It calls out to you. But, do not respond to its invitation. The tree cannot hold you with one arm. It cannot hold you like God longs to hold you during each season of life.

SECTION 1
Introduction to Life

In the beginning, God created the heavens and the earth.

God gives life … in the context of a fallen world. In this setting, your body or your human interactions cannot be immune to pain. Pain is a reality. Nevertheless, life should not be lived with apprehension or fear. As God allows pain, He also supplies a rich measure of His provision. He is faithful to meet you at the point of your need. Knowing God holds you during your difficulties is a critical step; you have moved on to the dance floor. Understanding God's agenda is like hearing the music of the orchestra. Yielding to God's lead is like being swept from your feet into the motion of the dance.

As you read from this first section, you are preparing for the dance. It may be tough to think about dancing when life is not going so well. But, God makes dancing possible. He allows you the privilege of experiencing your pain in the rich framework of His supply. He wants you to recognize all that He brings to bear on your behalf.

Section One is a story. It is the whole story of life. It is also one story within that whole. Notice God. Notice life. Notice the wisdom that makes sense of God's intent with life. Place yourself within this matrix to discover that your life is completely within the scope of God's sovereign watch. He is in control. His provisions are found within a dependent relationship. Recognize Him as your great I AM.

FROM ABOVE AND BELOW

From now until forever, forever is forever. The end of forever will never be known. Now imagine moving in the other direction; a forever without a beginning. This forever is mind-boggling. It's more inconceivable than imagining a forever without an end. The forever without a beginning is exclusively God's. He alone knows this forever that has already passed. He has always been. He is and will always be. He is forever and forever. Although He cannot be fully known, what is known about God brings reverent awe.

In the beginning, God speaks and all things come to be. He made all that can be seen and all that cannot be seen. Look at the endless heavens. They hint of God's omnipresence. Their breadth is a wonder to behold. The countless stars clearly resonate His omnipotence. They discharge light and heat to transform a black and cold universe. His omniscience is marvelously expressed on earth. The largest to the smallest living forms have life because of His wisdom. Every part of His creation echoes His glory. He is great, and He is good. He is over all, in all, and through all. He is Three, and He is One. He is the God of creation.

With His voice, He brings light to the darkness, shape to the formless, and substance to the void. The light breaks the darkness to form the day and retires to return the night. God sees His creation and calls it good. He separates the waters of the earth; one above and one below. The resulting expanse is established as the sky. God sees His creation and calls it good. He separates the waters once more to make dry land. On this land, He brings life in the form of plants that cover the surface of the earth. The waters of the earth are gathered into seas. God sees His creation and calls it good.

In the expanse of the sky, God forms two lights to reign. One reigns over the night. The other reigns over the day. Together they mark the seasons and bring predictability to the measurement of time. Innumerable stars are placed in the sky to provide company for these two celestial rulers. God sees His creation and calls it good. He fills the waters with every kind of living creature. They are complex, and they are simple. They are incredible and beautiful. They move across the breadth and depths of the waters. God also fills the sky with every kind of flying creature. From the majestic to the negligible, they move across the sky's breadth and heights. God sees His creation and calls it good.

God fills the vegetation-infested land with living creatures. They are diverse in shapes and forms. Their variety and numbers are a mystery for the ages. They are expressions of life that crawl across the ground. God sees His creation and calls it good. To rule over the fish of the sea, the birds of the air, and the creatures of the ground, God forms man. He makes man and woman in His image and likeness. They reflect His glory. They are not like anything God has previously created. They are exclusive because they receive breath from God's own mouth. They are created to know the forever that has no end. They are created with fellowship in mind. God sees His creation and calls them very good. He loves them very much.

AN ANGEL'S EYE

From above, I have watched the wonder of this creation. I have joined all the angels to marvel at the wisdom that spoke all things into existence. The billions upon billions of stars that stretch billions upon billions of light years across space compel me to be in awe. God is indeed worthy of His glory. As I travel through this wonder, I cannot contain my anticipation. I will soon behold with my own eyes the creatures that walk with God. They are His precious love. When God is with them, time seems suspended. Their exchange is a dialogue that leaves a heart full of joy and laughter. The creatures that walk with God find satisfaction in the Creator. The Creator finds an object in these creatures to receive His perfect love.

The angels do not have this type of exchange. We are created with tasks in mind. God calls angels to accomplish what He wills for His Glory. Angels are not conscripted to provide this service. We only respond to God's magnanimity. He is Great, and so, we find honor in the call to execute His desire. But, some have not maintained this exchange. They have savored the power and position granted by God to facilitate their service. Now, they love what they have more then the God who gave these things. They see a potential in themselves. They have embraced an idea that they can be like God. They have shared this poison with other angels. They have started a rebellion.

The rebellion of the angels is underway. Many unimaginable things have transpired with the acceleration of hostilities. I am surprised at the number of angels who have bought Lucifer's deceit. He speaks madness, but his persuasion is masterful. If he aims to be a god, he can say his training came from being a prince; a prince of lies and deception. Those who have joined Lucifer are completely convinced victory is within reach. So, they press forward. They are fools, but some are also my friends.

As I arrive in the Garden of Eden, I have mixed emotions. I look around in complete amazement. The creation of God truly reflects His glory and wonder. All that has been said about this perfect place is right. It is the focal center of God's great ambition. But, rumor has it that Lucifer's campaign will soon move across this domain. The thought makes me ill. As Lucifer attempts to increase his dominion, he believes humanity is important to his cause. He covets them as a prize. He plots and schemes to attain what he longs to destroy.

A clearing catches my eye. Finally, the middle of the garden is just ahead. As I approach, a familiar voice breaks the beautiful melody of the birds. The voice calls again, "Francis, Francis, over here." A sharp turn to my right reveals an unbelievable sight. My old friend Edgington calls from a branch overlooking the middle of the garden.

"Edgington, what are you doing here."

"Quiet," he responds. "Come ... sit with me." The invitation is awkward. Sure, Edgington is my friend, but he has joined the rebellion. I am not sure how to respond. But, I did not deliberate. My steps to Edgington carry a torn heart.

"What are you doing here?" I insist as I pull myself onto the branch?

"It's good to see you, Francis. How have you been?" His embrace rekindles the warmth of our fantastic friendship. A flash of memory recalls Edgington's service before God. He honored God. He did everything other angels do. He served God with excellence. At that time, there was no hint of his present course. But then again, who could have predicted any part of this rebellion?

With a deep breath, I sigh, "How have you been, Edgington?" Could he see my sincerity? Was my broken heart evident? Did he sense my absolute disgust with those who follow Lucifer?

"I've been just fine," he responds. That's it? Is that all he is going to say? Well, what did I expect him to say? Should I believe him?

"What are you doing here, Edgington?"

"Francis, from below I have wanted to see the garden for myself. Everyone talks like this is the most amazing place in all creation. Everyone says the garden will be an important battlefield. Well, I wanted to see why. I want to see God's odd love for Adam and Eve."

"You shouldn't be here, Edgington."

"Yeah, well neither should you, Francis. If I know you like I think I know you, you're here for the same reason I am. One day your curiosity may get the best of you, Francis."

"Yeah, like it got to you, Edgington."

"I am doing what I think is important. I am weary of God's monopoly on being a deity. I totally believe that anyone can be like God. Maybe if you're fortunate, you yourself will see Lucifer ascend the throne of the Most High."

"Stop, that's blasphemy! Listen to what you are saying. Your ideas are insane, and I cannot listen to your wickedness. I cannot believe you were once my friend. I cannot be here with you."

"Nonsense. What you cannot do is accept the inevitable future."

"Edgington, did you forget who holds the future? Are you now blind, deaf, and stupid? What chance do you think Lucifer has against our Creator?"

"God cannot hold on to His domain forever. We fight to liberate everyone from God's lies."

"What lies?"

"The lie that He is the only one who is and will ever be. This is the true blasphemy."

"STOP! Your wickedness is too much. I cannot be here anymore. I am sorry my old friend."

"No, no, I am sorry, Francis. You are my friend. No more. I will say no more about this matter. Please, stay. Seriously, why don't we share this great spot? We will both walk away with the experience we came looking for."

I did stay. But, why did I? As we sat next to each other, neither said a word. I was very uncomfortable. Edgington and I had so many experiences together. But now, where was the meaning of our relationship? My mind produced a hundred thoughts on behalf of my heart. But, this did not matter because the mouth failed to execute a single prompt. All I could accomplish was a forward stare into the middle of the garden. Even then, my eyes did not register what was happening within the space of my sight.

The middle of the garden is an incredible place. Although God created an endless universe with many marvels, He reserved this spot for two very unique expressions. In the middle of the garden, God placed two trees. They were not numbered with the countless trees created to provide food for Adam and Eve. These trees had another mission. One tree is called the Tree of Life. Its fruit would provide the means to render Adam and Eve immortal. They could eat from it and know the forever without an end. The other tree is called the Tree of the Knowledge of Good and Evil. Its fruit is forbidden. This is the one and only prohibition God placed on Adam and Eve. Nothing else in all creation is withheld from them.

EDEN'S BATTLE

The movement of living creatures within the garden could not draw or hold my attention. My mind drifted from the past to the future with no concern for the present. Why did the rebellion have to start? I speculated how the rebellion would end. I wondered what would become of my friend Edgington. So many variables and scenarios rushed through my mind. Could I fight against my friend if the need emerged? I did not know. As I pondered, I failed to notice what Edgington found curious.

"What do you see, Edgington?"

"A serpent is moving into the branches of the Tree of the Knowledge of Good and Evil."

"Really?" Initially, I saw nothing peculiar. Creatures of many forms may have visited these two trees with great regularity. Certainly they were free to do so since the single prohibition pronounced in all creation applied only to Adam and Eve. "Why so much interest in a serpent?"

"Francis, the serpent is considered the most crafty of all the creatures God made to crawl across the ground. We take pleasure in their aptitude. Maybe we find a kindred spirit in them. Certainly, I am impressed that this one moves with great indifference across the branches of this most significant tree in all creation."

"Nonsense!" Did I just say that? Why do I get so agitated? Did Edgington hear me? If he did, I did not break his focus.

Before I could explore his fascination with the serpent, Edgington slapped my shoulder. "Francis, look, over there. It is Eve. Wow! She is everything that has been said about her. How amazing that she was created from Adam's rib. And, look ... there. This is definitely a great day for us. Adam is following her into the garden. His walk is magnificent. God truly gave him a great position in the garden. What an amazing moment! I have waited forever to see these two with my own eyes. The creatures that possess the likeness and image of God are indeed a great prize."

"They are amazing, Edgington. But, do not call them a prize. They are the creatures that walk with God. He has a special relationship with them, and they are not His trophies."

"Okay, already. Lighten up, Francis."

Silence followed. Did Edgington have more words to follow his rebuke? He said nothing. He just stared at the walking creatures as if enchanted by their presence. I, too, was enchanted. Together, we watched as Adam and Eve went about their day. Life for them seemed a simple celebration; one of enjoying all earthly creatures and the other of savoring the company of their Creator. This is the harmony God had intended. This is the perfection of life God spoke into existence.

My heart was experiencing great joy and amazement. This was truly a remarkable moment. I looked at Edgington with a smile hoping this moment would move him as it moved me. But, he was not smiling. On the contrary, his face cringed in a scowl. Foam was dropping from his chin, and a low growl began to carry across our space. "Edgington!" Was this my same friend? He seemed so different. "Edgington!"

"Quiet, you fool. Look at the tree in middle of the garden. The serpent is speaking to Eve." Edgington was captivated by the serpent's opportunity with Eve. Why? I did not know. But, really at that moment, I did not care. I was in shock with Edgington. He was not the same anymore. I looked back at the middle of the garden to see Adam move close to Eve, but he did not interrupt.

To me a speaking serpent is no surprise, but why was Edgington so captivated? I could not imagine what he was sensing. Then, to my amazement, I saw Eve reach into the tree to pluck a forbidden fruit from its branches. Edgington began to growl and spastically bounce. What was happening to my friend? My head turned to record a brief glimpse of his commotion. But, I could not be concerned with him now. Very quickly, I turned back to Eve. I could see her holding the fruit with an open hand. What was she thinking? Did she realize how close she stood to catastrophe? As she held the fruit, I could see her resolve slowly crumble. She moved the fruit to her beautiful lips. Her mouth opened and drew a deep breath. Then, she ate.

Edgington immediately exploded into cheer and maddening screams. He dropped from the branch and began to run. I screamed his name attempting to penetrate his euphoria. "Edgington! Edgington!" My effort was to no avail. Edgington did not turn. The brief effort ended as he disappeared among the countless trees in the garden. I turned back to the tree in the middle. Now, I could see Adam holding the fruit. Was he preparing to discard the fruit and confront the infraction? He looked at Eve with his beautiful eyes. Slowly, those eyes dropped to the fruit. He took a deep swallow. Then, his resolve followed Eve's. Soon, the fruit landed on the ground with two bites torn from its body.

I buried my face in my hands and began to weep. Anguish overtook me. Shock paralyzed me. What had I just witnessed? Was I dreaming? Could the events of this day be a mere fabrication of my mind? I waited for someone to awaken me, but eternity had already recorded this tragedy in its pages. The passing of time only marked the production of more tears. Shock was moving into grief. I opened my eyes and dropped my hands. Peering through my tear-filled view, I looked into the middle of the garden. I did not see Adam or Eve. But, in the Tree of the Knowledge of Good and Evil, a stately serpent was moving slowly to the ground. The serpent had no expressions. It moved as it always moved. The present picture in the middle of the garden did not reflect the true aftermath of a fierce battle I had just observed. Only the single fruit lying below the Tree of the Knowledge of Good and Evil bore witness to the carnage in Eden's Battle.

The grief that began in the garden persisted along my entire journey home. Word about Adam's sin spread quickly. Before I could reach God's throne room, the angels had assembled to hear the Creator's response. I joined the masses of battle hungry angels. We waited with baited breath. When would God call for a retaliatory strike? Not a single angel wished to settle for anything less than total victory. Thoughts of annihilating every agent in Lucifer's army seemed almost as sweet as destroying Lucifer himself. But the Creator's plan derailed our craving for an immediate strike.

God was not standing at the apex of the angels' frenzy. He was instead walking in the garden. A cool breeze and the melodic sound of birds set an ominous tone for the task at hand. God's voice that brought all things into existence now called out across the garden, "Where are you?" But it produced no results. The silence was deafening. To whom did God call? Neither Adam nor Eve emerged. The trees, created by God to provide food for the creatures that walk with God, were now hiding them as they attempted to escape such a walk.

Finally, Adam called out. Covered with leaves from the trees of the garden, he and Eve approached their Creator. Adam said he was afraid because he was naked. The evidence of his infraction was clear. The next few moments demonstrated that God did not have annihilation in mind. He pronounced consequences to those who participated in Eden's Battle. God started by cursing the serpent. It would lose all legs and slither along the ground. From its belly, it would eat the dust of the ground and live in enmity with humanity. Eve would have pain giving birth to children. She would long for her husband, and he would rule over her. With Adam, God cursed the ground subjugating him to hardship in the quest for food. Adam's brow would measure the pain of his labor.

The reality of these pronouncements was immediate and final. The consequences endure to the end of the ages. They serve to remind humanity that only one infraction in the Garden of Eden displaced a Holy relationship. Every man and woman who will walk the earth will walk in the shadow of this pain and hardship. Nothing will be done to remove its sting. Humanity must never forget Eden's Battle at the tree in the middle of the garden.

A NEW REALITY

The consequences are just the beginning of God's battle plan. He moves quickly to facilitate life for Adam and Eve in light of their new reality. He gives them garments of skin to escape the shame of their nakedness. Seeing the potential liabilities from their knowledge of Good and Evil, God removes them from the Garden of Eden. He banishes them for their own protection. He knows living in the garden would allow Adam and Eve an opportunity to eat from the Tree of Life. God cannot let Adam and Eve know the forever without an end in their fallen state. So, they are marched to the garden's edge. God places angels to guard the path to the Tree of Life. A sword of fire endlessly flashes back and forth sealing the way to the middle of the garden.

Now, the tears belong to Adam and Eve. As they make one step into their newly devastated world, wailing joins crying. "Creator … Father." The names of God are shouted amid the cries of pain to bring some mooring against the avalanche of emotions. But, God does not stand with them. The anguish of Adam and Eve's heart is immeasurable. Shock chokes breath from their lungs. God will not ease the trauma of their consequences. God cannot amend His battle plan to accommodate their weeping.

The angels of God have watched this exchange. We know God is completely wise. His steps are perfect. As He spoke to Adam and Eve, His Love stayed His Holy wrath against their infraction. His battle plan clearly places importance in their restoration. God is not sidestepping the battle. He is not stalling. From my perspective, the offensive is underway. God has begun the end of Lucifer and sin. The creatures that walk with God will now only be known as the creatures that walk. But, someday, they will walk with God once more.

When will that day come? The angels have waited for that day with great anticipation. They have confidence in its arrival. Without a single episode of doubt, they faithfully execute every point of God's commission. They know victory can be had with a single command from His throne. Victory is inevitable. The outcome is not in question. But, Lucifer does not accept this reality. He clings to his own deception. With crafty desperation, he drives his campaign along a new battlefront. He hopes to rob God of Adam and Eve. He believes accomplishing this objective will place him on a path to his own victory.

The world outside of the garden is indeed the new battlefield. It is the platform on which Lucifer wages a decisive campaign of deception. He deploys his agents to sever Adam and Eve's dependent relationship with their Creator. Where Adam and Eve consider their labor a toil and pain, Lucifer builds a case against God in their hearts. He whispers into their ears, "If God loves you, why would He allow you to suffer like this? Remember how wonderful life had been in the garden? You are being robbed! You are missing what rightfully belongs to you."

Lucifer's deceit is effective. Adam and Eve fondly remember the garden's provisions and peace. They remember not having to labor. They remember the pleasure of walking in the garden in the cool of the day. They feel they have lost everything. They feel displaced. Lucifer masterfully persuades them to hope for the recovery of these losses. So, Adam and Eve begin to long for what they once had in the garden. This longing quickly outweighs the longing they once knew for God. Lucifer knows humanity's sin places them in opposition to God. He works to make the new enemy of his old enemy a new ally.

Over the course of time, Lucifer claims one life after another with his deceit. As this war rages through the pages of time, every passing day records Lucifer's advances. His forces have had sweeping victories. Lucifer targets humanity's trust in God. His agents crouch at the door sniffing out every opportunity to snare humanity in their web of deception. They devour what they capture. Even with God's warnings, humanity does not listen. They do not escape Lucifer's plot. Humanity quickly drifts from their intimate relationship with God. Their hearts rapidly slip into evil. They forget what they had with God, but God does not forget. He moves forward with His battle plan to restore what He has lost.

My commander has assigned me to walk again in this world that God spoke into existence. The earth, sky, and sea are again familiar to me. They continue to resonate the sound of God's voice declaring creation as being good. The memory of God's ecstatic joy over humanity still rings in my heart. I remember His words saying, "Very good." How passionate were those words? But, humanity is not at all good. They hardly resemble what I saw in the garden before Adam's sin. Now, they only long for evil. They are consumed by its passion and driven by evil intent in their hearts.

As humanity's heart bathes in sin, God's heart fills with pain. He is sorry that He made them. He told the angels He would destroy all the living creatures of the earth. Many of us considered God's wish a foregone conclusion. But, one man found favor in God's eyes. He alone stood to capture God's heart and divert God's intent. He is the man known as Noah. His trust in God was not compromised by Lucifer's schemes. Noah remarkably manages to walk with God outside of the garden.

I have been assigned to guard Noah. What a fascinating opportunity to watch righteousness at work in the world of unrighteousness. Noah faithfully labored a hundred years to build a boat that would ferry humanity into the next phase of God's battle plan. The wisdom of God employed a great flood to surgically diminish Lucifer's deceptive hold upon humanity. This event inspired me to dream. Now, I can only imagine how God will achieve His final and complete victory over sin.

How would God restore humanity and bring an end to Lucifer's rebellion? With the passing of time, this mystery only intensified. As humanity multiplied and spread across the surface of the earth, Lucifer's campaign moved with equal advancement. God did not mobilize the angels to halt Lucifer's progress. Additionally, the sinful nature of humanity served as a magnet to attract Lucifer's legions. Because of this nature, humanity was easily swept away by his forces. Every individual, from emperors to slaves, fell victim. They become Lucifer's pawns to dispense his poison to every generation in every land.

Removing all restraints, sacred and essential elements of human life were hijacked to support Lucifer's cause. He transformed God's blessings of life, worship, love, relationship, sex, community, emotion, truth, and consumption. They had been created by God to enrich humanity. Now, they were elements used to curse God. These expressions of abomination and desecration twisted God's intent for His precious creatures. As a result, the rebellion tore deep into the heart of humanity.

The rise and fall of civilizations and empires provided many platforms for Lucifer. He did not miss a single opportunity to further his agenda. In contrast, God selected the smallest stage to promote His. One generation after another, God moved closer to the day of His victory by supporting a single strand within the fabric of humanity. He chose a people who would carry His mantle and make the way for His assault. Only God's sovereign watch could monitor the consistent advance of His ultimate plan. But, Lucifer and his angels were too intoxicated with their own victories to note God's strategy. Their momentum created a sense of invincibility.

ONE IN BATTLE

The angels of God have known that victory is near despite Lucifer's momentum. The earth may be overrun by evil, but evil cannot overrun God. The millenniums have not dissuaded my resolve. And today, that resolve will finally be substantiated. God's ultimate assault is being readied. Orders are calling angels to assemble in a garden called Gethsemane. Lucifer will soon see the wisdom and power of God. His unbridled arrogance will know a humiliating defeat.

Within the garden, the angels are in formation. Their numbers are unprecedented with each sensing the importance of this moment. Jesus, who knew no beginning, walks into the garden with three disciples. He does not acknowledge the battle ready throngs that stand to attention upon His arrival. How could He miss the clap of thunder produced by our synchronized step? Jesus' focus inward fails to record this fanatical affirmation of His command. He instructs the disciples to wait, watch, and pray. Then, Jesus walks further into the middle of the garden. The angels see the Father walking beside His Son. For one brief moment, I felt I was peering into the Garden of Eden to see God walking with Adam.

Jesus fell to His knees. He cried, "Father, Father, let this cup pass from me." The angels recorded this cry and responded with a feverish shout. They were ready to march against Lucifer and eager to start that march immediately. But, Jesus did not seem ready for that battle. He expressed agony but not confusion. He knew God's battle plan and understood God's agenda. He knew He was the final point of the single strand God wove through human history. He knew His purpose, but He struggled with yielding His will. Blood dripping like sweat measured the intense pressure of His private debate. Finally, the most powerful words ever spoken in a garden came from His mouth, "Not My will, but Your will be done." If only Adam and Eve had pronounced these same words in their garden.

The events after this moment passed in a surreal mode. Jesus was led away to experience the fury of human hands. His physical body was pulverized and shredded. Those who mocked and jeered His claims crushed His heart. Finally, He was hung on a cross. The angels longed to free their Creator from all of these human devices of pain. But, Jesus did not call out. He understood God's battle plan. His spirit did not waver. On the cross, He awaited God's wrath. He knew He would bear the wages of sin for humanity. He would be the sacrifice to set them free. The full fury of God's judgment against sin would fall on Him. The angels quickly realized that Jesus would not lead us to victory. He would be the victory.

His final words on the cross marked the end of humanity's hopelessness. God's plan exceeded all my imagination. The war is indeed finished. But, the angels are ambivalent in this moment. Certainly, God's single assault captured total victory. But, this victory comes at a great price. Jesus, who knew the forever without a beginning, cannot know the forever without an end. The angels were bewildered by Jesus' death. Although He said it is finished, Jesus was not. On the third day, a shout swept across God's dominion, "Jesus is alive." I joined the jubilation and cried joy-filled tears. Jesus' resurrection from the dead validated His claim to know the forever without an end. He single-handedly satisfied the expectations for humanity's restoration and now lives to claim its glory.

ONE LIFE WON

Although the victory is immediate, the conflict is not over. Lucifer and his defeated legions have not yet been contained. The wisdom of God employs a plan that allows them limited freedom. This same plan aims to bring an opportunity to the creatures that walk on the earth to walk with God once more. Jesus' sacrifice makes this opportunity possible. When a single human responds, God immediately restores His intimate relationship by granting a pardon.

God's Spirit abides with those who receive this pardon. The Holy Spirit of God facilitates humanity's privilege to walk with God outside of the garden. Lucifer is not pleased. His desperation is evident. He prowls and paces like a roaring lion seeking anyone to devour. He and his legions are determined to fight God to the end. So, they plot and scheme to sabotage God's advancements that have quickly spread beyond the historic single strand. He incites battles along the paths of the righteous where the creatures walk with their Creator.

Today, I walk along one such path. "Happy Birthday, Charlie!" The crowd has surprised Charlie on his 41st birthday. He smiles through a sincere laugh. He did not expect this. Last year, a large number of family and friends threw a very memorable party to celebrate his 40th. He reaches out to hug his wife placing a soft kiss on her lips. Two children move across the room.

"Happy Birthday, Daddy."

"Thank you, angel."

"Happy Birthday, Dad."

"Thank you, P.J." He gives each a big bear hug. As they step back, a small line of well-wishers forms to convey a special warmth. Charlie shakes each hand and returns each hug, but he does not completely engage the moment.

Longing for solitude, he moves through the expectations of the party. When the last guest leaves, he withdraws to his bedroom and flops on his bed. His wife is too consumed retiring the children to notice his absence. Charlie stares at the ceiling as tears begin to flow down his cheeks. Earlier that day, he received the worst possible news. His initial doctor's visit discovered a problem with his heart. He has not said anything to anyone. Today's appointment confirmed his worst nightmare. He has been given less than six months to live.

He cries out to God hoping to make some sense of his life. He thinks he is too young to die. He reflects on a robust tennis match played just yesterday with good friends. He raises his arms toward the ceiling as proof of his health. Surveying their form and strength, he stretches them to God and screams with his inner voice, "Father, please don't let me die." He presses one hand against his mouth to muffle his crying. The other hand slowly wipes tears from his eyes. Thinking about his wife, children, and friends produces more tears and more muffled cries.

"Francis!" I am startled to hear my name in Charlie's room. Looking around, I do not see anyone. "Francis, Francis ... it's me, Edgington." Edgington? Could it really be my old friend? I have not seen him since

Eden's battle. How many millenniums have passed since that day?

"Edgington, show yourself." Silence followed. I raised my voice. "Show yourself."

"Francis, I cannot show myself to you." Was this Edgington? The voice did not sound familiar. I remember a pleasant and distinct voice. This could not be Edgington.

"Edgington, how long has it been, old friend, since we last talked?"

"Francis, don't you remember? We watched Adam and Eve by the tree in the middle of the garden."

Wow! This was Edgington, but what happened to his voice? I changed the tone of my voice to support my sincere invitation, "Edgington, please … show yourself."

From the shadows of the dimly lit room, a form moved into the light. The form was grotesque, bulging here and there with many sores oozing a sappy slime. Could this be Edgington? "Francis, I knew you would not like what you see. I am disgusting to your eyes. Please, my friend, look away to spare me the full measure of this humiliation."

"Edgington, what has happened to you?"

"Since the last day I saw you, I have watched change overtake my form. All the legions under Lucifer's command have seen a similar change. Strangely, Lucifer himself does not change. He is as radiant as always. But, we are not so fortunate. When Lucifer wins, he promises to give his legions a glorious new form."

"Edgington, I cannot believe any angel led by Lucifer still thinks victory is within their grasp. You, my friend, have lost. The war is over, and you know it."

Edgington's body inflated and quickly moved slightly forward. He locked his eyes with mine as he raised his broken voice to say, "Francis, we are not done fighting."

I mirrored his posture and quickly shouted, "Well, Edgington, we are not done conquering."

Edgington's form shrank and eased back into the shadow. I felt justified but also sad. One day I will see my friend no more. The mangling of his form is just the beginning of his future. God will move against Lucifer and his angels casting them into a fiery pit. This pit will serve as their eternal home. The thought makes me very sad. But, I can easily accept God's actions. After all, He unloaded the full measure of His wrath upon His own Son on the cross. The cross and the pit are equal expressions of God's wisdom.

Charlie rolls over and slaps the pillow with his arm. The abrupt sound catches my attention. He begins to pray. "God!" The sound of his voice calling out to God is unsettling. "God, why is this happening to me? Why? Why have you forgotten me?" The praying does not interrupt the crying. "Father, where are you? Why don't you answer me?" I remember these words. God spoke them in the garden as He searched for Adam and Eve. Charlie continued, "How long must I pray before you hear me? Why do you not respond?"

Charlie's prayer carried the tone of an indictment. Was God on trial? Charlie rolled over and buried his face in the pillow. A furious muffled scream rose from the bed as his body convulsed. Edgington moved from the shadow to cast a smile through his wretched face.

"Francis, I have been on this assignment for sometime. My work with Charlie has been brilliant. Listen to him. He is releasing anger as he embraces desperation. His resolve to trust God is crumbling. Listen to him abandon his Creator. This is the moment I have been anticipating." Edgington laughed with pride to celebrate his perceived victory. Foam was dripping from his chin as his low growl overtook Charlie's crying. Edgington began to bounce.

"Don't think you have won, Edgington."

"Francis, Francis, Francis. Lucifer understands the weakness of humanity. They want a predictable life. When tragedy strikes, humanity cannot cope. Humanity is taught from a young age to grow up and stand on two feet. They are encouraged to be independent. And, they feel self-reliant when life is moving favorably. This is ultimately what they seek. Sadistically, God wants them to be dependent upon Him. He cannot let go of what He made. Do you know why He blocked the path to the Tree of Life? He is afraid that humanity will become gods. This would lead to their liberation from their precious Creator. Lucifer cannot overtake the path to the Tree of Life, but he has other plans."

As he spoke these words, Edgington watched Charlie like a vulture awaiting death. "Francis, I know this victory is mine. Our master plan is effective. We enable humanity's fabrication of a garden like Eden in their mind and heart. Here, in the middle of this garden, they cultivate a tree called the Tree of Self. This tree is an appropriate substitute to the Tree of Life because it provides for their needs. They eat its fruit and find some reprieve from the difficulties of their life. When humanity partakes of the Tree of Self, they take life into their own hands. They stop looking for God's hand and stop trusting Him. They abandon their dependency on Him."

"Edgington, you lie to humanity. They need God and you know it."

"Then why doesn't God help them like they ask? Humanity is responsive because they cannot see God working. We do not force their response. They are desperate for the fruit of this tree because God does not answer their cries. They seek this tree for comfort and satisfaction when God does not meet their expectations. Charlie has cultivated a nice tree. He is about to eat from its branches ... again."

"You deceive Charlie."

"Francis, call it what you want, but we call it a victory. Throughout the course of Charlie's life, many needs facilitate countless opportunities to journey on the path to the Tree of Self. Only one deviant step from the path of the righteous brings Charlie to this path to this tree. As humanity becomes more and more dependent upon this tree, they become more independent from God. We vigorously assist humanity with this process. God Himself provides our main advantage. He created humanity to be dependent. We just choose for them to be dependent on something other than God."

Edgington is right. God made humanity to be dependent. He longs to walk with them and to hold them like children to His bosom. When they experience pain in this world, they are quick to seek a solution from their Creator. When He does not move according to their wishes, they are tempted to question their relationship. What they do not see is God's hand working to meet them at the point of their need. They do not see God holding them in their pain. God may not move as humanity would like, but He intends to provide safe passage. He works through the Holy Spirit to guide their steps along the path of the righteous. These steps are only possible as humanity's spirit yields to God. They are asked to echo the words voiced by Jesus in the garden.

At the tree in the middle of Charlie's garden, Charlie must yield his will and return God's embrace. His faith must support his resolve to trust God. He must say, "Not my will, but Your will be done." Life from this point of obedience may be surreal. But, God is faithful. He will bring about His good. His plan is the key to humanity's victory in this life. Until the resurrected Christ returns to claim His domain, this is the victory God intends for the creatures that walk with Him. Until that return, the orders have already been issued to each angel. They are asked to stand ready. We are ready to return with Christ, but we do not know when. Lucifer knows our arrival is imminent.

THE VOYAGE OF A LIFETIME

Although he fell asleep on his bed, Charlie's crying did not stop. He awoke in his dream to a strange world of water. His tears created this world. He noticed his bed had been transformed into a ship, and apparently he stood as its captain. Wiping the tears from his eyes, he realized his ship was adrift. As he scanned the horizon that completely encircled his position, only endless waters graced his view. He called out across the waters, "Hello, Hello, is anyone out there?" There was no response. Was he alone? He certainly felt alone. He directed his face into the wind and began to consider his future.

Ships were not intended to be adrift. They were built with a purpose in mind. Before machines, the world of wind and water provided humanity with an opportunity to sail. A simple apparatus to capture the wind placed a ship in a precarious middle world uniting the wind above and the water below. In this balance, ships could move across the vast surface of "the ocean blue." Humanity cataloged this achievement to demonstrate their superiority over all creation. Ships could carry more cargo than any beast of burden, speed across the water at a pace exciting dolphins, and endure a distance further than the most obstinate camel.

Charlie remembered that in earlier days, ships journeyed across the ocean on great sails. The ship's grandeur was evident in the strength and brilliance of each sail that hung from its mast. He began to imagine little boys on small rafts standing in awe to see a ship move across their view. The sight of a grown man crawling across the canvas of a deployed sail must have caused envy and restless excitement. Preparing for a future on the bough of one of these great ships, the boys may have tried to sail their raft with an aged blanket. The motion of these ships inspired their fantasies and pacified their thrill-seeking appetites.

Charlie hoisted sail, and his ship began to move. The acceleration of the ship across the waters raised his heartbeat and compelled a nervous laugh. Yes, sails capture the wind and drive ships in their direction. These ships are designed to bring motion from the energy of the wind. However, sailing is not just about motion. Had humanity only learned to produce motion from the wind, civilization would not have harnessed this energy to bring meaningful direction to motion. Success was accomplished by steering that motion to the distant point, the port awaiting the ship's arrival.

The ancient worlds discovered the meaning of this motion. They hosted many ports along their waterways. Ships cruised in and out of port with the splendor of a male lion approaching his pride. Adding to this mystique, sailors hid a face of joy as they arrived and fought a face of uncertainty as they departed. The men who braved the world of water considered each voyage a great adventure. Their adventures were often legendary. But, many legendary stories were lost to the depths of the waters. Charlie reflected on the adventures of his life. Would his story also be lost?

Standing at the ship's helm, Charlie stared at the horizon. What lay in the waters of the deep? They did not seem concerned with his presence. Charlie noticed the wind-driven sail propelled the ship to break a passage through the rough waters. Did not a mule pull a farmer's plow breaking the earth in a similar way? The farmer places a seed and returns the soil. As a result, the spot hosts a product commemorating the farmer's visit. But looking behind his ship, Charlie noticed the waters retained little memory of his passage. The wind above and the waters below returned to their play. No evidence remained of the ship's passage in the midst of their endless frolic. The world of water produces no paths that have been or will be followed.

CARGO ESSENTIALS

The essence of sailing brings motion along one's own path. A boy on a raft with an aged blanket can achieve this simple challenge. But, Charlie felt something was missing. He wanted meaning to his motion. He needed to move beyond the essence of sailing. He needed the more mature steps of directing motion with a purpose in mind. The great captains of the ancient world were praised for their ability to reach planned ports. Their voyage was not luck. They were focused on their goal with courageous determination. Through storms and still seas, they diligently pressed toward that distant point on the horizon always checking and rechecking their crude navigation devices. The only luck in that day was the presence of wind to aid their progress.

Charlie wanted to be purposeful in his voyage. The news of his illness and the prognosis of his condition rattled his view of life. Now he was desperate to make the most of what little remained. He knew God provided a single vessel; one body to enable a voyage from birth to death. With the passing of one day, Charlie hoped for another to take its place. He knew yesterday always claimed each spent day. Also, he knew tomorrow always held each day that was anticipated. Each day provided the next segment of navigable waters moving his ship closer to the point on the distant horizon. Now, every day mattered as if it were his last.

Charlie could not let life be a mere expression of chance. Life was too precious. He knew he could not reach a desired port without steering his vessel. To move from the essence of sailing to the essentials of sailing, Charlie needed to make a simple decision to be purposeful with his life. Now, more than ever, he was desperate to be purposeful. The motion of a ship over the water is only purposeful when that motion is defined with a destination.

Charlie must not see any object in the material world as his primary destination. He has been guilty of this error. But, he understands the point on the distant horizon cannot be defined by material elements: jobs, families, homes, etc. He reflects on his university days when many decisions were primary destinations. What to major, who to marry and where to live were just some of the milestones on his path. Decisions of this nature moved Charlie across many possible expressions. Much thought, careful planning, and plenty of hard work helped Charlie. Although the material world employed his time and energy, Charlie needs to see these accomplishments and successes as mere cargo.

In truth, God's sovereign watch brought this cargo to his vessel. With an eager heart, Charlie scooped the cargo from the waters whispering a prayer of thanksgiving. God has always promised to meet Charlie at the point of his need. And, God is faithful to do so. His goodness even sent blessings beyond belief to accompany staple provisions to Charlie's vessel. But, how often did Charlie forget God's promises? How often did he fail to see God's hand providing good thingss for his voyage? Charlie must recognize that the waters before him contain a rich supply of cargo to meet his needs.

This cargo provides substance and flavor for Charlie's voyage. Each piece of cargo is maintained on board provided it has meaning. Once cargo is consumed, expired, or jaded, Charlie no longer wishes to carry its weight. It is pushed from the bough. In some cases, cargo is eliminated to make room for new cargo with greater importance or value. The material world is limited in this process. Charlie's vessel can only carry a certain measure of cargo. Full is full.

Charlie now realizes the error of his life. Cargo had become his focus. He remembers sailing only to find the most and the best from the vast oceans. All of his life, he pushed the structural limitation of his cargo hold. He, with good fortune and clever desperation, mastered the art of excess. He secured cargo to the sides of his vessel. He amassed, stockpiled, and hoarded. So large was his construction that an island seemed to rise from the water. His vessel was hidden within.

The firm structure seemed to stand stable against the waters at its edge. At its edge, the resulting shoreline seemed to establish a new boundary. Although this island wielded a defiant watch against the storms of the sea, Charlie discovered it lacked any foundation. The wind pushed and pulled the vessel's weight across the surface of the water. On his birthday, he realized his vessel could not be shielded completely. Death would lay its claim.

In hindsight, Charlie acknowledged this island did not bring complete relief from the forces of the waters. This vessel, like all vessels on the high seas, lacked a foundation. If only Charlie had known this truth. Cargo cannot fill that void. More is not better. Those who have accumulated great wealth, reached celebrated levels of fame, or exercised complete power will tell you something continues to evade their grasp. Elusive soon gives way to impossible. Charlie knows fulfillment cannot be found in his cargo.

A DISTANT POINT

If cargo cannot bring this fulfillment, what holds the key? Charlie is on a quest to discover this mystery. The waters of this great ocean provide ample opportunity for him to chart a course. Direction becomes imperative. He knows the captain sets the course. His eyes must be trained on the point on the distant horizon. To be a great captain, Charlie must embrace the fact that the vessel and its cargo are only necessities to propel the voyage: nothing more, nothing less.

Charlie must know that one day his vessel must be lost. This is when the material world breaks the seamless horizon into the eternal. When one looks at the ocean from the bow, the horizon draws a distant line marking a circle around the entire vessel. This is where the sky and water meet. Death, one point in this distant horizon, is the final point of Charlie's life in the material world. This is the point when Charlie loses his vessel.

At this point, the cargo also will slip through his grasp. The vessel and the cargo are not made with eternity in mind. They are material. They will return from whence they came. The captain is not so. He was created with eternity in mind. What happens to him depends on where the loss of the vessel and cargo occurs. For those who reach the desired port, the intentional point on the distant horizon, their arrival is celebrated with brilliant fanfare.

As the captain steps onto this port, the loss of his vessel is immediate. The captain will not notice this loss amid sounds of joy and celebration. Life's elusive quest for fulfillment is satisfied at the port. The eternal world will be like bedrock beneath Charlie's feet. The angels have known the splendor and mystery of this port. We have found its wonder limitless. However, Charlie must know one stark truth. This truth will become a beacon for determination and focus. This one truth above all will drive his navigation.

The truth is that only one port exists. Yes, One. Not two or three. Not many dotting the waterways of any world. Just one. Fortunately, it welcomes all who may enter. With no other ports, the vessels that do not find this port will be lost at sea. The captains of these vessels will not see the celebration given for a successful arrival. With no port to support a stand, the captain will drop into the abyss. There are no alternatives after this finish. The abyss imprisons the captain's soul with eternal torment and suffering. No rescue. No second chances. No hope. Who can grasp the finality of this one moment? Who can accept a separation from God with no end? Who can afford to fail?

This truth brings sober focus to the importance of reaching the port. But many captains employ intentional navigation for other objectives. For some, the allure of cargo preoccupies their voyage. They sail here and there hunting for more and more cargo. So many vessels sail after reported riches with the passion of Ponce de Leon's march to the fountain of youth. For others, no true direction marks their meaningless course across the waters of the ocean. For still others, tragedy or indecision marks their journey pressing over the same waters many times more than once and for all.

Some captains engage endless debate. They ask if this port really exists. Is it a myth conjured by those who would distract a captain's will? Others would say more than one port exists. Captains have stepped forward to say they have seen these ports. Who should be believed? Could there not be more than one port? Many others say all directions lead to the same port. This could be the mystery of the high seas. Still others know about the single port on the distant horizon. But, they choose to wait for a fairer day to change their course.

All that hinders their arrival will have no consideration. Only the ability to steer the vessel to this port bears the mark of success. All other achievements are considered inconsequential in the voyage of a lifetime. Look all around. The port is only one of many points on the distant horizon. However, only this one point has a port, and very few find it. All other points are the way of destruction. Charlie, as the captain of his vessel, must sail with focus. He must guide his vessel to this port with determination. Eternal life awaits him.

THE PURPOSE OF LIFE

Charlie considers this revelation monumental. It compels him to stare toward the distant horizon. He wonders why he is here. As he peers across the endless waters, he debates what really is important. His mind parades several items before his heart hoping to influence his contemplation. The heart holds cargo with affection. One item of cargo may have been used to define the purpose for his life: a job, a family, or a possession. With these items in place, the voyage is filled with purpose until Charlie hits a tragedy; the rise of a tempest. Then, the item is lost. The question returns.

Charlie screams, "Why am I here?" As the grief and shock subsides, he attempts to secure another item of cargo. Once again the platform is filled and the heart returns to its fabricated sense of purpose. As long as these items are in place, the question is quieted. However, Charlie has discovered life cannot be predictable. Charlie's last tempest destroyed his platform. The question returns with a vengeance. Before his illness, Charlie had attempted to connect one segment of purpose to the next desiring to keep the question at bay. But that plan can no longer have merit. Now what does he do?

Further consideration of this dilemma leads to a discovery. What Charlie wants in life seems to direct his conclusions about the purpose of life. Charlie ties the wheel and leaves the helm. He moves to the ship's stern and sits at the vessel's edge. He begins to weep once again. He has been sailing for 41 years. He will only sail a few more months. Yet, he did not grasp the purpose of life until this moment. Is it too late?

Charlie ponders the adjustments he would make if he could go back in time. But, he cannot go back. So, he determines to navigate his future course with purpose. He wants to make the most of what life he has left. Simple reason reveals to Charlie that the shortest distance between two points is a straight line. Where Charlie sits now is one point. The port marks the other. He decides his goal must be to sail this line marking his course. The length of the course cannot be Charlie's concern. Instead, the line itself becomes the goal to ensure Charlie's success.

The waters provide many mysteries to hamper Charlie's progress. The conductor of terror on the high seas moves like a crazed pirate seeking captains to devour. Agents of deception support him. They travel the oceans with the thirst to distract and discourage the captain's focus for this port. They are effective. Much of their effort is made through the cargo floating on the ocean. The agents of deception move to convince the captain that any piece of cargo is more important than the port. Other agents aim to intoxicate a captain with the charm of a deceptive illusion. If a port remains in the captain's mind, they work to construct false ports. Mirages of the high seas so convincing even the greatest minds and sincerest hearts plot zealous courses to these points on the distant horizon. The proclamation of a new way and the prospect of mystical ports must not compel Charlie to set a new bearing. Nothing to the right or to the left should alter his course to the front.

A still sea, a storm, or the lack of staple provisions cannot dishearten his intentional focus. The lack or abundance of pleasures cannot sway Charlie's resolve. In all circumstances, Charlie cannot be derelict in duty. He must give sober attention to the task at hand. The poor, the rich, the pained, the hungry, the homeless, the male, the female, the crippled, the robber, and the murderer have the same reason for living. They must find the port. This is God's ultimate plan.

STEPPING ASIDE

Finally, with Charlie's determination in place, he has only one question. Where is this port? He does not have a clue. He yells the question over the waters. But, only silence returns. He screams the question again and again to relieve his frustration. But nothing responds to his effort.

Charlie starts to weep again. He buries his face in his hands. He is desperate to discover this port. In this moment, Charlie takes a slow deep breath. Although he sees the futility of his life, he trusts God's wisdom.

Charlie will soon die. No option exists. As he considers this reality, the tempest rises to reflect the tragedy in Charlie's life. Charlie's vessel is mercilessly tossed about in the waves created by this storm. He drops the sails and throws cargo from the ship. He thinks about survival as fear overtakes his heart. His weeping increases. He grips the helm and peers through his tear-filled view. Across the turbulent waters, he sees an image. To his amazement, Charlie sees Jesus walking on the water. "Charlie!" Was Jesus calling his name?

If Charlie listens, he can hear. If he opens his eyes, he will see Jesus' story spanning every generation. His place in history is always evident. In creation, Jesus stood as the agent of wisdom's marvel. In the fall of humanity, Jesus stood at the grave of lost glory. In redemption, Jesus stood on the cross; a sacrifice to satisfy God's wrath. Jesus built this port with his blood and body. The sacrifice to satisfy God's wrath opened this pathway to eternal paradise. Prior to this provision, Charlie had no port or place to stand. Only the prospects of eternal torment awaited him.

Jesus knows the location of this port. He calls over the waters for captains to resign their command to Him. He wishes to stand at their helm to guide their vessel to His port. Jesus knows that the helm is the vessel's point of control. It commands direction. As long as Charlie stands at the helm, he bears the responsibility of directing his vessel. Consequently, he is expected to discover the port. When Jesus offers to stand at the helm, He wants control of the vessel. He wants to guide the vessel to the port on the distant horizon.

Jesus claims to be the way, the truth, and the life. He takes the helm with perfect resolve. The vessel's success to the port is assumed after this transfer of command. As Jesus assumes command of the vessel, He knows the direction. In truth, only He knows. The place of this port is a mystery. No captain will discover its location regardless of great effort or phenomenal luck. Outside of Jesus, no other means is available to find this bridge between the material world and eternal paradise.

Responding to Jesus' offer is the only decision a captain can make in the material world with eternity in mind. Charlie has this epiphany. Clearly, the voyage of a lifetime is a meaningful opportunity to experience God's ultimate provision; the port awaiting his arrival. Charlie wants to invite Jesus on board and engage God's ultimate plan. In the end, this is all that will matter. In the voyage of a lifetime, a ship is not as brilliant when it sails on the high seas as when it arrives into port. Jesus calls again, "Charlie … Charlie."

ONE LAST KISS

"Charlie, Charlie … its time to get up." A soft hand brushing his shoulder accompanied the voice calling his name.

"Where am I?"

"Where are you? You're in our bedroom. You fell asleep last night before I finished putting the kids to bed. I was really hoping we could have a private birthday party, but I decided not to wake you. You looked really cute and comfortable. Happy Birthday, honey." Emily placed a soft kiss on his lips and smiled as if he had no worries in the world.

"Honey, I am so sorry for not helping you with the kids. I was very selfish."

"Nonsense. It was your birthday. You have the right to be a captain for a day."

Charlie shot up in bed. "Captain? Why did you say captain? Don't you usually say king? Why Captain?"

"Charlie, are you ok? I just said captain. If you want me to say king, I will."

"I am sorry, Emily." He took her hand and brought it to his face. At that moment, words were not available to explain thoughts racing through his heart.

Emily reached across and grabbed a perfectly wrapped box. "Charlie, this is for you. I don't ever want you to forget how much I love you." She placed another soft kiss on his lips. As she pulled back, he moved forward attempting to prolong his opportunity with that kiss. He did not want anything with her to end. She smiled but seemed a bit confused. Charlie stared at the box as tears started to flow down his cheeks. His strong emotion caught Emily by surprise. With a tender voice, Emily asked, "Are you ok?" No, he is not, but how could he tell her? How could he tell her this would be the last birthday gift she would ever give to him?

She wiped the tears from his eyes and placed a soft kiss on each eye. She wrapped one arm around his back to grab her other. An incredible hug followed. He returned her hug and held her tight. For what seemed an eternity, his troubles vanished in that embrace. Although the tears continued, Emily could not notice. He whispered into her ears, "I love you, Honey. I know I am the luckiest man in the world to have you as my wife. No matter what happens, I want you to know I have always believed you were perfect for me."

Emily pulled back. Her face registered a quick surprise to see his tears. But the face instantly changed to reflect her confusion. "Charlie?" Her voice mirrored her face. They jointly communicated uncertainty. "Is everything ok?" He did not know how to begin, but he did.

"Emily, honey …." Charlie does not remember everything he said that day. He only remembers Emily beginning to cry. She cried for several days. He was thankful to be present to wipe every tear. But, he also realized he would not have this opportunity when she would need him the most. As he held her, he imagined her world of water and the ship she sailed. He knew only God could bring her comfort in that place. He prayed a strange prayer asking God to hold her and guide her voyage through this tempest.

The next six months passed very quickly despite every effort to slow the sensation of time. Seconds were held like breaths, and days were slowly etched as numbers on granite. As Charlie's health deteriorated, family members and friends huddled close. No one wanted to leave. So many times, he hugged those departing as if he would never see them again. He did not know. He looked into their eyes as if to hold his place in this world, but he could not hang on.

On his last night, Emily and Charlie cuddled in bed. They talked about several things. But, mostly they talked about the garden in their backyard. This was their special project during Charlie's illness. Emily needed something to distract her attention from his pain. This was working. "Charlie, I will always remember you sitting by the tree in the middle of our garden." This was his designated spot because he could not participate. "I so enjoyed your company. Thank you for loving the flowers I grew for you. Thank you for smiling. Thank you...." She began to cry. Charlie reached around to hold her in his arms.

"Emily, I love you. It's going to be alright." She nodded, but the crying continued. As Charlie brushed hair from her face, she peered through her tear-filled eyes long enough to see him smile. That's the last thing he remembers. Sleep overtook him, but it did not touch her. She would not let sleep rob her of a single minute with Charlie. Before the sun's light broke through the window, Charlie breathed his last breath. Emily placed a soft kiss on his lips as the final period in his story. "Goodbye, Charlie. I love you."

Charlie could not hear Emily. He only heard the sounds of joy and celebration upon his arrival at the port. He felt solid ground beneath his feet. His voyage in the material world was a complete success. I joined the other angels to celebrate this moment. I was the first to welcome him. "Hello, Charlie. My name is Francis. Welcome home!"

THE DAY OF MY FUNERAL

"Oh death where is thy sting, oh grave where is thy victory." These words were displayed on a large screen suspended over the stage in the sanctuary. Emily has seen these words before but they have little meaning for her now. She cannot completely embrace them because the sting of death has pierced her tender heart. The pain is great. No one could have prepared her for the experiences of life over the past six months. She never could have anticipated the difficulty of this journey. Pain met her every day to walk alongside her. As much as she wished or wept for pain to leave, pain only improved its grip with each passing day.

Today, the pain reached a new level. Her tears know no end. Her heart and mind are busy attempting to make sense of a life that is far from what she had hoped. From the balcony in the back, she watched the motion of life through her tear-filled eyes. She cannot believe how many flowers grace the stage in front. They are so beautiful to her. Charlie's casket lay in their midst. She stared without reservation at the cradle now holding the man she promised to love until death. Now, death holds Charlie, and he cannot know her love.

As she looked around the room, family and friends were preparing for the service. Charlie's parents are sitting on the front row just to the right side of the center aisle. Her parents sit just opposite on the left. For a brief moment, she had an amazing déjà vu. Her heartbeat jumped, and breath left her lungs. She realized Charlie once stood on that same spot where he now lay. He stood there to receive her as his wife ten years earlier. What a beautiful day that had been. To her, he looked dashing. He wore a grand smile, and his eyes were beaming with pride. The energy of that moment caused everyone in the room to smile.

She felt no one was smiling in this same room today. "Except Charlie." Her body flinched to register the shock produced by my words. She made a sharp turn to the right to see me standing by her side. "I am sorry. I did not mean to startle you. Is this seat taken?"

Emily timidly responded, "Yes … I mean no, this seat is not."

"Emily, my name is Francis. It's a pleasure to meet you." I am sure I caught her by surprise. She just nodded in disbelief.

"This large crowd sure makes it tough to find a seat. Do you wonder where all these people are from?"

"Yes, Francis. I have been sitting here wondering how everyone here knew my husband."

"Emily, some of these individuals are from Charlie's cherished yesterdays, and others return from forgotten yesteryears. A few have only heard of Charlie and never witnessed a single day he spent." She knew that. She believed the differences in the crowd could not erase the special place of honor each seat in the sanctuary provided.

"Francis, even if everyone knew Charlie differently, I think they all loved him the same."

"Oh, you are right, Emily. That is why this room is filled with emotion. Everyone considered Charlie a valued part of their past." Emily now anticipates his absence. She wipes tears from her eyes, and with those same eyes, she stares at the cradle holding his lifeless body. This somber gathering attempts to help her accept the reality of Charlie's death. This is what brings them together. This is something they have in common.

"Francis, it's going to be tough living without Charlie."

"Yes, Emily. I agree, but you are going to be amazed how God will provide for you. Can you see one thing that God has already provided?"

"What is that, Francis?"

A GOODBYE GIFT

"It's the gift that everyone brings."

"Gifts, I'm sorry. Did you say gifts … like to a wedding?"

"No, not like gifts brought to a wedding. This is not a gift one gives. Instead, it's a gift one receives. Today, these gifts are wrapped in a delicate embrace. They are savored and shared in this setting. The more one savors, the more their value. The more one shares, the more their value. The more one savors, the more one shares. The more one shares, the more one has to share. Surprisingly, this one item grows the more you give it away."

"Francis, you're making me a little dizzy."

"I'm sorry."

"No, you're fine. But, tell me what these gifts are."

"These gifts are from Charlie. He gave them throughout the course of his life. With each moment, word, and interaction within the frame of his life, Charlie gave liberally to many people. The more Charlie gave, the more Charlie could give. The volume of these gifts cannot be known. But, one thing is certain. These gifts are very unique to those who received them. These gifts are memories made with Charlie."

"Wow, you are right about that. Charlie touched a lot of people."

I noticed Emily looked around the room, but she did not process what she really saw. Her mind was engaged in a more formidable task. The mind was held by her heart to assist in searching its chambers. Her mind moved the eyes of her heart similar to your physical eyes scanning the room: to and fro, here and there, far and near. This induces a movement of memories; a significant procession passing as an endless stream in her conscious thought. Her heart reflects on these memories as if to feed the appetite of grief.

Grief is imperative. Grief is God's process of helping Emily's heart release the moorings that bind her to Charlie. Her days and years spent with Charlie will soon find closure. This is why funerals provide a place of comfort for hurting hearts. The comfort of those present is important. Comfort eases the process of saying goodbye. "Francis, I love every memory Charlie gave me, but I don't really understand how to say goodbye to Charlie."

"Do you remember saying goodbye to Charlie at an airport? The tears you shed there are composed of the same substance as these you now shed. As you said goodbye, you released Charlie from one point on the planet to another. You missed his touch, but relief soon came with a phone call."

"I hated that he traveled so much. But, you are right. I always knew he would come home."

"Emily, a goodbye at a funeral is this process refined to its ultimate point. This goodbye releases Charlie from one world to another. These tears share the sense of missing Charlie, but then push further to note that the missing will never find relief in this world. And so, this goodbye is understood to be loss. This goodbye is the final goodbye."

"Francis, I did say goodbye to Charlie."

"I know you did, Emily. But, did you understand the complete meaning of that goodbye? It's a lot like your goodbyes at the airport."

"What do you mean, Francis?"

THE TREE IN THE MIDDLE OF MY GARDEN

"Well, Emily, your perception of loss is important in the grieving process. Have you ever misplaced a watch? After a time of searching, your mind concludes that the watch is gone. You contemplate your loss and consider your options. Then, one miraculous day, you lift an object in your home to find your watch. Your celebration begins immediately. The perception of loss caused the grief. In actuality, your watch was never gone; I mean really gone. It was only hidden from your view. So what was the loss?"

"Wow, I remember losing lots of things like that. Some were found, and others are still missing. Charlie was so good at helping me look for things. But, I am not sure I understand what you are saying."

"Emily, a shroud of secrecy separates the material world from the eternal. This hides the object of your affection. As Charlie moved from one world to another, you will follow someday. If you and Charlie are both in the eternal world, where is the loss? The loss is perceptual."

"Francis, you are right." Emily was beginning to understand the meaning of life. She never considered Charlie's death in this way. Charlie has gone home to be with Jesus. That home will someday be hers also. But, for now, Charlie was gone. And, like at the airport, she has lots of tears.

"Oh, I am so sorry, Emily. I didn't mean to make you cry. Here, use this to wipe those tears." Her tears are so necessary. They affirm the memories of her heart. Tears are the tangible manifestation of the mind and heart's agreement. They measure the depth and value of memories. Those memories are Charlie's living gift. With them, more tears may await.

"Francis, I have been crying so much. I am not sure where all these tears come from." I did not say anything. She stared at the coffin because she longed to see the man who left her with so many wonderful memories.

THE SECOND GIFT

"Emily, do you know that Charlie gives another gift?" This gift becomes obvious to her if she could see the assembly's next similarity. "Emily, look down there. The posture of the living attendees is in direct contrast to Charlie's lying position. A common thread of life weaves the attending assembly into one fellowship." Emily began to scan the growing crowd. Although Charlie did not hold this thread any longer, only a thread-like line separates the individuals in the room from Charlie, the sitting from the lying. At any moment, anyone could cross this line. With this thought in clear focus, the second gift becomes visible. This gift is a mirror. Through this mirror, each person is compelled to see the true picture of life.

"Francis, I have been thinking a lot about life. To me, life does not make sense. You are born, and someday you die. In between, life is basically hard. Francis, I think life is just short and tough. That's it."

"Emily, you are right. In the scope of eternity, life on earth is indeed a brief expression, a mere breath. It is a vapor appearing for a moment. Too many people forget their days are numbered." As I spoke, Emily was swept into a reflective world. Sure, she thinks about Charlie. But, beyond this, she wonders what will compel her to break across the frail thread marking the border of two opposite worlds. Perhaps more absorbing, she contemplates what awaits her beyond this threshold.

As she looks around, she realizes everyone in the room will one day pass. People are mortal. She blurts out, "What is the second gift?"

"Emily, the second gift is the opportunity to see the true picture of life through a mirror." I know this revelation brought more questions to her heart. But she did not ask them. I have watched many individuals leave a funeral without the second gift. They do not see its value. It will remain an unclaimed treasure. Sure memories with Charlie are priceless, but the mirror helps reveal the priceless value of their own life.

Looking into the mirror, Emily reflects on her life. "Francis, I know the importance of life. For the last six months, I have lived every second like it was my last. I held on to each day refusing to let it end. Many of these people live like they have eternity to spend. They need to realize life on earth is short and precious."

"I am glad you agree, Emily. People die everyday without understanding life." I had seen Charlie's obituary article in the local newspaper. Daily, it records the new faces entering the eternal world. I become immersed in the information and wonder what kind of persons moved across the threshold. The brief article failed to provide the exceptional platform of a large biography. Tragically, so much of their story will never be told.

Nevertheless, these few words are the deceased's moment of print fame. They say a picture is worth a thousand words. In an obituary, a word may be worth a thousand pictures. The past and present roll by as a couple dancing a wonderful waltz. Beauty, captured in print, preserves a faint hint of the music that moves these dancers. My mind begins to drift into the motion of the dance; the past and present partner to provide a glimpse of these vivid and lively pictures cherished by loved ones.

"Francis, people die everyday. I never thought about it until I looked at Charlie's article in yesterday's paper. So many people were in the obituary section. Francis, I read every one. I wanted to read because I knew someone else wanted to tell the story of his or her loved one. I know I wanted the world to know about Charlie. But, the article only allowed a few lines."

"Emily, I am sure Charlie is happy with every effort you have made. I know he would think the world of your thoughtful words in the article." In many ways, the world did acknowledge respect for Charlie. The street makes that possible. Soon Emily will be driven down the street in a procession of cars following a hearse. Cars will turn their lights on to express solidarity with her grief. This temporary gesture is appropriate. At the sight of this modern march, those watching the procession are also thrust into a reflective wonder. Their mind recognizes the contrast in the day. Their world is about the immediate and busy elements of life. At that moment, they are fighting traffic and praying for green lights in a hurried commute to their next event.

On the other hand, Emily's world is solemn and still. She profits from a police escort eliminating all traffic and negating all red lights. In this privilege, time is not lost. One day Emily will need a similar procession; this world of the living yielding to the dead. What will that day be like for her?

MY DAY

"Wow, Francis. I have never thought about what my obituary would be like. What would someone write about me? In fact, what will the day of my funeral be like?"

"Emily, few people think about their own funeral." Emily did not grasp the value of a funeral. The deceased becomes momentarily resurrected in the words and emotions of those present. Sure, the agenda of a funeral is to bury the dead. But, the outcome recalls the essence of a life consumed over time.

This essence rises like the aroma from fresh baked bread. When this aroma fills the room, the life of the deceased becomes evident. Who lived to raise a great family? Who lived to amass wealth? Who lived for themselves? Who lived for others? Selected individuals will share their thoughts. They will use words carefully. Factual information passes almost without notice. They all attempt to affirm the deceased as one significant drop in the great ocean of humanity.

Looking out into the audience, Emily wonders what will be said about Charlie. What did they see in Charlie? Will they see what Charlie saw in himself? Will they see what God saw? Will they value the values Charlie employed to be his guiding principles?

"Francis, Charlie has been a great guy since his childhood. Can you believe we have been friends since second grade? When Charlie's friends chose to get the most from their young lives, he made a decision to invest his life to give the most. When his peers lived for the day and saw no tomorrow, Charlie chose to invest the day for tomorrow. For Charlie, the thought of being a blessing was more important than the thought of being blessed. Charlie lived with intentional focus. I know he was very intentional with our last six months. He always considered every moment we spent together ...." She could not continue. She began to cry because she realized Charlie knew how to love people around him in a very special way. "Francis, I'm sorry. It's a tough day. But, you are helping me see Charlie in a whole new way."

"Emily, I also want you to see God in a whole new way. God gives life. And, He takes life. He has a plan and a purpose for each and every day."

For Emily, today is the most important day. There is a call for a profound appreciation for time. Time is a commodity in the material world that quickly fades. Each day the clock ticks through one twenty-four hour period. The lungs take and release breath, the heart beats a steady stride, and the eyes record countless expressions of life. One unknown person said, "Yesterday is history, tomorrow is a mystery and today is a gift. That's why it's called the present." How true this statement! This gift, today, is filled with blessings. Emily cannot escape the numerous blessings embedded within the frame of her day.

In truth, Emily is like a black hole absorbing the universe as fuel to propel her life through each day. All created things are poised and waiting to be counted as blessings in her life. She may successfully catalog items of blessings not granted on a single day. Sure, today Charlie is on that list. But when she tries to catalog the blessings that are found in an average day, items both evident and not evident, she will exhaust the day before exhausting this list. No two days are the same as are no two lives. Each day, like each life, ebbs and flows. But each life, like each day, is set in the context of a vast ocean of blessings.

"Francis, I wonder what God thinks about all this? I mean each day is fleeting, and everyone will die one day." She is right. Some will die on Monday, others on Tuesday, and others still throughout the week. Regardless of which day one dies, on that day, the day will be called today. Today is the day she will perish. Today, on that day, will be her last.

"Emily, on that day, one step will be taken to cross that frail line separating life and death. The breath of life will fail to flow through your body. So many functions taken for granted in the past will be silent. The heart will no longer beat, and the eyes no longer serve as the window to the soul. This mystery of life becomes the mystery of death. But, do not be dismayed. When you entered this material world, you came with nothing. When you leave, you leave with nothing." Little did she realize that I have witnessed great kings and mighty emperors fitting their graves with riches intended for the next world. Sadly, the only next world those riches entered were the greedy hands of grave robbers or the astute gaze of a modern archeologist. On the other hand, I have seen Charlie ushered from depravity to the glorious treasures of heaven. What a contrast. Charlie is swimming in the midst of God's boundless riches while his earthly body is confined to the rigid compartment of a comfortable coffin.

That coffin sits in the focal center of this beautiful chapel. People gather to pay their last respects. But how does one accomplish this task? Do they enter to acknowledge Charlie's new found fortune or concede the new loss of an old friend? "Emily, you cannot miss the meaning of this day. It approaches as an unavoidable sunset on the distant horizon.

Although many employ any means to delay this day and others live in fear of it, I invite you to consider this day as a great and glorious day."

ARE YOU READY?

"Wow, Francis. I can see it is a great day for Charlie. He is enjoying eternity with his Creator. I can't imagine what would be a better blessing. Francis, this is definitely Charlie's best day here on earth. He left with the greatest of all riches. God is so amazing."

"Emily, God makes this possible for everyone through the sacrifice celebrated each Easter. Do you remember celebrating Easter? Your little girl always wore such a beautiful new dress. At church, you and Charlie watched the new faces arriving for their annual pilgrimage. And who can overlook the Sunday sermon predictably bringing to mind the old, old story of the cross. Easter celebrates the blessing of Christ given to humanity. The cross measures as the unprecedented pinnacle of God's unconditional love. The Easter miracle makes all other blessings from God seem as child's play. Yes, eternal God has masterfully provided for your greatest need."

As Emily listened to me, I could not help but remember the day of Jesus' death. He did not have a funeral. No one stood to pronounce His selfless generosity to the masses. No article cataloged His passing. Now, my memory is filled with the phenomenal transformation of my grief to joy when Jesus rose from the dead. Jesus is now the Savior of the World.

"Emily, understanding the gift of eternal life through Jesus is imperative for everyone. As you accept His provision, you enter a union with God forged in the blood of Christ, an unbreakable bond with eternal resiliency. To accept brings the title of Christian. Look into the mirror to see the eternal world awaiting you. Are you ready?"

WHAT IS LIFE?

"Francis, I know Jesus as my Savior. As David says in Psalms 23, 'I will dwell in the house of the Lord forever.'" Sure, she understands this truth. But, the question regarding life has always plagued her. She often sat on a vista below a star-lit sky. Here, her eyes searched the panorama of endless space to find opportunities for insight, clarity, and definition. In those moments under the stars, she found inspiration for the purpose of life and determined to pronounce its meaning. What happened from this inspiration is unknown. But, with inspiration requiring expression, she left with eagerness. The world was before her awaiting her arrival. Life was pushing forward, and death seemed a distant concern.

These same questions of the heart have another result at this funeral. Here, her questions have a slightly different dynamic because of the object of her sight. The stars provided a canopy of endless sight. But, Charlie's coffin is a space with clear limitations. As she reflects, an impenetrable wall is built to cage her carefree spirit within mortality. From this perspective, she accepts the reality of death. The questions of the heart find desperation with this acknowledgment.

"Emily, many people view life through a limited lens. They conclude life is great when things are great. On the other hand, they say life is not so good when things are not so good. Why do they let the expressions of life establish their view of life? By doing so, they are caught up in life's unnecessary roller coaster of ups and downs. They cannot let circumstances cloud their sight of God's sovereignty and confuse His design. God's design has eternity in mind." I have watched God work through the millenna to support the steps of those who wish to walk with Him. But never have I seen God spare a single individual from experiencing trials and difficulties. The paths of the righteous travel through mountains and valleys alike. He promises to make paths straight providing clarity of direction. When a Christian does not keep his or her eyes on the path, life is evaluated without regard to eternity.

In the best of times, they believe life is great. They are lost in the blessings that fill each day. So many things in the material world exhaust their precious and limited attention. Their voracious appetite for life seems fulfilled. The euphoria of answered prayers fails to note the one to whom those prayers were sent. They become intoxicated with the scent of self-sufficiency. Who needs God? Who needs God when everything one needs in life is more than adequately present? The material world blinds individuals to the eternal in the best of times.

In the worst of times, their prayers are expressed to God as cries without end. In the midst of their difficult situations, they are tempted to jettison all hope. What, why, where and when become anthems around which their attention completely rallies. What is going on? Why is this happening? Where is God? When will God save me? Life produces a volume of tears. When they are too weary to wipe those tears from their cheek, a trail of salt remains. This trail provides a fitting memorial for their grief of life.

Solomon paints this vivid picture. He pictures life as a cruel creation or impossible obligation. While considering the many images and expressions of life, he saturates his picture with a sobering sense of despair. He considers the days of man upon the earth with contempt. He considers the prospects of not being born more desirable than having been born. Is this God's design of life? No. Solomon's conclusion of vanity is limited in its consideration. He only sees life within the frame of the material world. You cannot accept this limited view. Life is not vanity when one sees God's design. Look very carefully.

"Francis what do you think about life?"

"Emily, the question regarding life seems too elusive until life itself is first defined from God's perspective. If life were comprised only of your days here on earth, you would miss the meaning of the creation miracle that placed God's breath in your lungs. Clearly, God gave humanity life with eternity in mind. With this consideration, life needs to encompass birth to eternity in its definition. The best of times or the worst of times in the material world should not alter this view of life. Death is a mere portal or a bridge to the eternal. It is not the end. The sum of life on earth cannot equal the smallest fraction of eternity."

Wow, I could see Emily's countenance change. She began to grasp that life in the material world was a limited platform. She knew God intended a whole lot more with His brilliant creation of life. Emily cannot see what I can see. Eternity provides a complementing and more reasonable stage on which life can display God's dazzling intent. She has not seen a fraction of the wonders I have seen. I have not seen a fraction of wonders God spoke into existence. But for now, God is not calling Emily to see all this. He just wants her to see His intent for life. The mirror at this funeral helps Emily see this truth by allowing a gaze across the threshold of life and death. She needs to consider the days on earth as only a beginning. She needs to consider eternity as the forever without an end. She needs to take joy in knowing she was created to know the forever without an end. This is life.

"Wow, Francis. That's amazing stuff about the eternal. Thank you for sharing this truth with me. My understanding of life has really been transformed. I will no longer look at life from the perspective of the material world. I will not let problems or blessings in this material life blind me to God's sovereignty. Thank you, Francis."

"You're welcome, Emily." She stood and reached forward to give me a hug. Her right arm moved around me to meet her left. A tight squeeze conveyed the new found comfort of her heart. As she returned to the front of the sanctuary, she was surprised her eyes produced no more tears. She leaned on the casket.

Her dad placed his arm on her back. She dropped her head on his shoulders and cast an involuntary stare at the flowers. "How are you, Baby?" he said with the tender voice she remembered from her childhood.

"I'm fine, Daddy. I am at peace."

"Honey, that's wonderful. We are all going to make it through this." He pressed his arm into her to convey his support.

"Daddy, did you know the man that sat next to me in the balcony?"

"Honey, your mom and I saw you sitting there. We were thankful you were getting a moment to yourself. But, no one sat next to you."

"Are you sure? You didn't see the man that spoke with me?"

"Honey, there was no one." She got quiet. Her face reflected her confusion. Then, a smile burst across it. Her father watched this metamorphosis. He too experienced a moment of transformation. First, he felt sad for her, and then, totally confused.

"Honey, why are your smiling?"

"Yes, Daddy, I am smiling. I have a lot to smile about. I know where Charlie is."

"Honey, Charlie would be so proud!" Emily's dad wrapped his arms around her and held her tight.

She quietly whispered into his ears, "Daddy, we are all one day closer to being with Jesus."

SECTION 2
Under the Tree

P S A L M S   3 7 : 3 1

The law of his God is in his heart; his feet do not slip.

Can you see Emily smiling? Her smile is genuine as it comes from the depths of her heart. Proverbs 15:13 says, "A happy heart makes the face cheerful, but heartache crushes the spirit." The great tragedies of life had produced heartache, but she now knows cheer. Emily has been transformed. What is the reason for her change? In her opportunity with Francis, her eyes were opened. She now sees her circumstances as being within God's sovereignty. She yields to Him and depends on Him to guide her steps. She has mouthed Jesus' words, "Not my will but Your will be done." Life may still be surreal for her, but it is not out of God's control. Emily is finding rest in God's wonderful embrace.

As you read from this second section, God wants to move you to His rest. This part of the book is very different from the first. Francis, Emily, and the other characters from the first section are silent. They will not return. But, God's wisdom is not silent. Familiar characters of the Bible provide profound insight from their own lives in the pages that follow. Read any chapter you desire in any order. Each chapter celebrates one single element in the dependent relationship God desires from you. He is speaking directly to you.

When the heart feeds on God's truths, it will express His delight. Job 23:12 says, "I have not departed from the commands of His lips; I have treasured the words of His mouth more than my daily bread." Get ready to smile. The heart is about to feast.

HOPE IN HOPELESSNESS

What lies within the frame of one life? No one can know. With each day, life moves with time. The potential expressions of life in this movement are as innumerable as the stars in the heavens. So many possibilities exist. Each moment you live waits to direct the course of your life. The complex world of possibilities will not reveal what the next moment brings. Nevertheless, you seem able to assimilate your new circumstances. Somehow, you manage to maintain an expression of life you believe to be normal or familiar.

But as you know, no life is normal. You seem to forget that each day holds equal potential to be the day your world turns upside down. Tragedies, disasters, calamities, accidents, misfortunes, failures, adversities, and heartbreaks can engulf your life at anytime. Where do these bandits hide waiting for the perfect moment to strike? Where do they recruit their unlimited agents to administer their bad medicine? The smallest virus or the largest hurricane seems to obey their every wish. Their attack moves your life from the normal to the inconceivable. You never would have guessed what you now face. Your world lies in ruin.

What happened to you? Did a car accident take your child? Did you go through a divorce? Did a fire turn your dream home to ashes? Were you told you have a terminal illness? Did you lose your job? Are you on the brink of bankruptcy? Did a close family member die? Did your boyfriend breakup? Ultimately, what happened to you is immaterial at this level of pain. Everyone who shares this type of pain joins a fraternity of deeply hurting people. The world is full of them. Their circumstances may be different, but their burden of pain is the same.

ONE PAINFUL LIFE

The honorary leader of this fraternity may be a Bible character named Job. Job knows this burden of pain. His suffering compels his friends to join an extraordinary vigil. Job 2:12-13 says, "When they saw him (Job) from a distance, they could hardly recognize him; they began to weep aloud, and they tore their robes and sprinkled dust on their heads. Then they sat on the ground with him for seven days and seven nights. No one said a word to him, because they saw how great his suffering was." This is great suffering. This is extreme friendship. Although Job's friends recognize his pain and feel greatly for him, they could not join his fraternity.

Job's story is extraordinary. He probably lived 1800 years before Christ. For generations, his story was communicated verbally to inspire people living in a difficult world. Finally, an unknown writer was inspired to pen the book of Job. He secured this powerful story to serve as God's standard for those who suffer righteously. Readers have been inspired by its message for thousands of years.

In the beginning, Job is said to have had community renown, great wealth, and many children. Job 1:2-3 says, "He had seven sons and three daughters, and he owned seven thousand sheep, three thousand camels, five hundred yoke of oxen and five hundred donkeys, and had a large number of servants. He was the greatest man among all the people of the East." Job was an exceptional man. He was a model citizen, a successful businessman, and a perfect family man. His pre-tragedy story would command the subject of a highly publicized biography.

The book of Job makes a short but powerful introduction. Job 1:1 says, "In the land of Uz there lived a man whose name was Job. This man was blameless and upright; he feared God and shunned evil." His dedication to God is unprecedented. Throughout the book, Job defends his pure commitment to God and blameless state before God. His spiritual discipline is profound and evident. What man would claim to be free from lust? Job did. Job 31:1 says, "I made a covenant with my eyes not to look lustfully at a girl." He tells his friends that such a failure would require judgment and result in destruction.

Job not only cares to uphold his own spiritual aspirations, but he also cares for his children's spiritual well being. He employs the exercises available to him by sacrificing on their behalf. He is proactive in their spiritual affairs. His love for each child could not be overstated. Seven boys secure a strong family heritage. Three girls provide many other fatherly joys. Job meets everyone's need. His wealth is more than sufficient. The book of Job records frequent feasting by Job's children. They had a great life. Job had a great life. But, Job is not known for what he had. He is known for what he lost. From a high platform of success, Job's world fell. To say he was crushed after this fall would be an understatement.

The first two chapters of Job document the details of his tragedy. Satan asks God for permission to strike Job. With his opportunity, Satan completely takes Job's worldly possessions. All of his sheep, camels, oxen, and donkeys are lost to thieves and natural disasters. A strong desert wind rushes upon a house that holds Job's children. The house collapses, and not a single child is spared. Only four of Job's many servants escape death to provide Job with their eyewitness accounts of each event. One by one they arrive. One after the other, they tell their story. Job listens. His heart and mind have no reprieve. He is being dismantled.

Job's four tragedies cover various agents of destruction: attacks by outsiders, fire falling from the sky, and a mighty wind. Both man and nature are guilty of administering his pain. The choices of men and the chances of nature stand trial for these crimes against Job. He is their judge and jury. His mind and heart deliberate. They race to comprehend his fate. How could such calamities visit simultaneously? The chances of such occurrences are mind-boggling. How great are his losses? Can any scale measure the loss of ten children?

Satan is convinced that more pain should be inflicted. Job's mind and heart lay in waste after Satan's first strike. Now, Satan is given permission to bring pain to Job's body in a second strike. Job 2:7-8 says, "So Satan went out from the presence of the LORD and afflicted Job with painful sores from the soles of his feet to the top of his head. Then Job took a piece of broken pottery and scraped himself with it as he sat among the ashes." Sores transform Job's physical body into a hideous form. The pain brings a level of misery that compels a wish for death. Satan's masterful strokes have captured Job's heart, mind, and body in a checkmate. The game of life should soon be over. Job's wife articulates Satan's goal and advantage. She calls Job to curse God and die.

This is how Job's friends find him. As they sit with him for seven days, do they silently catalog Job's pain? Do they meditate on them in disbelief? If you were to search these events, you would find one or more mirroring your pain. Job can relate to your story. Job's pain may appear to dwarf your pain. But, remember, pain at this level is all the same. What happened to him and to you is immaterial. If you have experienced this level of pain, you can do what Job's friends failed to do; join Job's fraternity.

A LAMENT

Perhaps you know the fraternity song. Listen to a few verses:

Job 3:11-18

"Why did I not perish at birth, and die as I came from the womb? Why were there knees to receive me and breasts that I might be nursed? For now I would be lying down in peace; I would be asleep and at rest with kings and counselors of the earth, who built for themselves places now lying in ruins, with rulers who had gold, who filled their houses with silver. Or why was I not hidden in the ground like a stillborn child, like an infant who never saw the light of day? There the wicked cease from turmoil, and there the weary are at rest. Captives also enjoy their ease; they no longer hear the slave driver's shout."

Job 3:20-26

"Why is light given to those in misery, and life to the bitter of soul, to those who long for death that does not come, who search for it more than for hidden treasure, who are filled with gladness and rejoice when they reach the grave? Why is life given to a man whose way is hidden, whom God has hedged in? For sighing comes to me instead of food; my groans pour out like water. What I feared has come upon me; what I dreaded has happened to me. I have no peace, no quietness; I have no rest, but only turmoil."

Job 6:2-6

"If only my anguish could be weighed and all my misery be placed on the scales! It would surely outweigh the sand of the seas— no wonder my words have been impetuous. The arrows of the Almighty are in me, my spirit drinks in their poison; God's terrors are marshaled against me. Does a wild donkey bray when it has grass, or an ox bellow when it has fodder? Is tasteless food eaten without salt, or is there flavor in the white of an egg? I refuse to touch it; such food makes me ill. Oh, that I might have my request, that God would grant what I hope for, that God would be willing to crush me, to let loose his hand and cut me off!"

Job 7:1-6

"Does not man have hard service on earth? Are not his days like those of a hired man? Like a slave longing for the evening shadows, or a hired man waiting eagerly for his wages, so I have been allotted months of futility, and nights of misery have been assigned to me. When I lie down I think, 'How long before I get up?' The night drags on, and I toss till dawn. My body is clothed with worms and scabs, my skin is broken and festering. My days are swifter than a weaver's shuttle, and they come to an end without hope."

Job 7:13-16

"When I think my bed will comfort me and my couch will ease my complaint, even then you frighten me with dreams and terrify me with visions, so that I prefer strangling and death, rather than this body of mine. I despise my life; I would not live forever. Let me alone; my days have no meaning."

Job sings verse after verse. His pain inspires his heart to compose. He carefully selects words and images to convey the depth of his desperation. Desperation clearly alters his view of life. He believes that death would give him what life fails to provide. Job, the man who has reached the pinnacle of a fulfilling and balanced life, believes that dying at birth would have been better than his present state of pain. Can you believe that? He concludes that the sum total of life's joys does not equal the present value of pain. He is in a miserable state. The staples of life, food and water, are replaced with the staples of pain, sighing and groaning. Peace and rest are lost in the carnage of his circumstances. Even attempting to sleep is futile. The weight of pain is too great for Job. God, the object of his great devotion, is now seen as the governor of his pain-filled state.

As you read Job's lament, you may discover that some words and images reflect and echo your own inner voice. Job does not sing an alien song. Everyone in the fraternity sings along. Pain assembles a choir. Is this a new revelation to you? Do you feel no one knows your pain; the words to your song? Your proficiency in singing may lead you to believe you have a solo. Maybe your pain leads you to feel that you are alone in a dark room. Your pain blinds you. Your desperation makes you deaf. Look around. The room is full.

The Bible proves that others shared Job's song. David sang this song. Psalms 38:6-10 says, "I am bowed down and brought very low; all day long I go about mourning. My back is filled with searing pain; there is no health in my body. I am feeble and utterly crushed; I groan in anguish of heart. All my longings lie open before you, O LORD; my sighing is not hidden from you. My heart pounds, my strength fails me; even the light has gone from my eyes." David's heart is all too familiar with the words. He sings the words to communicate his own pain. Words and images are once again carefully employed.

PAIN MOVES YOU

As you reflect on the words and images, you discover that the song moves the singers along a common path. Pain pulls and pushes each individual. The steps are clearly marked. First, hope gives way to less hope. Then, less hope gives way to being hopeless. Finally, hopeless delivers the weary traveler to the destination, hopelessness. This is the bottom from the top. How can you know that you have arrived? Ask Job. He sees his hope vanishing. He will tell you he has no comfort. He has no sense of support. He has no relief. He has no wish but death. Reread Job 6:8. It says, "Oh, that I might have my request, that God would grant what I hope for, that God would be willing to crush me, to let loose his hand and cut me off!" Hopelessness makes an effort to separate life and the Creator of life.

How strange. From this state of hopelessness, Job is asking that his life be crushed by God's hand. Job 19:2-10 says, "How long will you torment me and crush me with words? Ten times now you have reproached me; shamelessly you attack me. If it is true that I have gone astray, my error remains my concern alone. If indeed you would exalt yourselves above me and use my humiliation against me, then know that God has wronged me and drawn his net around me. Though I cry, 'I've been wronged!' I get no response; though I call for help, there is no justice. He has blocked my way so I cannot pass; he has shrouded my paths in darkness. He has stripped me of my honor and removed the crown from my head. He tears me down on every side till I am gone; he uproots my hope like a tree." Is God responsible for Job's present circumstances? When Job moves from hope to hopelessness, a change occurs. Job is changed and his view of life is transformed. Proverbs 13:12 says, "Hope deferred makes the heart sick, but a longing fulfilled is a tree of life." Job is very sick.

Consider the dynamic world of hope. When you hope, you hope in something or for something. Hope must have an object. Have you ever hoped your car would last a few more months before breaking? Your hope is in the car. Have you ever hoped for a contract to be accepted on a house or apartment? Your hope is in the approval process. Have you ever hoped a girl would say yes to your invitation for dinner? Your hope is for a date. Hope builds the anticipation. In these matters, if the hope is dashed, the object of your hope may be questioned. For example, a rejected dinner invitation by a girl moves you from hopeful to less hopeful. Multiple rejections from the same girl may move you to hopeless.

Multiple rejections from multiple girls may dump you into hopelessness. You question the object of your hope. Are girls worth the trouble? As long as you are in hopelessness, you may never try again. What has happened? Look closely. You have been transformed in this movement. The girl(s) is (are) not to blame.

Neither is God to blame for your hopelessness. Job did not blame God. His spiritual depth fostered his response to adversity. At "ground zero," where Job's world fell apart, he worships God. Job 1:20-22 says, "At this, Job got up and tore his robe and shaved his head. Then he fell to the ground in worship and said: 'Naked I came from my mother's womb, and naked I will depart. The LORD gave and the LORD has taken away; may the name of the LORD be praised.' In all this, Job did not sin by charging God with wrongdoing."

How do you respond to your "ground zero?" You may have a desperate hope God will respond in your critical situation. When God does not respond, remains silent, or appears absent, do you conclude your hope in God is futile? In your desperate state, you wonder why God did not respond. What have you done wrong? Your hope was properly cradled in your great faith. You may have been the model Christian in your world. But, hope is now lost. Like you, Job and David had a strong devotion to God inspiring and rallying followers. But now, their tragedy has altered their spirit.

Look at David's account. Psalms 42:3-5a says, "My tears have been my food day and night, while men say to me all day long, 'Where is your God?' These things I remember as I pour out my soul: how I used to go with the multitude, leading the procession to the house of God, with shouts of joy and thanksgiving among the festive throng. Why are you downcast, O my soul? Why so disturbed within me?" David's world has been inverted. He has lost hope.

The noblest saints and the lowliest sinners stand on equal ground along this path moving hope to hopelessness. Each and every individual takes the same steps of descent. How does one travel in the direction of hopelessness? Notice David's words above; "These things I remember." This one simple phrase captures the propulsion system at work. This is how one moves to the undesirable destination of hopelessness. No one marches willfully. Each one is moved. Can you see it? In your troubled world, you have lots of difficulties but only one option. One item remains within your control. In your out of control world, you are able to choose your thoughts.

When you choose to remember your losses, as did David, you propel yourself towards hopelessness. Lamentations 3:17-20 says, "I have been deprived of peace; I have forgotten what prosperity is. So I say, 'My splendor is gone and all that I had hoped from the LORD.' I remember my affliction and my wandering, the bitterness and the gall. I well remember them, and my soul is downcast within me." Affliction, wandering, bitterness, and gall would individually comprise a severe dose of pain. Each one could easily carry an individual to despair. The writer has selected these words and images to convey a powerful picture of hopelessness.

Take for instance the words "gall" and "wandering." Gall is a bitter herb, a poison. It is a final blow to a tragic situation. Any resolve to persevere under your circumstances crumbles with its toxicity. Hope begs for an antidote. Life screams a silent cry as the body's immune system stands helpless. Wandering is the absence of an anchor for life in the midst of tragedy. A reference point for sanity is nonexistent. Wandering implies that no rest can be found. Life is adrift. No person, place, or thing can bring relief in the weary journey to hopelessness. The writer of Lamentations is very accurate with these four words. He describes the affects of pain. The writer knows each word intimately. He claims to "well remember these things." With each review of his life, his soul is moving. The more he reflects, the more he is downcast.

Individuals believe they can return to hope through self-effort. They attempt to forget the pain by suppressing its reality. Many people prescribe activities and meditations aimed at freeing the mind from these concerns. Many more people actively participate giving testimony they have found hope. But their hope is false. They have only stumbled upon a mirage on the road to hopelessness. Their effort to forget will be as successful as holding your breath underwater. Soon, you will have to breathe and admit your pain is still present.

SEEING THROUGH REALITY

But the writer of Lamentations is not finished. He does not end in his despair. He makes a profound declaration resulting in an immediate change. As he is swept away in the raging torrent of his collapsing life, he pulls the ultimate Houdini. His next few words in this passage reveal that he finds hope. How did he do that? Imagine Houdini being handcuffed and placed in a barrel. This barrel is dropped into the Niagara River destined to find the Niagara Falls. While the barrel moves closer to the falls, you think Houdini's fate is doomed. How could the great Houdini escape this difficulty? The crowd holds their breath. Then the unthinkable happens. To everyone's amazement, Houdini shouts from the riverbank. He is not only saved, but stands triumphant on a large rock. How is this possible? Who knows? The audience only knows that the great Houdini continues to amaze everyone.

The writer of Lamentations pulls off a similar feat. He moves from the doom of hopelessness to the bedrock of hope with one phrase. At that moment, when fate wooed death, hope arrived. How is this possible? Lamentations 3:21 says, "Yet this I call to mind and therefore I have hope." This phrase is his key. He chooses to think about something other than his troubles. By doing so, he is transformed. He still has the reality of his troubles, but a new reality has just been introduced. How does the new reality affect the old?

The writer is not forgetting the old reality. He masterfully manages both. He does not superimpose one reality over the other. Imagine two pictures being superimposed. Such an activity would distort both and cause confusion. The writer of Lamentations has another trick up his sleeve. He masks one reality with the other. A magician will tell you his trade is not magic but only illusion. He has mastered the skill of directing your attention to what he wants you to see. You, the viewer, perceive only one of two realities presently employed by the illusionist. You cannot see the other reality he desires to hide from you. The reality you are allowed to see masks the other. In a similar fashion, the writer of Lamentations is recalling to mind a new reality. What he now chooses to remember begins to mask his previous thoughts. The troubles are not gone. They only fade.

Imagine looking up into the sky on a clear night. The space above your sight is filled with countless stars. Imagine each star represents your affliction, wandering, bitterness, and gall. The more you look up the more your spirit moves down. This is the first reality. When the sun comes out, the stars disappear and the sky turns to a vivid blue. This new reality brings warmth and life to the soul. But, where is the darkness? Where are the stars? They are still there! Look up. The stars have not changed one bit. The darkness has not moved. Stare hard. Peer through the blue ceiling. The black sky and the countless stars yield to the sun. Nothing has changed but what you see. One reality, the sun, has masked the other, the stars.

In your world, one reality may be the troubles of life, the stars of a night sky. The other reality can be found in Lamentations 3:21. Reread the passage to notice what "this" is recalling. Lamentations 3:21-24 says, "Yet this I call to mind and therefore I have hope. Because of the LORD's great love we are not consumed, for his compassions never fail. They are

THE TREE IN THE MIDDLE OF MY GARDEN

new every morning; great is your faithfulness. I say to myself, 'The LORD is my portion; therefore I will wait for him.'" "This" in the passage is God.

The writer moves from remembering his circumstances to remembering God. He willfully engages a new reality to embrace God. The writer of Lamentations is convinced God is faithful in troubled times. He declares that the Lord is good to those who hope in Him. The new reality of God's person brings hope. The message is clear. God is the object and the source of hope. His love preserves your life. The writer of Lamentations says you are not consumed with God. You are saved in the midst of your inferno. Look at a fire. When fire burns an object, only ashes remain. The ashes seldom hold the identity of the object. Ashes are ashes. Burn several objects in a single fire. Each is reduced to ashes. The identity of each object is destroyed by fire. As your world burns to ashes around you, God's love protects you. You will not join the ash heap. You will not be lost. Hope in hopelessness makes you the phoenix rising from the ashes. You will taste the victory given to Shadrach, Meshach and Abednego (Daniel 3).

THE LORD'S PROVISION

The writer of Lamentations said that the Lord's compassion never fails. Compassion is God's love helping those in need. The helping nature of God does not have an end. He never stops. He helps when no one else can or will. Do you remember the first few days, or even months of your difficulty? You may have found aid and comfort from different individuals. But as time passed and your troubles persisted, the best intentions of these individuals could not endure indefinitely. People say they love you, but they return to their lives. Only God can go the distance.

The writer believes these considerations from God are new each morning. The new morning paints several wonderful images. The morning is a blessed time. To see a morning in that day was considered an accomplishment. With the morning, the mystery, danger, and uncertainty of the night are over. In the morning, the earth seems replenished as if it experienced a good night of sleep. The dew on the ground, the coolness in the air, and the start of the Sun's journey across the sky compel a feeling of delight and anticipation. Within this morning wonderland, God's promises seem replenished. The delight and anticipation of God's intervention covers life with a fresh layer of hope.

The morning has another great picture to offer. Imagine a campfire. In the evening, the fire burns with a brilliant flame. Warmth and light stretch from its core to embrace many standing within its reach. As the wood is consumed, the fire settles into a hot nest of embers. Overnight, the embers cool. When morning arrives, a blanket of ash covers the pit. The embers are silent. The morning chill calls for a new fire. You may conclude a new fire seems hopeless on this site. But, an experienced camper knows different.

To birth a new flame, a new site is not necessary. The old pit is not hopeless. The sleeping embers are awakened with a stick. As the stick moves the embers, signs of life appear. Gray embers breathe. Soon, the gray embers are magically transformed to red. The pit glows with warmth. A small flame rises as fresh wood is added to the pit. Eventually, the fire returns to its previous glory. Hope has been manifested from hopelessness.

The seasoned camper is not surprised by the results of his effort. He knows the potential of the pit and the process needed to bring about the results. In this way, the pit is faithful to perform to its potential. Faithfulness is a measure of God's character. The writer of Lamentations identifies God's faithfulness as great. Psalms 71:19-22 says, "Your righteousness reaches to the skies, O God, you who have done great things. Who, O God, is like you? Though you have made me see troubles, many and bitter, you will restore my life again; from the depths of the earth you will again bring me up. You will increase my honor and comfort me once again. I will praise you with the harp for your faithfulness, O my God; I will sing praise to you with the lyre, O Holy One of Israel." God's great faithfulness has been evident throughout the course of human history.

The writer of Lamentations claims the Lord as his portion. The word "portion" communicates a substantive supply in the context of a meal. Imagine facing hunger in an adverse setting. Mealtime is tough if uncertainty surrounds the experience. At the table, each portion is distributed from the whole. If there is not enough food, some individuals will receive no portion. So, you sit and wait. You know that food is available. But, you do not know if you will receive any. In his uncertainty, the writer expresses profound confidence. The Lord is his portion. The Lord will supply what is required for life. The material world may be experiencing scarcity, but sufficiency prevails with God. In this certainty, the writer is content to wait patiently for the Lord. Philippians 4:19 says, "And my God will meet all your needs according to his glorious riches in Christ Jesus." The Lord is able to meet you at the point of your need.

Job has no problem with this claim. He is constantly hoping in God. God's character does not disappoint Job's hope. In the end, a new flame burns for Job. Job's worldly possessions are restored. He is blessed to have twice what he had before his tragedies. Fourteen thousand sheep, six thousand camels, a thousand yoke of oxen and a thousand donkeys graze in his fields. His extended family members give him gifts of gold and silver. Most of all, Job fathers seven more sons and three more daughters (Job 42:12-13). Job has a great finish. Job 42:16-17 says, "After this, Job lived a hundred and forty years; he saw his children and their children to the fourth generation. And so he died, old and full of years."

The story of Job is inspiring. His life is a revelation for those who journey on the path to hopelessness. Job hopes in God. You may have heard someone say, "When you are down, you have no place to look but up." This is very true. When you look up, see the sky. Your two realities await you. Will you see the darkness and the stars representing your pain? Or, will you see the sun and blue skies representing God's provisions? If God is the reality you embrace during your tragedy, He should overwhelm any opportunity you may have to see your difficulties. Try looking at the blue sky to see stars. You will find this exercise an impossibility. As you drive, walk, or look out your living room window, let the blue sky remind your heart that God is in control. He is your hope. He holds your life in His hands. When you cannot see the darkness and stars, remind your heart that God is caring for your needs. He will.

Sing a new song with Job, David, and others who claim God as their hope:

Psalms 145:1-21

"I will exalt you, my God the King; I will praise your name for ever and ever. Every day I will praise you and extol your name for ever and ever. Great is the LORD and most worthy of praise; his greatness no one can fathom. One generation will commend your works to another; they will tell of your mighty acts. They will speak of the glorious splendor of your majesty, and I will meditate on your wonderful works. They will tell of the power of your awesome works, and I will proclaim your great deeds. They will celebrate your abundant goodness and joyfully sing of your righteousness. The LORD is gracious and compassionate, slow to anger and rich in love. The LORD is good to all; he has compassion on all he has made. All you have made will praise you, O LORD; your saints will extol you. They will tell of the glory of your kingdom and speak of your might, so that all men may know of your mighty acts and the glorious splendor of your kingdom. Your kingdom is an everlasting kingdom, and your dominion endures through all generations. The LORD is faithful to all his promises and loving toward all he has made. The LORD upholds all those who fall and lifts up all who are bowed down. The eyes of all look to you, and you give them their food at the proper time. You open your hand and satisfy the desires of every living thing. The LORD is righteous in all his ways and loving toward all he has made. The LORD is near to all who call on him, to all who call on him in truth. He fulfills the desires of those who fear him; he hears their cry and saves them. The LORD watches over all who love him, but all the wicked he will destroy. My mouth will speak in praise of the LORD. Let every creature praise his holy name for ever and ever."

THE BRILLIANCE OF A FRETLESS LIFE

Why didn't the skeleton cross the road? Because he didn't have any guts! Why don't cannibals eat clowns? They taste funny! Wow! You easily recognize these as bad jokes. They are totally ridiculous. Fortunately, I only tell these jokes to make a comparison. A great comedian is paid millions of dollars to deliver jokes. Their jokes can cause you to roll in your seats with laughter. You laugh so hard you soon forget to breathe. This is the power of comedy. I aspire to that. I would love to help people experience these moments. But my world of joke telling and that of real comedians are worlds apart.

In life, you experience many worlds. You may live worlds apart from where you should. No, earth is not one choice among several celestial bodies. Yet, your world may not be as brilliant as other possible worlds. Listen to the difference between a good joke and a bad joke. What do you notice? One brings laughter and the other brings a disbelieving chuckle. What about life? Is life bad or good? When you encounter your day, how do you respond? Are you filled with laughter? Or, do you respond with a disbelieving chuckle.

I am not proposing your beautiful life is a joke being played out. Instead, I believe there may be a brilliant contrast between your world and the world God offers. One world is far apart from the other. God's world is far from fretting. The brilliance of a fretless life is a world where challenges, worry and anxiety lack power. Fretless (by the way) is not the difference between the guitar neck and the violin neck. Sorry, I know. Another bad joke.

Psalms 37: 1-2 says, "Do not fret because of evil men or be envious of those who do wrong. For like the grass, they will soon wither. Like green plants, they will soon die away." David, the writer of this Psalm is helping you understand the world of fretting. By watching evil or wrong doers, you experience discomfort. They tend to take their world by storm. Their world seems void of the natural laws governing your world. They seem to have an advantage. David gives a clear charge: do not fret. The evil men and the wrong doers do not last long. This is David's opening observation.

Lying on his bed, David surveys his own life. He is calling an end to fretting because he knows its power. Follow the journey of David's life. You will find that David had lots of opportunity for anxiety and lots of reasons for fretting. When David, the "to be" king, was anticipating God's promise of a throne, Saul, the present king, was creating all kinds of grief for him. The evil men and wrong doers were all around David. David speaks from experience: "Don't fret! Don't fret!" This is a simple instruction with a very powerful principle.

You probably lie on your bed reflecting on your day. What do you think about? As you think, your heart begins to beat faster, the breathing begins to race, and the anxiety starts to take grip. Sometimes it seems, no matter where you start, you always find yourselves in the same anxious spot. Have you been there? Why is the bed such a fruitful place for thought? The bed was designed to be a place of rest. Instead, rest is lost in the weary exercise of worrying.

FRET PHYSIOLOGY

The Hebrew word for fret (*charah*, Khaw-raw') brings an image leading you to David's intent. It is the image of something beginning to glow, to grow warm, or to kindle. At a campfire, you may watch the flame of the fire slowly die. However, just the slightest breeze across the campsite brings new life to the fire. You will see the embers brighten and intensify. Sometimes, a finger of flame will emerge from the hot cavity of the fire pit disturbed by the breeze.

That is the way fretting works in your life. The brain may be the fire pit. The issues and people are elements within the pit. You start to think about all the things happening in your life. The pain of waiting or the agony of worrying builds an energy that grows the longer you linger in its company. Think of waiting as something taking movement, from being still to having life, energy, and vitality. The issues and people in life consume your hope and joy to generate this growing energy.

My favorite image of fretting is that of a child needing to go to the bathroom. Have you watched a child in this state? They first try to ignore the need. Soon when their need becomes more pressing, they begin to move; slowly at first and then with odd steps back and forth. The sound of these steps disappear amid a growing cry, " I need to go to the bathroom." Then, bouncing up and down in one spot is the next stage. Finally, the bouncing is rejoined by all the previous elements. The little child begins to wiggle, squirm, and jump. That's it! That is what fretting looks like inside you. For the child, there is only one solution, with or without a bathroom.

Do you get the picture? How well do you respond when things are challenging, consuming your mind, and ripping at the soul? What kind of picture do you see of yourself? Fidgeting? Wiggling about? Do you have an anxiousness to do something or make something happen? Do you want to find relief? Fretting is just like the embers glowing or like a child needing a bathroom. Fretting is the evolution of waiting-to-waiting not so well. It encourages action and anticipates resolution. Fretting comes as the result of your response to needs and wants in your life.

We all have needs. Basic to survival, life could not be lived without these elements. We need food, shelter, and clothing. Additionally, there are other needs, maybe wants if defined properly. In our life, these things make the experience of life much more meaningful, or maybe just more colorful. So, we wait, and wait. In this process, life creates the platform for fretting. Needs and wants in and of themselves do not create fretting. They are elements that facilitate fretting. They interact with time to produce fretting. With the campfire, time is the breeze. With the child, time is the eminent necessity of needing a bathroom. If I had needs and wants, and time was not a factor, then my needs and wants would not have the effect that leads to fretting.

Several years ago, a magazine reported the results of a study researching "emotional quotient." We may all be familiar with "Intelligence Quotient or IQ." A person's IQ served as a predictor for success. If a person did well on this intelligence test, high IQ, they were assigned a high potential for success in life. Emotional Quotient, or "EQ," is not a test. It is a simple task to determine whether children could wait. Here is how it worked.

One five-year-old was brought into a room. The child was asked to sit at a table. A stack of marshmallows was placed on the table. The person conducting the test would say to the child, "I'm going to leave the room. I don't want you to do anything with the marshmallows. When I come back, I will give you a marshmallow." This was the simplicity of the study. The test person would leave, and a team would watch the child from a viewing area. Guess what would happen?

Some children did really well. They just sat and looked at the marshmallows. Others would fidget in their chairs. Others could wait, but they could not be still. They would sit on their hands. Others would get up and walk around the room. They would walk around the table. Or, go under the table; anywhere as long as it was not near the marshmallows. There were some children who would go up to the marshmallows and pick one up. After looking at it, they would put it back. Then there were some children who would take the marshmallows and lick it. Hoping no one noticed, they would return the marshmallow to its place. A few children ate a marshmallow.

The children were given an EQ score based on their activity in the room. The children, who did not touch the marshmallows, were given a high EQ score. The children, who ate the marshmallows, were given the lowest EQ score. The activity between these parameters received corresponding scores. For years, scientists watched the children. They discovered that the high EQ rating children were far more successful in life than the children with the low EQ rating. The validity of this test may be debated. But its hypothesis seems to validate a principle: people who learn to wait are building for success.

WAITING ELEMENTS

Regardless of your situation, all the factors of life inviting the waiting process seem to share a common ground, time. The children were asked to wait. This involved time. Fretting cannot accept the factor of time in the equation of waiting. Time is the space between the start and finish line. So you run. You run faster and faster, but you cannot soon run any faster. The more time you need in waiting for something, the more desperate you become. You want time to hurry. You want things to just get there! You want to graduate quickly. You want to get married quickly. You want to get over a health issue quickly. You desperately want what you wait for, but you defiantly do not want to wait. Fretting is the product of not accepting the time factor God has placed in the things He has promised. Think about that. Fretting is your unfavorable response to the time factor that God has ordained.

So you must wait. Yes, God's desire may be for you to have certain things, but give it time. How well do you do when waiting is the present order of business? David recognizes when you are waiting, you can see evil people and wrong doers. These people are not focused on God but arrive at things you long for. By watching them, you are tempted to do something. Watch youth squander their purity because they will not wait. They say everyone is doing it. Watch people cheat on their taxes because they will not wait to reach monetary goals. They may rationalize that prosperity could expand their opportunity to give to God.

Needs and wants expressed as difficulties and challenges in your life may be a number of things. It may be finances. It may be school. It may be friends. It may be family members. It may be your social activities. It may be work. It may be your spouse. It may be your children. It may be your car. It may be your neighbors. It may be your house. It may be your health. It may be the absence of these. It may be a unique combination of these. It may be what may be. Who knows what it will be? But one thing seems to be very true, it will be. Waiting is part of life.

David is right on the mark when he says, "Don't fret." Fretting is like some level of activity experienced by the children who just couldn't sit still in the study. A lot of times, you are just like those little children. Have you noticed that in your life? God tells you to wait on something and you are pacing around. He tells you to wait on something and you are "touching it" hoping He doesn't mind too much. And some of us jump right in and get way ahead of God. Waiting is God's vehicle for testing and building your faith. Waiting is God's opportunity to see the substance of your relationship with Him.

The Psalmist makes application of this idea. Psalms 130:5-6 says, "I wait for the LORD, my soul waits, and in his word I put my hope. My soul waits for the LORD more than watchmen wait for the morning, more than watchmen wait for the morning." A long march to dawn tested the resolve of any night watchman. But, they waited. Waiting is showing your love for God. Waiting is an invitation to a unique relationship with God that stretches your resolve and intensifies your dependency upon Him. Waiting is not about time. Waiting is about trust.

You cannot adjust time. You cannot make it go faster or slower. You cannot make it stop. Time is independent of you. Clearly, trust is the dependent variable inviting your participation. You can determine if you will trust or not. Do you trust God? Do you? Consider one example. You may not be married at a time when almost all of your friends seem to be. Girls sometimes say, "Always the bridesmaid, never the bride." Maybe not being married makes you really anxious at times. You may be 18, 22, 27, 30 or even 40, 50 or 80. If this is your issue, regardless of your age, you may think you have waited long enough. What children? How long do you have to wait? In all of life's issues, you want to determine the time variable. Out of desperation you call to God saying, "God! What about me?" The thought process kicks in and you produce ample argument to prove your case before God.

Think about your trust relationship with God right now. Think about your faith, your ability to take this great God who created the universe at His word. David, in Psalms 37 says, "Do not fret because of evil men or be envious of those who do wrong; for like the grass they will soon wither, like green plants they will soon die away." Compare that to what Psalms 1:3 says, "Blessed is the man who does not walk in the counsel of the wicked or stand in the way of sinners or sit in the seat of mockers. But his delight is in the law of the LORD, and on his law he meditates day and night. He is like a tree planted by streams of water, which yields its fruit in season and whose leaf does not wither. Whatever he does prospers." David is making a brilliant contrast for you. He is showing the difference between individuals who trust God and those who follow evil individuals. Do you see the comparison in these two extremes, grass and tree? They are worlds apart.

CORRECT WAITING

Are you like grass or are you like a tree? In Psalms 37:7, David continues, "Be still before the LORD and wait patiently for Him. Do not fret when men succeed in their ways. When they carry out their wicked schemes." David spells this out. How do you respond to fretting in your life? The answer is like dousing water on the flame and embers attempting to glow. David says the right response to fretting is to "be still." Are you good at being still? Sometimes it seems like a joke for me to think about being still. I have difficulty being still. Being still? Wow!

My dad had a great punishment for me growing up when he wanted my total attention. Spanking could not have had as great a result as his special brand of punishment. I had to kneel in front of my dad. The kneeling posture had to be right; high and straight. If I failed to maintain the correct kneeling posture, he would encourage my whole-hearted participation with a firm tangible reminder. My dad wanted to communicate something very important to me. Being still gave me the chance to think through what was happening.

God isn't trying to punish you. He is trying to make a point with you, be still! Psalms 46:10 says, "Be still, and know that I am God. I will be exalted among the nations. I will be exalted in the earth." The whole idea behind being still is captured in the opportunity for you to collect your thoughts, to realize the true picture of your circumstances, and to get the true picture of God in the midst of those circumstances. What does it mean to know that God is God? Take a moment to survey the implication of this passage. God had no beginning. He has no end. He spoke all things into being. He is all knowing. He is all-powerful. He is the only God. He is Holy. He is kind. He is faithful. He is… and is and is and is and is…. As you are still, you detach from your pressing circumstance, and more importantly, you attach to your eternal Maker.

Psalms 37:7 backs up this idea. The writer said, "Wait patiently for Him." Not just "wait." This waiting is a mandate with specific clarity. He is telling you how to wait: patiently. How do you know you are waiting correctly? In realty this may be simpler than it would seem. If you are waiting with the object of your waiting in mind, you will become stressed the longer you wait. Say your boyfriend needs time to think about your relationship, and you wait for him to call. Say you are hungry, and you cannot wait to have food. Say you own stock, and you are hoping it goes through the roof. Say you are waiting for a job, and you are checking your email every hour for a message. This is waiting with object-centered waiting.

Once a phrase filled my mind that championed the wrong kind of waiting. The misguided phrase that I believed was from God stated: If God wills it, let it be so, if He won't, let it go. Like the rhyme? My mind and heart rehearsed this motto. Then one day, a picture came to my mind that really opened my eyes. I saw a child at a grocery story shopping with her mom. She held up a package and said, "Here mommy, can you buy this for me." Defying her mom's refusal, she continued to hold the package. Not until the checkout lane did the child release the object. That was the final point. The object had to be released. My phrase had a built-in flaw.

It implied the object of my waiting had been held in my hand until it was denied. I gave it to God, but it remained in my possession. My affection was directed to the object. How often are you like this? You pray for something: my car needs to be fixed, my house must sell, my son needs to break free of his addiction, and the list goes on and on. For some of these things, you may not get what you ask. Nevertheless, you hang on to it until God is forced to finally say no with necessary punctuation. The agony of the object-centered waiting leads to fretting.

Wait, but wait correctly. If you wait with God in mind, the waiting period and process builds you as you wait. This is how you can tell you are waiting correctly. The better you are waiting the better you see God at work and your heart's affection draws to His. When you wait with God in mind, God-centered, you release the object of your waiting into His capable hands. This waiting produced a new phrase: "God's will, God's way or no way."

The people of Israel are a great case study on waiting. They had prayed and cried to God for several generations to be delivered from slavery. But, when they were released and in the wilderness, they longed to be back in Egypt. Why? Because! They prayed and waited with an object-centered attitude. Sure, they wanted freedom. But, they wanted freedom on their terms. Exodus 14:11-14 says, "Was it because there were no graves in Egypt that you brought us to the desert to die? What have you done to us by bringing us out of Egypt? Didn't we say to you in Egypt, 'Leave us alone; let us serve the Egyptians'? It would have been better for us to serve the Egyptians than to die in the desert!" Moses answered the people, "Do not be afraid. Stand firm and you will see the deliverance the LORD will bring you today. The Egyptians you see today you will never see again. The LORD will fight for you; you need only to be still."

Catch this last phrase: "You need only be still." WOW! Why be still? Follow the previous few words. God is at work. He is the great I AM. His plan will be greater than anyone could have imagined. God promised to deliver them. Furthermore, they were told they would never see the Egyptians again. God was not only solving an immediate problem, but he was freeing the Israelites for good. What a promise. How could they handle their dilemma?

They are pressed against the waters. The great Egyptian army is moving toward their position. Certainly, several ingenious leaders could have stepped forward with battle plans. Move the women and children near the water, send the men to the front to meet the Egyptians. By standing against the Egyptians, Israel is being asked to do something quite extraordinary. The thundering sound of horses can be heard. The great chariots of the Egyptian army are battle hungry. The people have known the pain of an Egyptian slave-master's whip. Will they soon know the poison of the Egyptian sword? Pharaoh and his armies are drunk with a passion to return the Israelites to Egypt. For the people of Israel, the waters are at their back. A massive army is before them. Hopelessness and fear mark their every turn. The sights and sounds of desperation fill the air. They cry out to God and to Moses. God clearly says wait and be still. Wait? Be still? That is it?

Can you relate to their plight? When have you felt like this? Issues in your life seem to place you in this type of grip. Picture the circumstance in your life producing conditions that make desperation your only option. Your backside is blocked by an impossible physical hindrance. Your front side hosts an army of great challenges: everything you face seems to build against you. When you keep your eyes on circumstances, you move to hopelessness with ease. You become fearful, and as a result, you begin to pace and scheme. Regardless of what your lips may say to God, your eyes are guiding your heart. The Israelites are directed by Moses to watch the Lord fight for them. Who could have imagined what God did? The Egyptian war machine encountered a force from God that easily crushed them. God was not playing games. Be still Israel. Be still. When they obeyed, they could see God bringing incredible victory.

When you cry out to God in a God-centered waiting experience, you can have confidence that God is working on your behalf. Psalms 27: 13 says, "I am still confident of this: I will see the goodness of the

LORD in the land of the living." You may not see the supernatural events seen by the people of Israel in the wilderness. But, you can have full assurance God is acting on your behalf as passionately as He moved in the midst of the Israelites. The prophet in Isaiah 30:18 says, "the LORD longs to be gracious to you; he rises to show you compassion. For the LORD is a God of justice. Blessed are all who wait for Him!" This passage clearly marks the spirit of God's attention in response to your waiting. He is not passive.

GOD MOVES WHILE YOU WAIT

Can you see the picture here? God longs to be gracious to you. Can you understand this longing? Consider this thought. Do you remember your first consuming crush? Do you remember waiting for Christmas to arrive? Individually, anyone of these longings is very intense. Imagine combining all the longings in a lifetime. This would be very intense. The intensity of a longing is only as powerful as it affects attention. Great longing may produce great focus. God's longing is powerful and perfectly intense.

God also rises to show you compassion. Have you ever been lazy on the couch? You ask for the remote. Someone responds that the remote is on top of the television. The television is only a few feet away. You ask them to get the remote for you. You are lazy and they are lazy. No one moves. Finally, you decide to move. The effort feels monumental. If someone jumps up to retrieve the remote for you, how wonderful would you feel? The example is very, very trivial, but it makes a simple point. God rises for you.

If you explored this truth in a deeper God-centered way, you may realize God moves because you cannot. Imagine now that you are in a hospital bed. You ask for the remote. Someone must respond because you cannot get out of bed. When you realize this reality, God rising on our behalf is the only option you possess. Now, the wonderful feeling produced by someone rising on your behalf has meaning.

God is the God of Justice. When Isaiah is calling for you to wait on God, he is calling you to wait on God's nature. The nature of the world is different. You want the world to do right. But, over and over again, the world seems to exploit wrong. When wrong is done, you want justice. The pictures of injustice in the world compel the masses to cry out. You cry out to those who enforce the laws of the land. Police officers and judges apply their trade attempting to respond to your need. But justice is not guaranteed. When Isaiah calls God the God of Justice, he makes a powerful statement about justice. It's a guarantee. God will do right.

With these truths, waiting seems more palatable. But Isaiah does not promote "waiting made easier." Sure the above truths ease the waiting process, but ease is not Isaiah's goal. He ends this thought with "Blessed." Those who wait on the Lord are blessed. In the midst of the waiting process, the waiter is blessed. Imagine the people of Israel. The Lord longs to be gracious to them. He rises to show them compassion. He is their God of Justice. Have you ever considered Israel as being blessed in the midst of their wilderness? The wilderness experience is a blessed journey. Isaiah 30:18 attempts to instill confidence in God.

The people of Israel were filled with fear at the water's edge. But fear was not intended to be the present order of business. God calls us to be strong in His presence. When you wait, fear attempts to derail your resolve. You must stand firm, be still, and know that He is God. Paul says in 2 Timothy 1:7, "For God hath not given us the spirit of fear; but of power, and of love, and of a sound mind." (KJV) Affirming the movement of God's Spirit, Paul says items will be manifested in you: power, love and a sound mind.

After Jesus' departure, the disciples manifested what Paul declared. Jesus told them to wait. The disciples waited as their first act of obedience after Jesus' ascension. They may have been tempted to do much more. Their Lord had risen from the dead. They had seen His very presence, heard His voice, and touched His body. Perhaps they wanted to tell someone. Who would they tell? What would they say? They had so much excitement following the ascension. Yet, in the midst of all this excitement, they were asked to wait.

Their excitement may have been accompanied by some fear. What if those who crucified Christ hear that a group of his followers were meeting? An army may amass to greet them as Jesus was greeted at the Garden of Gethsemane. How long were they to wait? What were they waiting for? Their instruction was to wait. As they waited, they were God-centered. Acts 1:14 records their resolve to wait with God in mind. Verse 14 states, "They all joined together constantly in prayer, along with the women and Mary the mother of Jesus, and with his brothers." When their waiting was complete, the vigilant manifested power, provided through the Holy Spirit's spiritual gifts. Love was evident in their practice of sharing with one another. Sound mind was present in Peter's Pentecost message.

Whatever your situation, do not fear. Whatever your challenge, do not fear. Whoever is against you, do not fear. Basically, the message is do not fear. Fear works like a fuel. If time is the breeze that brings life to the embers, fear is like pouring gasoline into the heart of the fire pit. Fear propels the fretting process and ignites improper action. Trust God and know where He stands in the midst of your turbulent world. Here is an image that Isaiah painted to help Israel understand. Isaiah 41:13 says, "For I am the LORD, your God, who takes hold of your right hand and says to you, Do not fear; I will help you."

God is holding you. Have you ever experienced a great physical pain resulting from a quick and sudden injury? Suppose you stubbed your toe as a child. Do your remember the pain? Remember how that pain consumed your complete thought? The world around you was unknown. You may have cried out for your parent. Where were they? When the pain diminished, as pains mostly do, your world comes back into focus. Strangely, you feel arms wrapped around you. You realize your parent is holding you. They have been holding you since you began your cry. I picture God holding me. Even when my life pain is so great that I do not or cannot acknowledge His presence, He is there, faithfully. Can you feel His strong hand? This is the precious picture I see when waiting is my calling.

Isaiah adds one more incredible image in verse thirteen, "For I am the LORD, your God, who takes hold of your right hand and says to you, Do not fear; I will help you." God is holding your hand. Once I spoke to a hurting teen. Difficulties from his childhood left him feeling like he was in the dark; no light present to bring understanding to his turbulent world. He wanted some light. He cried out to God to move him from the darkness. As I spoke with him, I quickly realized that long-term counseling would be required. In the short term, I asked him to seek the hand of the Lord.

In a completely dark room, you cannot see your hand before your face. The fear produced from such a room is quite intense. Often, a desperate longing to escape into any light pushes the heart. But, when someone is in the room with you and holds your hand, your heart calms. God holds your hand in this way. He can easily push the darkness from the room. For the moment, this may not be His will. Nevertheless, He is there for you. He can see where you cannot. He provides His presence. He gives His assurance. I asked the teen to consider the power of this truth in his dark world. What about you? Can you see God holding your hand? What a beautiful picture you and God make. Don't keep your eyes on your situation, object-centered, but move your eyes to God and trust His incredible hand of power. When you do, you are able to be still.

TOUGH AND BALANCED

One of the greatest examples of patient waiting may be with trees. Do you admire trees? Their beauty and size amaze me. My neighbor remembers when all the trees in our neighborhood were planted. For decades they have occupied the same spot. They have never moved. What an amazing thought. Lie down next to a tree to discover the space they have always known. Have you ever seen a tree fret? Can you imaging a tree fretting? A tree does the two things very well that God wants us to do: "be still," and "wait."

The Methuselah tree found in California holds the claim to the oldest tree in the world. It's about 5,000 years old. This tree was alive when the pyramids were built. You may think to survive this long the oldest tree would be grown in the most nurturing, protected, and pleasant environment possible. But in reality, the environment is quite different. The tree grows in the shadow of the Sierra Nevada which blocks weather approaching from the West. The annual precipitation is less than 12 inches; most coming as snow. The summer has about six weeks of warmth. The soil for this plant is not dirt, but Dolomite. It is a limestone-substrate with hardly any nutrients. Growth is very, very slow. The oldest tree in the world grew in a place that was not pleasant.

Picture yourself like a tree in Psalms 1; firmly planted by streams of living water. The Psalmist is not painting a picture with difficulties. He is not looking at your circumstances but focusing on the source to which your roots attach. He is aware your source of life is from the Lord. You draw from Him. The streams of living water aim to depict the vitality of your relationship with God. Philippians 4:19 says, "And my God will meet all your needs according to his glorious riches in Christ Jesus." In light of this truth, the Psalmist is correct.

Look again at the picture of the planted tree. Notice the Psalmist says the tree is firmly planted. Trees should not move very easily. Their roots are intended to bring stability. The roots provide strength. Winds can prove devastating to a tree. High wind brought forth in a storm can challenge the strength of any tree and push them from their place. If the roots of a tree are strong, firmly planted, then the tree will stand in any storm.

When you wait, you must see the strength of your relationship with God. This strength will hold you steady. The storms in your life may be producing powerful winds. Winds that push hard against your face driving breath from your lungs. Psalms 27:14 says, "Wait for the LORD; be strong and take heart and wait for the LORD." Strength and courage facilitate waiting. When you wait with God in mind, how can challenges and issues move you? They must push against God holding you.

If you don't wait, you begin fretting. Those embers that begin to glow when the wind blows over them are doing something. You cannot fret for long without something resulting. You have to deal with fretting or fretting will deal with you. The product of fretting is found in Psalms 37. Verse 8 says, "Refrain from anger and turn from wrath; do not fret— it leads only to evil." Look at every word that the writer uses to bring understanding. He says, "Don't be angry, don't be wrathful." The wrong product of fretting is the product that involves anger and wrath.

Anger may be an imbalance in your life. Anger sometimes is the result of things not going the way you want them to go. It's a question of trusting God. In a movie, a wife is laying in bed with her husband who suffers from schizophrenia. She attempts to have an intimate physical experience with him. Influenced by his medication, he does not reciprocate. Frustrated, she leaves the bed. She goes into the bathroom and throws her fist into the mirror screaming as the mirror shatters. That was anger! She may have felt she did not deserve this difficultly in her life.

There is a balancing act between humility and pride. A healthy element of pride in your life is embodied in each individual. You are a precious expression of God's wisdom in creation. Humility in your life acknowledges you are dependent on God. The imbalance may occur when you are object centered. When you are stressed out on the humility side, you say, "I don't deserve this! I don't deserve waiting all these years for this! Life should be better than this." Or, if you get pulled over to the pride side, you may say, "I deserve this, God. Why has God not delivered this yet?" Imbalance may be the order of the day in an object-centered waiting experience.

The Psalmist is calling you to be careful! He is concerned about anger and wrath. When fretting is encouraged by anger and wrath, you will be tempted to take matters into your own hands. If fretting is the movement from being still to having energy, then the Psalmist is correct to say fretting leads to evil doing. Watch the process. You are asked to wait. You cannot stand the time factor. You start to think about the object of your waiting. You fail to trust God because you stopped watching Him and started watching the clock. Soon you want to do something to make something happen.

COLLATERAL EFFECTS

When fretting gets to action, you are usually trying to do things without God. If you allow fretting to continue, it begins to grow. Anger and wrath builds because you stopped talking to God and started talking to yourself. Eventually, you take matters into your own hands. You will do this or that. Whatever it takes, until that which you want is yours. In this process, you always push towards that which you long for in your object-centered waiting. Pushing will lead to your own pain. Stop! Just be still.

When I was in elementary school, my brother and I decided to catch birds in my backyard. We took a plastic clothes hamper; the kind with holes. We propped the hamper up with a stick and tied a string to the stick. We ran the string across the backyard and into my sister's bedroom window. We put bread all around the hamper and then inside it. Returning to my sister's window, we waited. The birds came to eat the bread. First they were all around the hamper. And then, as if scripted in a movie, a single bird went under the hamper.

We pulled the string and the stick fell. The clothes hamper dropped. The trap worked perfectly. My brother and I ran through the house to the backyard. We couldn't believe it! We caught a bird. As soon as we hit the backyard, we noticed the bird was ballistic inside the hamper. We first attempted to calm the bird, but our presence only made matters worse. It bounced from side to side, often with forces that rocked the hamper from the ground. Finally, we noticed the bird had caught its neck in a hamper hole. We quickly decided to release the desperate bird. Lifting the hamper, the bird was free. Before long, the freed bird was dead from the cut around its neck.

This is the image of what fretting means when it leads to evil. God sometimes sees you under the pressure of waiting. It may seem to you like a cage. You start fretting. Soon you are going ballistic. Decisions become confused and desperate. As a result, you bring harm to yourselves and maybe to people around you. The objects of your waiting seem more and more hopeless. You try this and then that. You move and move and move. Your loving God looks at you and says, "Be still! Be still!" God watches you in the same way I watched the desperate bird. All your desperate movement is only producing pain, evil.

With fretting, you have an uncertain, dark, and, miserable view of life. Without fretting, you can be in a place where gloomy hopelessness gives way to sunshine. Sound like an unbelievable contrast, two worlds not the same. In Psalms 37: 1-6, the Lord paints this great picture of a life without fretting. Look at the words, "Do not fret because of evil men or be envious of those who do wrong; for like the grass they will soon wither, like green plants they will soon die away. Trust in the LORD and do good; dwell in the land and enjoy safe pasture. Delight yourself in the LORD and he will give you the desires of your heart. Commit your way to the LORD; trust in him and he will do this: He will make your righteousness shine like the dawn, the justice of your cause like the noonday sun." This is the brilliance of a fretless life. Look at the contrast between the world of fretting and the fretless world.

In biblical times, "Dwell in the land" spoke volumes. The people could dwell in a land given for their children's children. "You will enjoy safe pastures." The shepherd's job was to provide safe pasture. Shepherding came with some difficulties when providing safe pastures. In many ways, the people of this time were like sheep living in the midst of physical danger from predatory entities. They did not know from day to day how secure their home would be. They didn't know if someone would come to conquer, pillage, and destroy. God was promising them safe pastures, a world apart from their reality. The promise of safety was a world apart from the uncertainty of each day.

God says, "I will give you the desires of your heart." He makes a promise that acknowledges what is on your heart. This is not intended to be a "name it-claim it" passage. If you look at the context of the passage, the writer uses strong words that are relationship based: delight in the Lord, commit your ways, and trust in Him. When you are God-centered, you release your expectations and yield to God's. Your desire becomes His.

The fretless life has one more element to its picture: sunshine. The Psalmist says you will shine. What was hidden in darkness will be revealed in the light. He says your righteousness will be like light and your judgment like noonday. Gone are the gloomy clouds that obstructed your point of view. In time, He will roll away anything that covers your righteousness and honor. Noonday is the sun overhead, the brightest sun, with little to no shadows confusing the revelation of your righteousness or judgment.

The world promised by God in God-centered waiting is brilliant. It is worlds apart from the world of fretting. In the latter world, you picture yourself being enslaved to fretting. You have been captive in a foreign land. And like the Israelites, you may have been praying to be delivered. God desires to release you. He has given you a description of the "fretless promised land." The course has been set and you are asked to follow. Will you take the steps necessary to leave this world of fretting and enjoy the world of the fretless? The first step like every step in following God requires that you trust Him. If you follow the journey of the Exodus, the people of Israel failed to trust God repeatedly.

What brings success? Reaching the world of the fretless is closely tied to this passage. Stated previously, trust is the key to the fretless life. It serves as the water that extinguished the embers within the fire pit. This trust requires all your heart. Not a token, trivial, or half; but a whole. This is where the people of Israel failed. They did not commit their whole heart.

Have you ever watched a child at the edge of the pool? The father stands in the pool slightly back from the edge, holds his hands up and calls out. Jump. Jump! The child is being asked to trust the father. His invitation is extended with grand anticipation. Will she jump? If there is a trust relationship, the father's invitation is returned with a wholehearted leap. Her eyes may be closed, but her heart is completely open. If the trust is whole hearted, there is no provision for any part of her body to remain at the pools edge; jumping requires transferring all the weight from the edge to the air. Trusting God is similar. Now, will you leap?

TRUST COMPLETE

The voices of two instructors finishing their check-list were drowned by the revving of prop engines, one under each wing of the plane awaiting our entry. The sound of these motors brought sober awareness to my absurd undertaking. My instructors claimed they had packed my parachute with the same care and expertise as their own. I could not be sure. I had not seen the chute packed or conduct any tests. In fact, my eyes did not examine one rope or stitch before the pack was issued. I realized there were no personal guarantees. I had trusted two individuals whom I barely knew. Upon boarding, the plane door was closed eliminating my options to turn back.

The plane rumbling down the runway successfully lifted my heartbeat. Shooting into the sky, the ground quickly dropped beneath my sight. My instructors were smiling, laughing and talking. I did not join or listen. Only the sound of engines entered my ears. Wondering how many jumps they had experienced before this one, I returned a superficial smile. This was my first. I did not know what to expect. All I knew were the basic procedures outlined and memorized in jump school. Over and over again my brain attempted to rehearse these steps. Focus seemed to be the key. One deep breath after another attempted to proclaim my belief: I can do this.

Jump school could not have prepared me for all the sensations. The air cooled as our climb reached higher into the sky. The scenery was amazing. The puffy white clouds were now far beneath the plane. The blue skies stretched under us to caress the green pastures beneath. The ground was very, very far away. The roads seemed as strands of thread laid on a table. My heart was beating very fast. As we neared the jump zone, my breath was slow and difficult.

Finally, the plane door opened. The wind invaded. Its rush within the cabin stirred my heart and collapsed my stomach. Fear pounded my forehead pressing against my resolve to jump. I quickly entered an altered state of consciousness. One firm pat on my back gave the sign to engage my rehearsed procedure. Following one instructor, I crawled out onto the wing of the plane at thirteen thousand feet with not much more than a pack on my back. My breathing immediately changed to compensate for the rush of the wind upon my face. Each breath was short and shallow. A nod from the other instructor started a rhythmic count and motion allowing all members of the jump party to release the plane in unison: two instructors, a cameraman, and me.

They say the rate of descent is one hundred and twenty miles an hour. They say that everything moves in slow motion. They say the sensation of falling is hardly noticed. They say the thrill is unforgettable. They are right. I looked up to see the plane falling upward from my view. No sensation of motion. Only the rush of wind registered. I had lost track of breathing, but I had not lost my breath. The free fall was only thirty seconds, but it seemed endless. Then, the instructor gave the signal to pull the rip cord. I cleared everyone with a two-handed cross-wave, reached to the right side, and pulled.

My life depended on what would happen in the next second. The entire science and sport of parachuting intended to alter my descent rate. Almost as quickly as the cord was pulled, a strong jerk jolted my body. Instantaneously, I lost one hundred miles an hour of velocity. With a large red canopy deployed above me, I was relieved. Ropes attached to the edge of the canopy were also attached to my back and shoulders. I sat suspended in a harness that provided a seat from which my feet dangled five thousand feet above the ground. No one was in sight. When I looked down, I saw the clouds two thousand feet below me. Now, the wind was a cool breeze moving from below to above.

Sitting above the clouds gave me an opportunity to review all the experiences in this incredible event. My body was subjected to acts inconceivable a hundred years earlier. What I experienced did not make logical sense. My decisions removed me from the safety of a plane to the certainty of risk. Deadly consequences were possible. At the moment my grip released the metal brackets of the plane's wing, all reservations about my absurd undertaking had lost their opportunity to override the decision to jump.

My experience was textbook. The canopy ride to the ground took a really long time. At every point, trust was at work. With the jump, my trust was complete. Why do I choose to trust? What makes trust possible? How does trust work? Who do I trust? These questions accompanied my slow and gentle glide to the ground. Without trusting, this ride would not have been possible.

PATHWAYS

Countless situations of life may bring about these same questions. In these moments, you have an opportunity to see the dynamic process of trust at work. In this case, I chose to trust because I wanted the thrill of jumping. In the end, I realized that skydiving was more about trusting God than about trusting the man-made apparatus employed in my experience.

God asks for your complete trust. How will you respond? Proverbs 3:5-6 says, "Trust in the LORD with all your heart and lean not on your own understanding; in all your ways acknowledge him, and he will make your paths straight." This passage addresses the four questions about trust. First, why do I trust? The choice to trust is driven by the goal of the process. It is the outcome that compels you to trust God. In this passage, the outcome or goal is a straight path.

The Hebrew word, *yashar*, is translated here as straight, implying a straight path. The Lord is offering to mark your journey in life. He is fully capable to bring about what you have not or could not manage for yourself. Would not a straight path be great? If your life is typical, you are probably dealing with uncertainty, ambiguity or confusion related to direction. You are most likely frustrated or weary. You are uncomfortable with uncertainty. You may be desperately seeking direction from the Lord. You could be thinking where is this straight path? You were probably ready for it yesterday.

So much energy is spent discerning direction. Trails can truly be a challenge. You check for a beaten path, markings carved into a tree, or painted signs to decipher if you are on the right path. Sometimes they are poorly marked. Or, the ground fails to retain the impressions made over time. Stop along the path to ponder. Questions seem to bring even more uncertainty to uncertainty. In the heart of this deliberation, how wonderful would the discovery of a straight path be?

How about your life? Are you confused about direction? Did you lose the trail? Have the signs vanished? Or, are the options too numerous? Would you like to just sit and ask God to take you to your next destination? With trails marking your journey through this life, a straight path would eliminate any need to decipher direction. A straight path would remove the grip of uncertainty and move you forward with confident steps.

You may be wishing for supernatural direction, something miraculous to interrupt uncertainty. The people of Israel had an incredible deal with God for direction in the Exodus. Are you familiar with their story? Their direction was administered by the physical presence of a cloud by day and a pillar of fire by night. The instruction was very simple. When the object moved, they were to pack up their tents, gather their belongings, and set a course shadowing the object of their guidance. They did not look to their right or left when direction was being offered directly in front.

Many generations later, Cyrus, the king of Persia, received a powerful promise for guidance. Isaiah 45:1-3 says, "This is what the LORD says to his anointed, to Cyrus, whose right hand I take hold of to subdue nations before him and to strip kings of their armor, to open doors before him so that gates will not be shut: I will go before you and will level the mountains; I will break down gates of bronze and cut through bars of iron. I will give you the treasures of darkness, riches stored in secret places, so that you may know that I am the LORD, the God of Israel, who summons you by name." These verses capture the amazing expression of God's involvement in the agency of direction. The Lord was willing to do great things to bring about His provision of a path. God is able to do as He pleases. Nothing or no one will stand against Him. Is this pledge exclusive to Cyrus?

No! In the spirit of Israel and Cyrus, God offers a straight path for you. Many scriptures speak of this type of direction. A survey of verses provides a clear and sound case for the Lord's direction in your life. Proverbs 4:10-11 says, "Listen, my son, accept what I say, and the years of your life will be many. I guide you in the way of wisdom and lead you along straight paths." Isaiah 48:17 says, "This is what the LORD says— your Redeemer, the Holy One of Israel: 'I am the LORD your God, who teaches you what is best for you, who directs you in the way you should go.'" In Psalms 32:8, the Lord says, "I will instruct you and teach you in the way you should go; I will counsel you and watch over you." The evidence of these and other verses completely support the hope and expectation of direction from the Lord.

You know how a funeral procession moves to the graveside with a police escort? This same effort is made for the living in other situations. Sports teams, dignitaries and VIPs receive a similar escort. Traffic is held and people are stopped. With this latter procession, bystanders become excited. They see this as an enviable privilege. For example, when the President of the U.S. moves through a city, all the intersections are secured and freeways are diverted. The process and precision of this task is a refined science.

You peer through the stalled traffic awaiting the motorcade. In most cases, you get only one glimpse of the one car for which all the labor is dedicated. This is the most secure ride in the world. Nothing impairs the path. How impressive to see a long line of dark vehicles moving at a uniform pace. They are flanked in front, back, and sides by police vehicles that create a spectacular sea of blue lights.

God moves you each day like an escorted dignitary along a straight path. Your procession through the day may not be physically as spectacular as a Presidential motorcade, but the best motorcade in the world does not have the level of care and attention afforded by God for every step under your feet. Why should anything that happens surprise or dishearten you? Why should anything worry you? Romans 8:28 says, "And we know that in all things God works for the good of those who love him, who have been called according to his purpose." With this perspective, you should see God's sovereignty and wisdom in your path.

In the abundance of options or in their scarcity, God offers to direct your steps. In any and all circumstances, God offers to make your path straight. This may not eliminate all of your troubles. But, you will know the Lord is with you. Each step you make in the journey of life can be with absolute confidence. Your confidence will be from God. He is faithful.

His straight path awaits you. Psalms 37:23 says, "If the LORD delights in a man's way, he makes his steps firm." You may be quick to ask, "How can I delight in God?" Earlier you read Proverbs 3:5-6. In this same passage, the Lord enumerates conditions for a straight path. The Lord is delighted when you trust Him, when you lean not on your own understanding, and when you acknowledge Him in all your ways. These three items help with the final three questions. What makes trust possible? How does trust work? Who do I trust?

TRUST BY NATURE

What makes trust possible? You are created with a capacity and propensity to trust. Watch any small child to see that this is universally true. Trust is a natural part of your day-to-day life. There is no difference between religious and non-religious people with regard to trust. You exercise trust on a continual basis. Take a moment to survey the use of trust today. From the moment you awoke, you trusted hundreds of things hundreds of times.

Did you check and recheck everything before you plowed through your morning? No, you trusted. Occasionally, items of the morning can be an issue with regard to trust. You may elect to taste orange juice before you commit to drinking a full glass. When the issue of trust is an issue, all objects are subject to checking and rechecking.

Just read about the attention given to facilitate a Presidential trip. Everything is checked. The food is checked for poison. The rooms are checked for surveillance devices. The venues hosting the President are checked for dangers. In contrast to this type of scrutiny, you have a built-in ability or aptitude for trusting without checking. You may find checking before trusting is often the exception and not the rule. Some may disagree with me. You may cite unhealthy or impossible applications of trust with certain things, certain individuals or individuals in general. I agree. In some cases you have a valid point. This is why the next question is important.

How does trust work? Trust is a dynamic relationship requiring all parties to do their part. If you exercise trust, you are placing your trust with the object or person of your trust. For example, the chair you sit on possesses your complete trust. It received your complete trust as you placed all of your weight on it. That transfer of weight could symbolize the transfer of trust. This type of trust is complete unless you are cheating by holding the table.

The chair must do its part. As you trust the chair, the chair must hold your weight. If the chair fails to hold your weight, your trust cannot remain with the chair. You will look for another. If the chair wobbles, you may not be able to place your complete trust in the chair. In either case, when your complete trust is not completely reciprocated, you do not have a complete trust relationship. This is the dynamic nature of trust, all parties doing their part.

In this way, trust becomes an important commodity. You may not wish to engage some objects based on fear. For example, those who are afraid to fly will not board an airplane. Those afraid of heights will not experience the view from atop the Empire State Building. Sometimes, distrust is fostered through an accident. In these experiences, the relationship is broken. For example, as a child, you may have fallen from a swing set, vowing never to return. Other times, difficult or tragic life experiences may have created your present apprehension to trust. An adulterous spouse, an abusive parent, or a lying business partner may make you think twice about trust.

People are not predictable. Their thinking is driven by their own set of needs, desires, and experiences. Complex thoughts and actions are involved in every situation. People are unpredictable. When we attempt to trust them, any number of scenarios develops. How can you best see this process? Observe traffic to make some sense of this complex world of interaction between individuals.

Drivers daily place themselves in peril. Metal and rubber are strapped to their body with the goal of propelling them at various speeds, often within inches of other vehicles. Trust is always at work. Drivers are compelled to obey laws created to allow maximum roadway success at minimum roadway provisions. Much of this works by design. Most drivers are actively involved in doing their part to make traffic work. They willfully comply with the laws. They can be considered trustworthy. They will reciprocate your trust.

However, laws are not always followed. Drivers can be ticketed for infractions. Some infractions may result in accidents. With all infractions, drivers are functioning with two possible intentions. In one case, a driver may fail to comply because of an absence of mind. They did not mean to break the law. Perhaps they were distracted by a crying baby or ringing phone. Although they did not comply, they did not willfully fail to comply. They can be considered somewhat trustworthy. Your trust will likely be reciprocated.

In another case, a driver fails to comply because of malice. When he or she enters the roadway, he or she is self-consumed, self-destructive, or aims to destroy others. These drivers do not care for anyone's welfare but their own. They drive with selfish carelessness. They are people who may be like you, but they willfully fail to comply. They can be considered not trustworthy. Your trust will not be reciprocated.

These are three types of drivers on the road. In the situations of life, trust sees these three types of individuals waiting to receive your solicitation. People are trustworthy, somewhat trustworthy, or not trustworthy. You cannot always know who is who. You cannot know how one will respond to any given situation. People are not predictable.

In the course of your life, how have you done with trusting people? Who has been trustworthy? Who has been somewhat trustworthy? Who has been not trustworthy? Do you see your parents? Do you see your children? Do you see your co-workers, your neighbors, and members of your church? Where do they all stand? How consistent have they been? Have you been hurt? Trust is a difficult element in human interaction. If you have difficulty trusting, you are not alone.

ONE GOD

Proverbs 3:5-6 calls for you to trust God. How difficult is this? Is He trustworthy? In Christianity, only one face graces the minds of those who call out. The world sees three: the Father, the Son, and the Holy Spirit. Christianity maintains they are one. This one face specializes in all the areas within the frame of your life. This trust in God is a singular trust for all the issues. You are not being asked to trust one god for this need and then move to another god for another need. One God is all you need. He is the great "I AM."

Consider the story of Moses. Through Moses, God visited Pharaoh with plagues intended to remove Israel from the grip of slavery. Pharaoh unsuccessfully called out to his god for help. None was provided. Pharaoh's son joined the list of losses suffered by Egypt during the liberation of Israel. The face of the "I AM" prevailed over the non-responsive face of Pharaoh's god.

Bible prophets have called into question the validity of trusting in gods who cannot respond. Habakkuk 2:18-20 says, "Of what value is an idol, since a man has carved it? Or an image that teaches lies? For he who makes it, trusts in his own creation; he makes idols that cannot speak. Woe to him who says to wood, 'Come to life!' Or to lifeless stone, 'Wake up!' Can it give guidance? It is covered with gold and silver; there is no breath in it. But the LORD is in his holy temple; let all the earth be silent before him." The people of Israel exclusively trusted and worshiped the great "I AM" within a very pluralistic world. They were convinced that their God was alive. They were criticized for believing all other gods were dead.

Trusting a supernatural god requires that your supernatural god be trustworthy. Being alive would be a minimum requirement for this consideration. In this case, the gods of other religions would not be trustworthy. The God of Israel is not only alive, but also reveals that He is trustworthy. Numbers 23:19 says, "God is not a man, that he should lie, nor a son of man, that he should change his mind. Does he speak and then not act? Does he promise and not fulfill?" Many other passages speak to the various expressions of the eternal God to humanity. God is: Light, Just, Able, Faithful, Wise, Strong, Truthful, Near, Righteous, Holy, Merciful, Sovereign, Flawless, Full of Compassion, Good, Our Refuge, Our Help, the King of all the Earth, The Rock, Lord, Righteous Judge, Exalted, Mighty, Giving, and God of gods.

These expressions of God's trustworthiness are throughout the Bible. Isaiah 25:1 and 9, says, "O LORD, you are my God; I will exalt you and praise your name, for in perfect faithfulness you have done marvelous things, things planned long ago. In that day they will say, 'Surely this is our God; we trusted in him, and he saved us. This is the LORD, we trusted in him; let us rejoice and be glad in his salvation.'" Trust in God is reciprocated. He is trustworthy.

The final lesson on how trust works is related to you. How do you trust? Trust is exercised in two ways. Some people give a hundred percent trust at the beginning of an engagement. They meet someone and immediately respond to his or her request for trust. Recently, I needed a place to stay for two weeks. A couple from my church responded to my need. After a brief introduction and conversation, they handed me a key to their house and left for their vacation. I could not believe their level of trust. They did not know me. But, they immediately and completely trusted me.

In another category, trust is given slowly. When trust is requested, a small piece of trust is given with the rest earned cautiously. This is clearly seen with a mother and her baby. Sure, everyone wants to hold her baby, but you have to earn her trust before she allows the baby into your arms. Soon, she may let you see the baby, a little bit of trust given. Slowly, she may let you touch the baby. After some time, she may let you hold her baby. Greater levels of trust may eventually allow you to walk around with the baby. Finally, she may let you be alone with her baby. One hundred percent trust is achieved.

Which category do you find yourself in? How do you give trust? With every situation, trust is only trust when you give one hundred percent. By its definition, trust needs to be complete. You cannot hold back in any way. Can you imagine trying to jump from a plane without one hundred percent trust? Can you imagine sitting in a chair without one hundred percent trust?

Proverbs 3:5-6 says that you must trust God with your whole heart. You are not being asked for ten percent, fifty percent or even ninety-nine percent. You are being asked for one hundred percent. Kings in the Old Testament are great examples of individuals who struggled in their trust relationship with God. Second Kings 21:19-24 records the trust relationship Amon established with the Lord. It was not complete. Verse 21 and 22 show some results, "He walked in all the ways of his father; he worshiped the idols his father had worshiped, and bowed down to them. He forsook the LORD, the God of his fathers, and did not walk in the way of the LORD."

After Amon was killed, his son Josiah becomes king. Second Chronicles 34:33 records Josiah's relationship; "Josiah removed all the detestable idols from all the territory belonging to the Israelites, and he had all who were present in Israel serve the LORD their God. As long as he lived, they did not fail to follow the LORD, the God of their fathers." Solomon did not fare so well. He was blessed with wisdom but lacked complete trust. First Kings 11:6 says, "So Solomon did evil in the eyes of the LORD; he did not follow the LORD completely, as David his father had done." Ironically, Solomon penned Proverbs 3:5-6 and failed to practice what he preached.

MORE CONDITIONS TO CONSIDER

You have seen the first condition in Proverbs 3:5-6; trust in the Lord with all your heart. Two more conditions are pending. Or, are they? Before you consider the next two conditions, think about this. Steps are needed to produce any desired result. Starting a lawn mower requires placing the control to the "on" position, holding down the throttle and pulling on the rope from the crank. Driving a car requires that you turn the ignition, place the transmission in drive and accelerate. In both of these examples, each action is critical to the success of the experience. Any one action could not by itself accomplish the experience. The omission of any one action would make the experience impossible. Each independent action is equally required to accomplish the outcome.

Upon inspecting Proverbs 3:5-6, my initial conclusion identified three similar conditions producing one outcome, a straight path from God. I believed the omission of any one could not accomplish the task. These three conditions are clearly delineated. The outcome of a straight path is in the balance. I am eager to accomplish all the conditions to achieve this outcome. Pondering this passage raises questions.

Could it be that I have not seen the true nature of this passage? Are these really three conditions for one outcome? The questions find some validity realizing conditions two and three are difficult, if not impossible. Think about condition three: acknowledging the Lord in all our ways. You will agree that each day is filled with many decisions. Picture decisions within the span of one day. Could you not see them like torrential rain falling from the sky? Decisions in a day are all connected in a web more intricate than any spider could have imagined weaving. Every decision seems impacted by previous decisions. Every decision aims to impact one or more in the future. With so many decisions, the challenge to acknowledge God in all our ways seems impossible. What if you missed one?

Think about condition two: leaning not on our own understanding. This condition seems equally impossible. Because you can think, you have a propensity to think. Your brain was designed to analyze variables in a given situation with the prospects of making decisions. The "What ifs" and "Only ifs" are poised to support the brain in its endeavor. The conclusions are evaluated to arrive at an understanding; your understanding. You employ this process because you want understanding. You try to make sense of life. You hope life will make sense. You constantly engage the thinking process with every issue that invades your life. Your brain is forced into this battle. This second condition is a condition that seems to contradict God's design for the human brain.

Only the initial condition articulated in Proverbs 3:5-6 seems achievable. Trust is a simple choice. Either you trust or you do not. It is your single choice directed in this passage to a single person, God. In every variable within every situation and every option preceding every decision, the trust dynamic does not change. Financial problems, difficulties raising children, deciding what college to attend, marriage trouble, loneliness, and many more life situations cannot alter this one question. Over the span of a lifetime the question remains the same. The question is always the same. Do you trust God? Yes or No?

With this consideration, Proverbs 3:5-6 comes alive in a new light. This verse does not have three conditions equally weighted. They are not independent actions equally required to accomplish an outcome. This is not like driving a car or starting a mower. The last two conditions in Proverbs 3:5-6 are dependent on the first. The first is the only one you have to accomplish. You cannot trust God with all your heart if you are leaning on your own understanding. You cannot trust God with all you heart if you are not acknowledging Him in all your ways. Accomplishing the first condition would make the latter two automatic. Omitting one or both of the latter two conditions would render the first condition bogus.

You can see this process with firing a gun. Pull the trigger. As you do, you have accomplished the only condition to firing a gun. But, two other conditions are automatically engaged. The hammer in the gun hits the shell of the bullet. The gunpowder in the bullet explodes propelling the bullet quickly to its target. The first action produced two resulting actions. The total process produced one outcome. Without pulling the trigger, you cannot have any action. By pulling the trigger, you have all the actions required for the product.

WHOLE, NOT PART

Trusting in the Lord with all your heart would release any need to lean on your own understanding. You would not have any need to understand because you would trust that God understands. Trusting God acknowledges that your mind, as complex and as wonderful as it may be, is too limited to grasp all that may be happening. You would praise God because His capacity to understand your complex life is far greater than your capacity or potential. Why try to make sense of something that is beyond you to understand?

Trusting in the Lord with all your heart would release any need to devise your own way.

When you think to draw understanding, you utilize understanding to produce possible scenarios. Within each scenario, a number of plans outline several avenues through your situation. If you are having trouble at work, you think through your situation to conclude a certain action, hoping for a good result. Or, you may conclude that this same situation is hopeless. In either case, your actions, your ways, are within your limited understanding.

If you trust God with your whole heart, your mind would resign the activity of producing your ways. You would follow God. He may lead you in ways that surprise you. His way may fall outside of your understanding. Trusting the Lord with all of your heart is one condition with two results and one outcome. This formula is needful because God wants to insure you are able (or willing) to follow the "straight path" He brings before you.

Consider the story of Noah. He is a classic model of Proverbs 3:5-6 at work. The story of Noah begins nearly at the end of the world. God is not happy with humanity. Genesis 6 records the unfolding drama. The hearts of men are completely turned away from God. The Lord is grieved, and His heart is filled with pain. The Lord's agony inflames Him. He wishes to destroy men, and all creatures of the ground and air. Then, the most pivotal word in history is recorded in the story. The word is "but." It changes the outlook of humanity by holding back the omnipotent wrath of God. The word appears because of Noah. He was not like all the others. The passage says he alone found favor with the Lord. He had a trust relationship with God. This relationship helped him remain close to God in the presence of great sin.

God calls Noah and lays out the plan to deal with the wickedness. He will still destroy the world, but will spare Noah, his family, and selected animals from the earth. I am sure Noah was relieved. But, I am sure he was hurt, too. The world that was so sinful included his extended family and close friends. The trust process for this situation was beginning. Noah had to trust that this dreadful action was necessary. The cost was high. The trust process continued to intensify with the disclosure of the plan. The plan aimed to accomplish all of God's desires. How interesting is the challenge of killing everything in the world except a few specific things? After the destruction, the world had to support the life spared by God. The plan had to be perfect.

God spoke the plan to Noah. The plan was unimaginable. What raced through Noah's mind as he listened? He must have wondered what God would do. God would flood the earth and crush breath from everything that had breath. He would bring waters from the sky as rain. The waters would cover the earth until every creature failed to find a place to stand. Waters would rise twenty feet over the tallest mountains. In anticipation of this cataclysmic phenomenon, God asked Noah to build a boat large enough to support the life stowed on board. Building instructions followed with specific details. With the plan fully disclosed, Noah had only one choice, to trust or not to trust. God was waiting.

This is where you see trust at work. If Noah thought to gain his own understanding of the plan, several things may have proved difficult to digest. First, what was rain? Some theories believe rain had not fallen before Noah's time. These theories stem from the belief that a firmament stood above the earth storing water. The passage speaks of the heavens breaking forth, bringing waters sufficient to cover the earth. The deep was also to yield its storehouse of water, springing up to join the waters from above. Noah could not have known where all the water would come from sufficient to cover the vast surface of Terra Firma.

More questions may have flooded his mind. Will everybody have to die? What if people change? Why a boat? Would a boat work? Why so big? How much time do I have? Why not build near the water? Would it not need to be tested? Do I have to get the animals? Why so many animals? What if the animals attack my family? How about the neighbors? What will they think? How much will this cost? How long will it take? When is the flood coming? What if I die before it's finished? What about this? What about that? What about this and that?

How many questions attempted to invade Noah's mind? By the time God spoke to him, he had lived five hundred years. He may have known a thing or two about life and the world. Nevertheless, entertaining the questions would have produced conclusions and scenarios based only on his understanding. Then, he may have been tempted to lean on that understanding.

By leaning, Noah may have been tempted to go his own way. He may have tried to talk to the people to get them to change. He may have moved his family to the nearest and tallest mountain. He may have decided to use a different wood or alter the design. He may have elected to build a smaller boat hoping to help only his family. He may have done this. He may have done that. He may have done this or that. So many decisions may have been before him. Really, only one decision needed to be addressed; did he trust God?

Noah proves why Proverbs 3:5-6 is important. Noah was asked to do something very unthinkable in every way. Everything about this plan from God seemed beyond his own understanding. Yet, Noah trusted God. Because Noah trusted God, he followed God's plan. Noah's steps were prepared to overcome the obstacles of his own understanding and the options of his own ways. As a result, he did not lean on his own understanding. He did not go his own way. Noah acknowledged God in all of his ways and with all of his thoughts because he trusted God. For over one hundred years Noah complied with God's will. The straight path supported each step he would take. He did not turn to the left or to the right. He only looked straight. Noah had complete trust in God. His trust was reciprocated. God's faithfulness brought about a brilliant and perfect plan to save Noah and his family.

DO YOU TRUST?

What do you think about God's plan for you? What unbelievable situations dominate your world? You must completely trust God to follow Him. When you trust Him, He gives you a straight path to make following possible. In some cases, or maybe in most cases, the plan He gives does not seem to make sense. You may conclude you have a better plan. In exchange for your complete trust, you receive one step at a time. Step by step, you will begin to experience the straight path of God's faithfulness.

Can I put you in Noah's shoes? Stand next to me. Fold your arms in front of you. I am standing behind you now. I ask you to make your body stiff like a board. I place my hand on your back and ask you to fall backwards. Just before you act, you hear my promise to catch you. You trust me, and so you fall back. I catch you and my audience applauds. You smile and breathe a sigh of relief. Sorry, that was just a warm up. You are not in Noah's shoes just yet.

I pull a blindfold from my pocket. Your sense of sight attempts to make sense of the blindfold. I ask if I can place the blindfold over your eyes. For the sake of the exercise you agree. I have now removed your sense of sight. I take your hand and ask you to follow me to another part of the stage. Here, I ask you to climb a platform you may have seen earlier. I tell you there are five steps. You make each cautiously holding my arm to steady your progress. When we arrive on the platform, I move you to its outer edge. Just in case you have forgotten, I remind you where we are. You nervously smile and laugh joining the nervous commotion of the audience. There you stand, at the edge facing the audience with me standing by your side. You cannot see, but you know what is seen.

Then, I place my hands on your shoulders and turn you, positioning your back at the platform's edge. As I hold you, I can feel nervousness. I try to say words to ease your fears. While I hold your shoulders, I ask you to fold your arms. At this point, I remind you where you are. I let go. Your nervous laughter now turns to a quiet cry beginning with a "ooooh" and ending with "Moses." I speak to you letting you know I am here. My voice is directly in front of your face. When I let go, the sense of touch was lost. You do not feel my hands on your shoulders or on your back as earlier. Your sense of smell and taste seem useless at this moment. You cannot use them to help you understand anything about your situation. So, you are left with one sense, hearing.

You carefully listen. You hear the audience making various sounds registering their disbelief with your present situation. They only reinforce your fears. When you listen some more, no more sounds are distinguishable. Finally, my voice breaks through your growing desperation. Relief? No, not really. I have just asked you if you trust me. Do you? You give a halfhearted nod. Do you really trust? My voice, in front of your face, says something you could not have imagined. I ask you to fall back. You enter some level of shock screaming "What?" You hear my voice in front of you, but it fails to provide any assurance. With me standing in front, you have no idea what waits behind you if you comply. Your sense of hearing fails to help you understand what is happening. At this moment, all of your senses are rendered useless.

Now you are in Noah's shoes. Here on this platform, you do not have your own understanding. You cannot devise your own ways. To do anything but fall back, would acknowledge that you do not trust me. You cannot trust me in part. A small step back would remove you from the platform. A small step forward would break your pledge. I interrupt your debate about the situation to ask, "Do you trust me?" Finally, the only question having merit in a trust relationship surfaces. You ask, "Will you take care of me?" Now we are at the doorstep of complete trust. When you walk through, you leave your understanding and your ways there. You ask again as if knocking a little harder, "Will you take care of me?" I assure you that I will.

You take a deep breath. You resign all of your own understanding. You release all of your ways. You begin to completely trust. You acknowledge me in all your ways as you begin to shift your weight. That is what I have asked from you. You are moving toward the unknown. The audience noise grows with hysterical anticipation. You slowly realize you are now crossing the point of no return. Your weight is committed. Gravity reaches up and pulls you toward the ground. Your breath is lost. You just want your trust reciprocated. Your safety depends on what happens in the next second.

To your surprise, amazement, and relief, something breaks your destiny with doom. You quickly reach up and pull your blindfold. All of your senses return. You use them to quickly determine the source of your rescue. Four strong individuals have provided a cushion to catch your stiff body with a soft bed of arms. You laugh hysterically while smiling at the individuals. They place your feet on the ground and lift you to a stand. You quickly reconstruct the event. Step by step the picture is coming together. Your breath is fast and your heart is racing. You are in awe. The audience shouts, claps and cheers. They do not clap for me. They clap for you for your trust. They are impressed and excited. You have demonstrated complete trust. Your trust is complete.

Now, let's go back to your reality. As you read this, what are your situations? Is God asking you to trust Him? Will you picture yourself folding your hands, making your body stiff as a board and falling back into His provisions? He will catch you when you give Him your complete trust.

CONTENT MEANT

Do you remember being taught how to pray? The process can be amazing to witness. Perhaps you have children going through this process. A friend gave me an unforgettable glimpse into this world. Their family dinner provided my introduction to a unique brand of prayer. Among other things, I observed children promote the activity of prayer with great excitement. The four-year-old girl says, "Daddy, daddy, we need to pray." Her excitement was easy to see. Dad agreed, "Oh yes, honey, let's pray."

She prays, "God, I want to thank you for my mommy and my daddy. I want to thank you for my sister. I want to thank you for Moses. I want to thank you for the birds and I want to thank you for our car and our house. I want to thank you for Ms. Schnyder at church and … I want to thank you for…." As she continues, mom and dad look at each other. Their eyes are asking, "Who will stop her?" Mom steps in. "Honey, we need to go ahead and thank God for the food so we can eat." "But I'm not done praying," cries the little girl. Mom explains, "Well, I think God is ready for us to eat, so we need to finish the prayer, okay?"

In these experiences, you discover how precious children are in prayer. As she finishes, I smile faintly recalling how simple prayer should be. She sees me smile and immediately asks dad, "Let's pray again!" The process may seem silly or trying to parents, but the child is sincere. For her, each episode of prayer is engaged with excitement, joy, and authenticity. Prayers from children have an honest and powerful tone. At times they may say, "God, please make daddy stop screaming at mom." Or, "God, take care of grandma because daddy says she is with you now." Or, "God, please give us money. We need to pay our mortgage bill." This is communication. The child's words are from her heart. Her words seldom move through the mind. She prays what she feels and knows. She does not seem to notice those in her company as she speaks freely with God. She realizes that she is center stage before God. She uses every ounce of the spotlight to celebrate this privilege in His presence.

When you pray, your words seem to start from the mind. You think and therefore you ask based on your understanding or rationalization. If the prayer starts from the heart, you move it through the mind aiming to construct its potency. You may inadvertently or deliberately attach specific words and phrases to note your fervor before God or to impress those present in your company. Jesus speaks about prayer. He gives two examples to teach us how to pray. Matthew 6:5 says, "And when you pray, do not be like the hypocrites, for they love to pray standing in the synagogues and on the street corners to be seen by men. I tell you the truth, they have received their reward in full." Again in Matthew 6:7, He says, "And when you pray, do not keep on babbling like pagans, for they think they will be heard because of their many words." Awareness of those present or the abuse of words is not proper for the exercise of prayer.

When you learned to pray, you were told God is your audience. You learned you should communicate the needs in your life to Him. You believed God could hear. Sometime along the way, you seemed to have "grown up." Prayer grew into an involved process requiring more thought. You learned to package a prayer. You eventually believed the package was more important than the heart that initiated the prayer. How much do children really understand to be so eloquent in prayer? Mom says, "Now honey, don't forget to pray in 'Jesus' name, amen.'" The little girl responds, "Oh yes, in Jesus' name——aaaaaamennnnnn." What does she really know? In my experience, this same child looked at her mom later and said, "Mommy, Moses is here today, can Jesus come tomorrow?" She then laughs and smiles at me as if I knew what she meant.

You have learned how important Jesus' name is to a prayer. His name alone makes prayer successful. You use this protocol to place a stamp on your prayer package. Imagine a box represents your package for prayer. Write all your prayer requests on small cards. Take these requests and place them in the package. Kneel before the Lord placing the package in front to symbolize God's throne before you. All children, teens, college students, single adults, married adults, and senior adults have needs. Regardless of your station in life, all people share one common and inescapable need for prayer. And so, you pray, "Lord, these are my prayers—in Jesus' name....amen." You stand and walk away. It's done—isn't it?

A LINE THAT BINDS

There's only one problem. This package you sent to God has items that are really, really important to you. Their importance captivates you in a very powerful dynamic. The powerful dynamic has nothing to do with God. It has everything to do with you. In fact, it has only to do with you. You cannot stop thinking about your prayer requests. You worry about them. You see the box over here before the throne of God. You live on the other side in the material world. But, a part of you stayed with the box. You start to think in your heart, "What has God done with my requests? What is He going to do?"

Attempting to peer into the spiritual, you agonize over the fate of your request. You cannot escape the shackles binding you to your prayers before God. Children do not seem to pray like this. They pray and seem to forget. They pray words from their heart and fail to hold on to those prayers. After their prayer, they engage their next event as if they had never prayed. Strangely, you have evolved into a prayer exercise that stays connected to the request. What changes this practice? Try to see this praying process like fishing for fish.

The great world of fishing hinges on finding that perfect spot on that perfect lake. I have sat in a boat. Traveled at the break of dawn across the waters of an isolated lake. Baited my hook. Cast my line, and waited. Holding the fishing pole, I stare at my line that disappears into the water. A soft conversation with my host does not divert my attention from that point where my fishing line enters the water. The morning moves into the afternoon without a single sign of a fish. Nevertheless, obvious determination holds my attention to the fishing line. I want a fish. In this process, the hours pass. Although I live above the water, my heart lives those desperate hours below the water. Thoughts surveying the possibility of fish below the water fuels my steadfast vigil.

If only I could see below the water. If only I could see the fish, then my heart would not be so anxious. What if I am in the wrong spot? What if I used the wrong bait? What if, or if only, I had some knowledge of the world under the water. I would do something. I would do anything. But, I sigh realizing I can do nothing. That is fishing. The fishing line is paramount and the process cannot be cheated. When you pray, you cast your prayer into the throne room of God. You give it to God, but you cannot seem to disengage from it. There is a line called expectation that connects you to that prayer request. When you are wrapped up in that line, praying is difficult!

To be successful in prayer, you may need to try fishing with a twist. Cast your line into the water. And then, cut the line. How crazy does that sound? Sure, the fishing world will never adopt my suggestion. But, this absurd suggestion paints the perfect picture for prayer. This suggestion is exactly what prayer is asking. The simple act of cutting the line of expectation affirms God's design in the prayer process. Cutting the line is how you can disengage. Look at prayer in this new light. Yes, the requests are important, but the outcome need not be.

Philippians 4:6 says, "Do not be anxious about anything, but in everything, by prayer and petition, with thanksgiving, present your requests to God." The successful exercise of prayer requires three things. The first is "do not worry." The Bible gives this as a clear command. Do you hear this simple call? Are you interested in obeying God? Yes? So, you obey. You resolve not to worry. You give your prayer requests to God. You walk away, and for that brief moment, you experience success because there is no worry. This fact brings some sense of excitement. You breathe a sigh of relief. Then almost without notice, worry grips your heart. Why did worry reengage so quickly? The Apostle Paul in this passage said that prayer should not involve worry! Because you worry, did your prayer fail?

WORRY WART?

Previously, I asked how you learned to pray. Now I ask how did you learn to worry? Where did worry come from? Did your parents sit with you at the dinner table and say, "Now, honey, this is the way you should worry. Will you just repeat after me?" Were you coached to worry? My dad coached me in soccer. He was my first soccer coach. I clearly remember his ball control drills and practices aimed to improve our skill. I don't remember him or anyone coaching me how to worry. Nevertheless, today, I am an expert at it! This is the mystery of effortless acquisition. If only other things in life were this easy to acquire.

In Matthew 6:25-29, Jesus says, "Therefore I tell you, do not worry about your life, what you will eat or drink; or about your body, what you will wear. Is not life more important than food, and the body more important than clothes? Look at the birds of the air; they do not sow or reap or store away in barns, and yet your heavenly Father feeds them. Are you not much more valuable than they? Who of you by worrying can add a single hour to his life? And why do you worry about clothes? See how the lilies of the field grow. They do not labor or spin. Yet I tell you that not even Solomon in all his splendor was dressed like one of these."

In this passage, Jesus is a graphic and colorful teacher drawing pictures that communicate. Step into the shoes of this gospel writer. See what he sees and feel what he is trying to say. Jesus is standing before a group of people. He may have glanced over to see birds milling in the grass nearby. He may have pointed to them and said, "Who fed those birds today?" The birds have never prepared their own food. People are not so fortunate. To eat, you are bound to a process that is worlds away from the good fortune of birds.

Money is needed for food. You work for money. You buy food at a store. How often do you take food items and slave over a stove to produce something edible? It takes work to eat. Most people engage this process daily. Occasionally, you can take a short cut and stop by a restaurant. In Jesus' day, there may have been no such option. If a person got hungry, they knew labor was involved to prepare food. The people listening to Jesus were all too familiar with this labor. They knew that birds did nothing to eat.

Jesus may have also glanced over to see a field of brightly colored flowers. He may have compelled His listeners to look. They saw awesome color and beauty. They saw exactly what you see today. Flowers with brilliant yellows, purples and blues. Do flowers work for their appearance?

How do they get so brilliant? In making this observation, Jesus is making a comparison that may not be so obvious to you today. What do you notice?

When I look today at a crowd in a sports arena, the team color becomes clear inspiration to paint the stands with dazzling results. Scan a crowd at the mall to see color that spans the entire color spectrum. Now, think back to Jesus' day. Clothing was not so colorful. People may have worn drab clothes because color was an exception and a luxury. Jesus' comparison is powerful. He boldly compares the flowers of the fields to Solomon, the richest king of Israel. In this comparison, Jesus says Solomon could not contend with the magnificence of a single flower. Wow! Jesus is right! God clothes the flowers in grand fashion. If God can take care of the flowers and birds in this manner, He can take care of you.

This thought should ease your anxiety. This insight into God's power and faithfulness should compel you to abandon your expectation. Don't worry. He will meet you at the point of your need. When you pray with this thought in mind, you experience some confidence in your prayer. Are you at that moment free from the grip of worry? Can you walk away from your prayer? No. The line of expectation remains. Knowing that God can respond does not change the fact that He has not yet responded. When you are honest, you realize this view of God did not eliminate your connection to the outcome. The heart is still gripped by expectation. What will God do?

DON'T HOLD ANYTHING BACK

The second thing required for a successful prayer exercise according to Philippians 4:6 is "bringing everything to God." I consider this requirement a great privilege. You do not have this same privilege with most people in your life. As a Campus Minister, I previously had the joy of working for a university president I believed in. The president's office was accessible to me. He was not only the president but also a friend from my distant past. Occasionally, he and I met to discuss chapel themes, guest speakers, or ministry objectives. What an honor to be in his office and sit in front of his desk. Each visit was thoughtful and needful. Can you imagine setting an appointment with him to ask which color pencil would best accent the color of my office? He would graciously show me the door. His busy schedule is mindful of my needs but understandably lacks time for trivial questions.

I often asked my superior what items should be brought before the president. Some things did not need his attention. On the contrary, everything in your life needs God's attention. Nothing is meant to be in your life without any hope of His assistance and involvement. Everything is clearly meant to be everything. No matter how trivial or small, nothing is out of God's consideration. In Philippians 4:6, God is writing a blank check. He wants to hear everything and anything. He is clearly saying He is approachable. When something becomes the object of a prayer, you are called to bring that prayer before God.

A British orphanage founder prescribed an experience in prayer that makes a clear case for the spirit of this passage. Brother Lawrence engages an exercise practicing the necessity of God's involvement in all daily matters. He went through the day communicating every decision to God as a prayer. No matter how big or small the decision. Which should I do first, brush my teeth or take a bath? Should I brush my teeth? Should I take a bath? Each and every decision met the same consideration.

This revelation should make you excited. You have many prayer requests. You are asked to place every prayer in the box. No reservation should remain with regard to the importance of each prayer. They are all equally summoned into God's presence. This knowledge should ease your anxiety. Walk away from the box. Try it! Do you feel some freedom?

Sure. But, if you are honest, a brief survey reveals you are still connected. The thought of God wanting everything is powerful, but those prayer requests are still important to you. You are still wondering how God is going to answer each of your many requests. Because the outcome is pending, the heart is still engaged.

"THANKSPRAYING"

The third thing required for a successful prayer exercise in Philippians 4:6 is "being thankful." How many of you are thankful to God? How many things are you thankful for? Take a moment to list your items. Begin with your body and move across your world until every single item has been cataloged. My guess would be that no end would be discovered to the number of blessings from God's hand in your life. You have so much. Clearly, being thankful in prayer is not a difficult request. It only requires a small effort. This small effort has a big value for the prayer process. Being thankful is a prayer necessity with two simple functions.

One function concerns your view of God. As you bring your prayer request to God, He gives you a solid sense of His goodness and faithfulness. He wants you to see Him as He sees Himself. He responds. He gives. He cares. He provides. He loves. He is approachable. Thanksgiving opens the eyes of your heart to these images of God. When you pray, your image of God is important. He receives your prayers. He is the one who accepts the responsibility for the outcome of your prayer. God is worthy of your thanksgiving. You enter His presence with a thankful heart. When you begin to grasp His provision, you conclude God is good. God is a good God. He is very, very, very good to you.

The second function of thankfulness in prayer concerns your view of prayer itself. When you are thankful to God in prayer, thanksgiving opens a vigorous and energetic prayer experience. Thanksgiving moves your heart with gratitude. Long before your prayer requests are spoken from your lips, you are swept into a current created by thanksgiving. Imagine a river raging past a rock. Stand on the rock and sense the current sweeping below your view. Drop a stick in the water and watch what results. The stick is quickly swept away. Effortlessly, it moves in the direction of the water and disappears beyond your sight.

Can you see thanksgiving serving a similar function? As you thank God, you are so amazed with Him. The Psalmist captures this image as he approaches God. Psalms 100:4-5 says, "Enter his gates with thanksgiving and his courts with praise; give thanks to him and praise his name. For the LORD is good and his love endures forever; his faithfulness continues through all generations." You need not be timid in your approach. You are eager because you realize how good God is. Prayer becomes effortless because thanksgiving supports the weight of the prayer by acknowledging God's goodness. Thanksgiving eases the passage of prayer from your view.

Does thanksgiving help you disengage from your prayer request? Almost. Certainly, thanksgiving revolutionizes prayer. But, you still have a connection to your expectation because you still consider the outcome as being important. You cannot wait to add your answered prayer to your thankful list. Although you may have successfully applied the three things listed above for a successful prayer exercise, you step back only to ask what is still missing.

CUTTING THE LINE

In the previous chapter, you read that only one choice is yours in the midst of life's situations. You can choose to trust or not to trust God. In this chapter, there is a similar single choice. It is not about the prayer. You are not left deciding whether to pray or not to pray. Clearly, when life presses hard enough, all individuals call out to God. It is not about bringing everything to the Lord or even about being thankful. At a minimum, those things are naturally present when circumstances or insights are supportive. Try lying in a hospital bed without bringing all of your needs before God. Try watching a sunset without being thankful.

The missing element is related to the outcome of prayer, the heart of your expectation. This is what fuels your anxiety. You must specifically aim to eliminate anxiety by severing your line of expectation. This brings you to the threshold of disengagement. Thanksgiving serves to bring you to this choice. Through thanksgiving your eyes are opened to who God is. The key to your choice is God. You must believe He is able to meet you at the point of your need. When giving thanks, you assess that God has thoughtfully and bountifully provided blessings in your life. With this belief, the stronghold of expectation becomes vulnerable.

The deathblow to expectation hinges on your single choice in prayer. As you pray, the choice is simply to trust God or not. You believe or you realize that God provides everything you need within the context of your life. He is the source of all your blessings. The Bible is full of examples of what God gives. He gives far more than you will ever know. He gives everything including life itself. Your life is full. The outcome to your prayer is not critical in this reality of God's complete provision. Thanksgiving supports this conclusion by rehearsing your awareness of God's provision. He completely provides. If you have a trust relationship with God, the choice to trust Him will be manifested in your life as contentment.

What is contentment? Contentment can be seen as the reflection that mirrors your choice to trust God. Do you trust God? Survey your life circumstances. Consider every nook and cranny of your world. Are you content? There cannot be different answers to these two questions. The two choices are wrapped together because God is the object of your trust and the source for your contentment. God helps you find contentment. Being content is accepting your life as being sufficient. God gives to you according to His great wisdom. He has given all He intends for you now and all you need in the context of your trust relationship with Him. The Palmist says, "The LORD is my shepherd, I shall not want." When you are content, you lack nothing.

Contentment is accepting that your life and your circumstances are in God's hands. God is all that you need. Isaiah 41:10 says, "So do not fear, for I am with you; do not be dismayed, for I am your God. I will strengthen you and help you; I will uphold you with my righteous right hand." God calls you to trust Him in the midst of your difficult circumstances. The trust is necessary to deal with the fear that accompanies unfavorable or traumatic situations. Fear encircles when you are in this place. When you are down or defeated, the circumstances of your life produce forces that press against your trust in God.

Picture diving into the waters of a Pacific reef. Blue skies join blue waters to bring tranquility to the picture constructed by your mind. Your world is completely acceptable until a swarm of sharks encircle your place. They are aggressive and hungry. They dart close and jet past. They are attempting to probe their fortune in finding you as their meal. Fear drives your uncertainty to the brink. You conclude that only a few moments separate you from your death. The Isaiah verse speaks volumes to this challenge. You are asked not to fear because God is with you. Think about this God who created all things. He created the sharks. He created the waters. He is by your side. You are not alone in the waters. He affirms your relationship with Him by reciprocating your trust. He clearly claims to be your God. He promises to provide strength and help to facilitate your journey through difficult waters. Even more, He places you in His right hand. What a powerful picture!

How can one see His hand at work in this dynamic picture? Water, sharks, and fear are there. Imagine the picture is placing you in the waters with the sharks within the confident support of a diving cage. Now the picture embodies the essence of this passage. In the cage, you are safe in the midst of the shark-infested waters. The cage makes a sport of an otherwise life-threatening situation. Here, fear is lost to fun. In this protective environment, you are easily content with your circumstances. The waters and the sharks are still present, but fear is gone. What encircles your waters today?

Isaiah calls you to be content in God's sovereign hand. Circumstances cannot nullify the reality of God's sovereignty. He is involved with every element of your life. He sees your life from His perspective. He knows you more intimately than you know yourself. He has counted the number of hairs on your head. God is amazing! Your life can never be beyond His power. When your circumstances are most difficult, your appreciation of God's sovereign watch is most intense. You must know He is able. He is able to do anything, everything, or nothing. Because you trust God, whether He responds or does not respond favorably to your prayer request becomes immaterial. And so, the line of expectation is cut. Finally, you are free.

SURVIVE OR THRIVE?

The line of expectation can only be severed with contentment. Contentment is translated from a Greek word, *autarkes* (ow-tar'-kace), meaning "sufficient in oneself, self-sufficient, adequate, or needing no assistance." Do not translate this word to mean you are sufficient in yourself. Paul uses this Greek word to show sufficiency not in himself but in God. In this consideration, contentment means that you are not dependent on the outcome of your prayer. You are independent from the results of your prayer request. Therefore, contentment gives freedom from anxiety and worry.

Philippians 4:11-13 says, "I am not saying this because I am in need, for I have learned to be content whatever the circumstances. I know what it is to be in need, and I know what it is to have plenty. I have learned the secret of being content in any and every situation, whether well fed or hungry, whether living in plenty or in want. I can do everything through him who gives me strength." Paul's secret is clearly stated here. He has a dependent trust relationship with God. He needs God's strength for the good times and the very difficult times in his life.

Too often, the strength you receive from God may not be noticed or appreciated during your good times. You seem to lose sight of it in the midst of your energy and excitement from the moment. During the difficult times, God's strength is your only hope. You desperately need His strength to even take and release each breath. Oh, yes, Paul had his list of difficult times. Read 2 Corinthians 6:4-10 and 2 Corinthians 11:23-31 to get a glimpse of Paul's life. What can you conclude about Paul's life? In the midst of all his circumstances, Paul's contentment moves him forward. He has a "can do" attitude. God provides the needed strength to do all things. God's strength propels Paul through all his circumstances. This strength is present not just to help him survive but also to thrive.

The power from God in the midst of your contentment is remarkable. Psalms 59:16 says, "But I will sing of your strength, in the morning I will sing of your love; for you are my fortress, my refuge in times of trouble." The Psalmist understands the beauty of this strength and its power to stand as a fortress. Have you ever wondered why life is so crazy? Did you ever think you would have to face what you now have to face? You may be in the middle of some incredible and unthinkable circumstances. Do not lose heart. Do not give up. Stand strong and experience the strength of the Lord. Be content.

A LIFE WORTH FOLLOWING

Joseph stood strong. His stand was epic: not just through one great difficulty but through several great difficulties spanning thirteen long years. His story begins in Genesis 37:1. Joseph is the favorite son of his father Jacob. Joseph's father treats him with special consideration by presenting a coat with many colors. In light of the earlier discussion on color in the ancient world, you can imagine that this coat made quite a statement. His brothers were not impressed. They really did not need another reason to hate their brother. One day, Joseph shares a dream with his brothers. The dream Joseph shares elevates him to reign over his brothers. If you have a brother you may be identifying with their growing anger and resentment. The Bible says, "They hated him even more."

Wait, the story continues with another dream. This time, Joseph gathers his brothers and his dad. Joseph shares that his family will bow down before him. Can you imagine the sight of this family conference in the living room? They are not pleased. Joseph's dad rebukes him. Have I already mentioned his brothers did not need another reason to hate Joseph? Well, this is one more. Their anger is building. After his brothers return to watch their flock in the fields, Joseph is commissioned by his father to check on their welfare. As Joseph arrives, his brothers brew a plot. They intend to kill him. You would think this is the end of the story, but this is just the beginning of Joseph's incredible story.

One brother steps in and convinces the others to spare Joseph's life. As a result, the other brothers drop Joseph in a pit and consider their options. This one brother has plans to break Joseph free and return him to their father. But, Joseph is not so fortunate. While that one brother is away, the other brothers seize the opportunity to sell Joseph as a slave to a group of traders headed to Egypt. Joseph is now a slave. His dreams may have been replaced by nightmares at this point. Can you relate? The idea that his abduction was a mere joke has definitely vanished. His grim reality is a very uncertain future.

The brothers agree on a plan to explain Joseph's fate. The father is told a wild animal has killed Joseph. The coat of many colors is offered to the father as proof of their claim. The coat is ripped and covered with blood. The coat of many colors has only one color seen by Joseph's father, blood red. His grief is great. The brothers have no opportunity to reverse their decisions. Their loving father is led through unnecessary pain. Their little brother is launched into unthinkable difficulty. Life will never be the same again.

In Egypt, Joseph is sold to the household of Potiphar, the captain of Pharaoh's bodyguard. At this point, the Bible records the secret of Joseph's plight: the Lord was with Joseph. Because the Lord was with Joseph, Joseph found favor in the eyes of Potiphar. Potiphar entrusted his entire household to Joseph's care and leadership. Potiphar never again concerned himself with household matters while Joseph stood at the helm. Nothing was out of Joseph's sphere of influence. Joseph did a great job. He prospered. Everyone noticed that Joseph was exceptional. Even Potiphar's wife did not miss the dashing young man in her house.

At an opportune moment, Potiphar's wife attempts to take Joseph for herself. She verbally calls him to engage her in physical relations. He says no. The Bible says this seductive temptress worked day after day to demolish his resolve to honor Potiphar and God. Joseph always said no. Finally, one fateful day, she grabs his clothes, and begs him. Please, sleep with me. Joseph refuses citing this sin would be against God. And he runs. She holds his clothes to prevent his exit. He leaves his garment to escape the scene of his temptation. Potiphar's wife begins a scheme to destroy what she could not have. She fabricates a plan to paint Joseph as the perpetrator.

When Potiphar returns, his wife shares that Joseph tried to seduce her. With the grandeur of a Hollywood soap opera, she explains the gory details of her horrific encounter. The garment from Joseph is offered to Potiphar as proof to her claim. Potiphar's anger rages against Joseph. He strips Joseph of his position and throws Joseph in jail. Joseph has no opportunity to reverse the decisions made by Potiphar. Yet, the Bible records that the Lord was with Joseph.

In jail, Joseph finds favor in the eyes of the chief jailer. Before long, Joseph was in charge of all the prisoners who were there. The chief jailer trusts Joseph. He does not concern himself with anything placed under Joseph's charge. In this place, Joseph meets two men who were servants in Pharaoh's court. The chief cupbearer and the chief baker are placed in jail for unspecified episodes that brought anger to Pharaoh. Joseph is their caretaker. After an undetermined number of days, both men had a dream that compels them to sorrow. Joseph discovers they are sad because no one could interpret their dreams.

He seizes the opportunity. Joseph volunteers to be their interpreter. One can only guess how he may have considered the meaning of his own dreams. What hope did he still place in those interpretations he rendered for himself many years earlier? Nevertheless, Joseph jumps into the dreams of the two who yearned for his thoughts. The two dreams produce two phenomenal results. Both men are given interpretations that prove true within three days. The fulfillment of the dreams placed the chief cupbearer back in Pharaoh's court; just as Joseph predicts. The other man is hung on a tree; just as Joseph predicts.

Joseph has asked both men to remember his deed on the day of their freedom, but both men fail to share Joseph's talent with anyone. No one comes to reward Joseph's expertise as a dream interpreter. No one comes to accomplish what Joseph had hoped would be his ticket from jail. This is important to Joseph. He shares with both men that he was unfairly brought to this place. Both men should have had sympathy and empathy for Joseph. But, neither helps. The Bible says that the cupbearer even forgot Joseph.

For two years, Joseph has good fortune as the chief jailer's chief helper. As a prisoner, he continues with faithfulness in all tasks marking life. Joseph dreams of freedom. His former station as a slave afforded a type of freedom foreign to him at present. He sits waiting for God to move. Then, Pharaoh reports a dream no one in Egypt could interpret. With Pharaoh's dilemma, the chief cupbearer seizes the opportunity to inform Pharaoh that a young Hebrew prisoner has skill in the art of interpretation. Say no more. Joseph is swept into Pharaoh's court after a good bath and a shave.

Pharaoh shares with Joseph, and Joseph renders an interpretation. Joseph identifies God as the source of his interpretation. With this interpretation, Joseph makes a commentary outlining a plan to save Egypt in the years to come. Pharaoh buys the interpretation and the plan. He asks what man could accomplish the tasks outlined in Joseph's plan. No one steps forward. Maybe no one has the opportunity. The Bible records that Pharaoh declares Joseph most capable. Immediately, Pharaoh takes action. There is no consultation with any members of the court. No second opinions are sought. Pharaoh takes off his signet ring and gives it to Joseph. He places royal robes and gold necklaces upon Joseph. He takes Joseph for a ride in the royal chariot and calls all Egypt to bow before Joseph. Pharaoh gives Joseph a wife. What a deal. Just yesterday Joseph is only dreaming of freedom. Now, Joseph is second to Pharaoh in all Egypt.

TRIED AND TESTED TRUTH

Yes, God works in mysterious ways. In the course of this story, a lot has been learned. Think about Joseph's journey. He has had several moves. He is hurled from the comfort of his father's house to the darkness of a pit. He is dragged from this pit to the shackles of a slave convoy. The slave convoy discards him in the palace of a great Egyptian warrior. Joseph tumbles from the prestige of this palace to the misery and obscurity of a jail. He catapults from the dungeons of this jail to the pinnacle of the Egyptian empire. What a ride? Wow! Joseph is amazing.

He never seems to give up.

Can you see what he now sees? He must have seen that cupbearer who forgot him for two years. He must have seen the chief jailer who gave him responsibility but did not help him with his false imprisonment. He must have seen Potiphar. He must have seen Potiphar's wife. Read the rest of Joseph's story. He sees his brothers and his father. In their presence, the dreams of his youth are fulfilled. He seems to have forgiven them all. What is the reason for his tremendous character and strength in the face of so much adversity?

What does Joseph teach? He teaches contentment. How you ask? Look closely and you will discover Joseph's thoughts about the course of his life. Genesis 41:50-52 says, "Before the years of famine came, two sons were born to Joseph by Asenath daughter of Potiphera, priest of On. Joseph named his firstborn Manasseh . . . and . . . The second son he named Ephraim . . . ." Names in the Bible have a significant role in story telling. Names convey much about the persons and events within the frame of a biblical story. Look at some easily recognizable examples.

What did it mean to change Jacob's name (Genesis 32:28) to Israel? What was the message in the names of Hosea's children (Hosea 1)? Joseph is no exception. With the names of his two sons, a powerful message is proclaimed to all who seek the secret to Joseph's success. Embedded within their names is the simple guideline for contentment. Joseph uses the names of his sons to declare the contentment he employed to move through his life.

Manasseh celebrates Joseph's success over the difficulties of his past and present. This name means God has made Joseph forget his troubles. Contentment accepts the troubles in ones life as allowed by God. They may be the product of bad circumstances or ill-advised decisions, but they are within the sovereignty of God. The Psalmist declares in Psalms 23, "Even though I walk through the valley of the shadow of death, I will fear no evil, for you are with me; your rod and your staff, they comfort me." The Psalmist is acknowledging the possibility of valleys. The Psalmist is willing to walk through the valleys. God does not promise to eliminate all the difficulty in your life. But, He promises to be with you and provide for you. He promises to meet you at the point of your need.

Contentment sees this. Throughout Joseph's story, Joseph is clearly acknowledging the presence and anointing of God in the midst of all his circumstances. The Bible records his constant awareness. He forgets his troubles as he goes. This practice is clear throughout this story because no mention is made of any bitterness. To forget the past means to let it go into the sovereign hand of God. He placed in God's hand any lost time with his dad. He placed in God's hand any lost days of freedom. He placed in God's hand all the things he missed out on. All of his previous troubles are forgotten.

This contentment principle also works in the present. He still has troubles. When he is with his wife and child, he may wonder if his father will ever know them. When he is at work, he carries a heavy weight. Joseph has the charge of a large campaign to save the Egyptian empire without the use of a sword. He moves against an enemy that has not arrived. So much pressure is riding on his shoulders. For seven years he must work to mobilize the masses to store grain. Then, after seven years, he will know if the Lord's anointing to interpret Pharaoh's dream was completely sound. But, when Joseph looks into Manasseh's face, he is called to forget all of his troubles, past and present. Joseph is content.

Manasseh also means God has made him forget his father's household. This is another great principle of contentment. To forget his father's household does not mean to push them from his memory. In the latter stages of the story he clearly receives his family with forgiveness. Nowhere in Joseph's story does he express resentment. Look at the places where Joseph weeps. In one place, he sees his brother Benjamin. Genesis

43:30 says, "Deeply moved at the sight of his brother, Joseph hurried out and looked for a place to weep. He went into his private room and wept there." He is not weeping tears of pain. His tears are tears of joy. He is overwhelmed with the sense of God's goodness in His life. He is feeling the beautiful fruit of having forgiven others.

As proof of forgiveness being complete in Joseph's life, he gives the choicest land in all Egypt to his family. His forgiveness is like that of Christ. Your infractions against God were far greater than any Joseph received from his family. When Christ forgave you, He did not just cleanse you from your sin. He forgives you and blesses you with a relationship with God. God did not hold your sins against you. He forgets them but not you. Contentment calls you to forgive others. You must strive to forgive as God forgives. This forgiveness is something Joseph applied as he went. If anger and bitterness were in the picture, you never see a single hint in Genesis. Joseph is content.

This type of forgiveness is important when you strive for contentment. In contentment, you accept God's sovereign provision for all things. You also place all things into God's sovereign hand. Forgiveness is a part of that. If God is sovereign over your circumstances, He is also sovereign over the people in those circumstances. You must "forget" them. Look at Christ as He hung on the cross. He looks at those who have constructed His situation. He feels the pain of their ambition. Luke 23:34a says, "Jesus said, 'Father, forgive them, for they do not know what they are doing.'" Forgiveness is something God has freely given to you. Forgiveness is something Christ shared in the midst of his troubles. Forgiveness is something Joseph applied as he went.

Why do you attempt to hold it from others? You should "forget." You should forgive others as you forget your troubles. The Bible calls you to forgive others as God has forgiven you. Luke 11:4 says, "Forgive us our sins, for we also forgive everyone who sins against us." Joseph is saying you cannot have contentment until you learn to "forget" those who have brought your pain. Manasseh reminds Joseph to keep the vigil of forgiveness. The name, Manasseh, brings to bear the "forgetting principle" in contentment. This is the first step to true contentment.

The second name, Ephraim, gives the second step. The name of Joseph's second son celebrates success in the past, present and future. This name means that the Lord has made him to be fruitful in the land of his suffering. At this point, Joseph has reached the top of his world. He could be the poster child for success. He is no longer a slave or prisoner. He is not just an average "Joe." He is "the man." But, do not think for one moment that the inspiration leading to the name of this child is only drawn after he ascends Pharaoh's court. Notice Joseph's journey.

He experiences success in every station of his life: in the pit, in the convoy, in Potiphar's house and in the jail. Joseph had success. In the pit, he is successful because he is not killed. In the convoy, Joseph's success is shrouded in the mystery of a Hebrew boy being bought by the head of Pharaoh's bodyguard. Joseph's success has a clear source; the Lord. The Lord is with Joseph in the pit, in the convoy, in Potiphar's house and in the jail. Joseph completely believes the Lord directs his journey. In a climactic moment in his story, Genesis 45:8 declares Joseph's belief before his brothers. Joseph says, "So then, it was not you who sent me here, but God. He made me father to Pharaoh, lord of his entire household and ruler of all Egypt."

The Lord is the common theme in each setting. He acknowledges the Lord on many occasions. Joseph has not forgotten Him. He also knows the Lord has not forgotten him. The sense of God's presence is important. It is the key to this step in contentment. Potiphar can see God is with Joseph. Genesis 39:3-4a says, "When his master saw that the LORD was with him and that the LORD gave him success in everything he did, Joseph found favor in his eyes and became his attendant."

GOD IS SO GOOD

With any and all difficulties, Joseph does not give you a lesson for only surviving but for thriving. He has had a lofty dream given to him from the Lord as a youth. When that dream seems the farthest thing from Joseph's grasp, he is gripping responsibilities and activities in his present reality with peculiar zeal. Joseph may consider his present situation a stewardship. The present is always wrapped in the package of your circumstances. The package should never affect your response to the call of steward. You are called to seek the Lord and prove a faithful steward in each station of life. You see Joseph's situations. Your present situation may also be trying. Are you determined to see fruitfulness in the land of your suffering? Be encouraged. Romans 8:28 records, "And we know that in all things God works for the good of those who love him, who have been called according to his purpose." God promises to work with you to this end.

You do not know what will be the good that will come from any situation. If you trust God, you cannot lean on your own understanding to determine what may be the possible good. God may work beyond the realm of your possibilities. You can safely assume being Pharaoh's second was not on Joseph's wish list. Also, God may work beyond the realm of your awareness. You may not know what God is doing, but reading Joseph's story reminds you God is doing something. Success in the land of your suffering is a work in process. And, God is at work.

For Joseph, the one brother who pleads his case pleads in a timely manner to save Joseph from death. God was preparing this brother to take this stand. How timely is the passing convoy. Imagine all the details involved in the convoy from its start. Who could see the convoy coming at that moment? God brought that convoy during the absence of the one brother who pled Joseph's case. If the one brother had been with the other brothers at that moment, he may have thwarted their plans to sell Joseph.

But, if they had not sold him, where would this story be? Connect all of these timely dots in the story of Joseph. Look at God's fingerprints scattered throughout each scene. Joseph knew God was at work.

God does not intend bad things, but He uses them to accomplish His good. He seems to make the best of each situation. Joseph does not just wish that situation away. Is wishing for a change in a situation wrong? Wishing is not always wrong. Joseph tells the two men with a dream in jail that he wants to get out of jail. In some sense Joseph affirms working for change. But also notice Joseph does not let this wish consume him. It does not cripple him. It does not deter him from being a faithful steward and making the most of his present situation. Contentment compels him to press forward through all situations in a faithful manner. Ephraim is the child whose face reminds Joseph to be a good steward of the present. The two steps of contentment move you forward.

Once you breach the threshold of contentment, the Lord is busy supporting the decisions that tangibly manifest your trust in Him. Contentment helps you see how responsive the Lord is to your prayers. Like you, Paul has needs. He prays. But, Paul is content knowing that God, in His way, will meet him at the point of his need. Although the outcome may be immaterial, I believe God actually responds immediately. In light of this, your previous anxiety seems totally in vain.

Are you familiar with the possible responses God gives to your prayer requests? They are evident in Scripture: Yes, No or Wait. That is it. And the response is immediate. Survey your recent list of prayers. Where did God say yes? Where did God say no? Where did God say wait? My prayer history is littered with many requests assigned to each of these three possibilities. If I do not receive an immediate yes or no, then I immediately place that request in my wait category. That is what God calls me to do. He asks me to wait.

One of my requests garnered this wait response from the Lord. After an evening worship service at a summer youth camp, I met a mom as she cried tears of desperation for her daughter. As we sat outside, she told me every night she waited for her daughter's response to God's invitation for relationship. The mom was devastated. She said, "Tomorrow night is our last camp worship. My daughter has not made a decision to become a Christian." Her desperation is compelled by the fact that she did not know how much longer she would live. She continued, "I have been diagnosed with cancer. I am very desperate to see my daughter become a Christian before I die."

Waiting is something she feels she cannot afford to do. She needed an answer from the Lord. She needed something. I asked her if she was content. Are you willing to acknowledge God's sovereignty in your situation? Do you know He is in control? Do you know He is mindful of your need? Do you know He hears your cry? Are you willing to trust God with your daughter? Are you willing to see that God has answered your prayers with a call to wait?

She had fought her anxiety with valor, she had brought this request to the Lord as one of everything in her life, and she had been thankful. She had followed the three things needed for a successful prayer experience. But she lacked being content. She lacked freeing herself from the expectation of her request. Her choice to trust God in this situation was the only choice she had not made. She needed to trust God. She needed to be content. She needed to be like Joseph because Joseph shows how content is meant.

GUARDING PEACE

What images come to mind when you think of peace? Do you think of peace as a symbol painted on objects across your world? Do you think of peace as a timeless greeting shared with your fellow man? Do you think of peace as the absence of war? When have you experienced peace? Did you have peace when your cancer moved into remission? Did you have peace when you got a job? Did you have peace while overlooking a mountainous panorama? Was peace waiting outside of your office building?

The right place, the right time, and the right set of circumstances seem to be requirements to paint the perfect picture of peace. But, what is peace? Is peace a feeling? Is peace something found or received? Is peace a sword made into a plow? Can you choose peace? Does peace choose you? Who needs peace? Who does not need peace? A countless volume of people, situations, and issues compel you to scream for peace. Whatever peace may be, peace is definitely desired by the masses of humanity. In response, the world makes many efforts to obtain peace. Their endeavor to create peace is extensive but not successful.

BY DEFINITION

The first consideration of peace by a dictionary places peace at bay when war is present. In light of human history, questions are raised concerning the effectiveness of any global efforts for peace. Proponents cite the "war to end all wars" as a modern memorial to the pursuit of global peace. Today, the world is entangled in wars that dot the planet. Perhaps you cannot relate to war. Take a single glance at the news to see the reality of this global crisis. Several countries are all too familiar with the daily activity of war. Peace fades from their landscape as millions of lives are shattered. And so are treaties to end those wars. The dictionary's second consideration of peace, an agreement or treaty to end hostilities, seems a lost cause amid the carnage of broken peace efforts throughout history.

So, the question of world peace marches on. If world peace is difficult, what can be said about national peace? Americans want borders to be safe. How certain is that peace? How sure are you that the next terrorist attack will be discovered in time? Experts have said they cannot protect everything all the time. How confident can you be in your government's pursuit of peace? The dictionary's third consideration of peace as public security is not a guarantee.

The dictionary's fourth consideration of peace as a freedom from quarrels pits one person with another. Every setting where two or more individuals live or work may attempt to establish and maintain this type of peace. If this utopia were achieved, the need for lawyers, doctors, police officers and counselors would diminish. Divorce courts would not exist. Sporting events would not be as exciting. Family reunions would really be a family affair. And, brides would finally have a real chance at their perfect wedding. But this peace is like dancing the tango. You cannot dance alone. You cannot assume your partner likes or even knows how to dance. Peace among individuals can be challenging to predict.

The dictionary's fifth and sixth consideration of peace as inner contentment, serenity or a state of tranquility is very appealing. This peace deals with individuals individually. Are you at peace? Can you imagine how many people long for this peace in their lives? But, is there such a peace? Is peace of this nature only a wishful fabrication? Is the pursuit of this peace foolishness? Jobs, children, neighbors, friends, family, politics, finances, crime, self-image, and much more wage war against personal peace. In this world, everything bears the potential to rob peace of its place in your life. So, peace may seem just beyond your reach.

HIS PEACE

Many people only know peace as a distant memory or farfetched fantasy. Nevertheless, people are willing to do anything for peace. Individuals engage possessions, counselors, substances, work or pleasure. These items provide a medium to harvest peace through compulsion or addiction. Peace under these circumstances is masterfully constructed, but momentarily held. The efforts seldom maintain peace because no one can predict or control circumstances. As a concession, many individuals seem to be okay moving from one experience of momentary peace to another. This peace seems to be compromised when rationed in such portions. Where can lasting and meaningful peace be found?

The Bible is not silent concerning peace. Peace is an angel's proclamation to the world on a silent night. Peace is a charge administered and a promise given to many generations worshipping the God of Abraham. Peace is central to God. He identifies Himself as the God of Peace. He blesses humanity with His peace. Psalms 29:11 says, "The LORD gives strength to his people; the LORD blesses his people with peace." Isaiah says His peace flows like a river. Solomon says God's peace with famine is better than strife with a banquet. The Psalmist says he will lie down and sleep in the light of God's peace. Peace is identified as a fruit of the

Holy Spirit in the New Testament. The Bible calls Jesus the Prince of Peace. His mission is pronounced as the "good news of peace" (Acts 10:36) and the "gospel of peace" (Ephesians 6:15). In John 14:27, the priestly prayer, Jesus says, "Peace I leave with you; my peace I give you. I do not give to you as the world gives. Do not let your hearts be troubled and do not be afraid."

What do you notice about this Jesus' peace? His peace is not the same as the world's. Initially, you agree His peace is not made through your effort. God knows you cannot make His peace. You cannot in any way produce the peace that abides. Your peace cannot endure. You cannot make the peace that withstands the pressures of this life. Additionally, His peace is not fleeting or wavering. It is not the product of circumstances, but abides despite your circumstances. This fact is very, very important. Jesus does not hide the fact that trouble awaits and exists in your world. John 16:33 says, "I have told you these things, so that in me you may have peace. In this world you will have trouble. But take heart! I have overcome the world." Jesus' peace abides in the midst of your trouble-ridden world.

Picture all of your troubles. Can you see the issues and individuals who rob you of your peace? Can you see your time, money, and productivity lost in your crazy, peace-less world. Where can you find peace? The answer is amazingly simple. Philippians 4:7 says, "And the peace of God, which transcends all understanding, will guard your hearts and your minds in Christ Jesus." Can you see His promise of peace? Philippians 4:6 is an instruction on prayer. The "and" in verse seven strongly links the two verses placing peace as God's response to your prayer. Peace is the true product of your prayer; the only outcome you should seek.

Remember the camp mom from the previous chapter? She wanted an answer to her prayer. She was restless and needed something concrete from God. She prayed for her daughter to make a life-changing decision at camp. She wanted results that day. When she tells God how and when to do something, does she not limit His sovereignty over her situation? When she seeks only the answer, does she not miss being content? When she is not content, she is not trusting God. When she is not trusting, she is not experiencing the peace God promises.

The mom finally claimed this promise and sought the peace of God on her final day at camp. She smiled and testified that she had peace regarding her daughter's future. She trusted God. She successfully sought to be content and now was experiencing the peace God provided. That night, her daughter accepted God's invitation. The camp mom was elated. Answers may not be so immediate for you, but you can immediately have what this mom had, peace. Do not look at your prayer process as only a channel for your requests to approach God. See prayer as a channel for God to provide you with His peace. Pray a lot. Then, abundantly seek peace, the true product of prayer. In this troubled world, you can certainly use all the peace God cares to provide.

Now look at your world again. What are your challenges? What are your difficulties? Is your life a complicated web of issues, feelings, and worries? Do minutes staring at the ceiling evolve into hours? What are your thoughts before you find sleep? At this time, life may be generating many prayers of desperation. Jesus said you would have troubles. Peter adds that you should not be surprised by your difficulties. 1 Peter 4:12 says, "Dear friends, do not be surprised at the painful trial you are suffering, as though something strange were happening to you." How unfortunate no one is immune to the issues and difficulties in the world. A marriage, a financial problem, a barren spouse, a rebellious child, or other insurmountable challenges can be overwhelming. They challenge your choice of contentment. Many times, a single skirmish, a small issue, can escalate into a major unrest within you.

The Texas Rangers, a famed law enforcement agency, have a saying, "One Riot, One Ranger." Early in Texas history, one Ranger was dispatched to address any single issue of civil unrest. An assumption was made that civil order will be restored upon the Ranger's arrival. The state's confidence in their Rangers is legendary. Unfortunately, God's peace has not reached such legendary status for its similar function in this world. His peace clearly distinguishes itself from the world's peace. When you voice personal unrest, God dispatches peace, immediately. He assumes peace will do its job in the midst of your unrest. He has confidence in this mission.

However, most people have mistakenly set peace as the goal for their journey through difficult circumstances. Sitting on a beach, hearing the waves, and feeling the touch of the sun are fantasies that embody their traditional view of peace. They believe peace is something experienced in the absence of difficulties. But, Jesus' peace is different. His peace has a distinct purpose. God's intent is very clear. He has a big interest to protect: your trust in Him. God sends peace. Every prayer prayed receives this same consideration from God. And, peace goes to work.

ON A MISSION

Can you see your difficulties attempting to perpetrate and devastate your world? Like waves crashing on shore, difficulties relentlessly pound your resolve to trust God and be content. Many times, you travel through a single day and never find relief. Your efforts to be content seem hopeless. The choice to be content should not be affected by these or any challenges. Peace aims to swing the momentum of the conflict. Peace is on a mission to help you win the battle to hold contentment and preserve trust.

In Philippians 4:7, peace is administered to your heart and mind. God's peace is very important to these strategic points. As discussed earlier, the mind is tempted to gain its own understanding in the midst of your difficult circumstances. The heart is tempted to create its own way.

For trust to be complete, the heart and mind must equally and wholly be yielded to God. As you take your issues and difficulties urgently to God, you trust Him. You chose to be content. The forces inherent in difficult circumstances push against your choices and a war ensues.

The heart and mind are involved in this conflict. They play a cruel game. With the mind, you think about the situation. You think about all the ways your situation can be changed. You use words like, "if only" or "what if." Remember the game. Soon the issues jump down to your heart. You feel all the injuries you have sustained. You are hurt! You are in pain! You feel this situation is not fair or right! When you get tired of feeling, your mind reengages the battle. Once again the mind wrestles and wrestles. When the mind is again tired of thinking, the heart returns to feel through the issues. The cycle repeats over and over. Back and forth, back and forth this battle rages for hours, days, or decades. Does this material sound familiar? The dynamic process played out before your decision to trust God is the same dynamic process that continues after you choose to trust God.

No matter the issue or difficulty, God sends peace to guard the trust you placed with Him. How does this guarding work? Picture individuals employed as guards. When guards work at a correctional facility, the security configuration is organized to keep prisoners in. The entire system is focused to prevent anyone from escaping. Guards are assigned the tasks necessary to accomplish this goal. As long as no one escapes, the endeavor is considered successful. Guarding has another component. When a museum is guarding a priceless painting, the security is configured to keep would be vandals and thieves out. Guarding here does not involve keeping the painting itself from walking away. As long as no one enters to disturb or steal a painting, this ongoing endeavor to guard is considered successful. Peace guards your heart and mind in both of these ways by monitoring the traffic of messages.

In the course of a difficulty, your heart and mind receive and send messages that aim to affect your trust in God. The heart's messages aim to express feelings. The mind's messages aim to bring understanding. During one difficulty in my life, I began to record these messages. The list attempted to capture the messages moving through my heart and mind. The messages were random and regular. Examples of such messages you might have are: I will never find a good father for my children, we will lose this house to the bank, or the health of my spouse is irrecoverable. Years later, I reviewed my list and realized most of the messages from those days were false or unfounded. But, at the time, I was completely convinced they were true. I remember making decisions based on this perspective. In hindsight, I realize the messages were used to destroy my contentment. With contentment defeated, my trust in God wavered.

As I took matters into my own hands, a sense of peace came with my new perception of control. At best, this sense of peace was only momentary. My decisions in response to my pressure undermined God's design for peace. If I spoiled peace's mission, I did not know at the time how I played the spoiler. How does God's peace guard your trust in Him?

When messages are traveling from the heart and mind, not all the messages are good and not all are bad. Left to yourself, you would have difficulty discerning which is which in the midst of your troubles. The guarding function of peace in Philippians 4:7 screens each message to determine which is good and which is bad. Peace will identify feelings and thoughts that are harmful to your trust in God. Likewise, peace will affirm messages that build your trust in God.

This guarding element of peace can best be seen in the functionality of a computer anti-virus program. With the advent of the Internet, a number of files rushing in and out of your computer from various sources skyrocketed. Specialized anti-virus programs became critically important to ensure the safety of your computer. If a virus gets in, the operation of the computer is affected. The anti-virus program reviews all files entering and exiting. The program must constantly be updated to keep up with the new harmful files arriving daily. When a file arrives or attempts to leave your computer, the anti-virus program checks its integrity and composition. If something harmful is found, the file is identified for discarding. You are given the choice to click and discard the file. The threat is gone with the discarded file. Your computer is safe.

Messages from your heart and mind are handled in a similar fashion. Travel from continent-to-continent, country-to-country, city-to-city, and house-to-house. Imagine how many experiences of pain and heartache are captured in the frame of one life? Imagine how many messages one lifetime produces? These messages are a natural product of life. Just as you are not immune to difficulties, you are not immune to messages traveling to and from your heart and mind. They are birthed in many sources. They are from people and situations. They are direct. They are implied. They are a product of your intuition and imagination.

Over and over again, as messages stream to and from your heart and mind, peace screens the traffic to protect your trust in God. Peace helps you recognize the infected messages. The means to this end may surprise you. Philippians 4:7 says this peace transcends all understanding. Initially, the verse seems to promote your inadequacy to understand God's peace. As the object of your contemplation, His peace is so wonderful you cannot fully grasp it. Verse 7 may be in full agreement with this view. God's peace is very profound. His peace thrives in the midst of your pain. Many in the world may be asking how that is possible. They, and in truth most Christians, are truly amazed at the end result of God's peace. The problems may still be present. The solutions may seem distant. But, peace stands a defiant watch against the winds of turmoil in your life. Transcending understanding in verse 7 captures the world's inconclusive deliberation attempting to know God's peace.

STRATEGIC POINTS

Another perspective may also be in order. The "understanding" in this passage may be the understanding produced by your mind regarding your situation. The messages generated by your mind aim to destroy your trust in God. Verse 7 may be saying that peace transcends all this understanding from your mind. Peace's mission cannot be thwarted by your mind. Peace destroys your mind's misled understanding in its path to victory. The verse spotlights insight into the battle plan employed by peace to guard your trust in God. As the mind produces messages, peace takes its stand. The Greek word for transcends, *huperecho* (hoop-er-ekh'-o), places peace above or superior to understanding. This peace is better, higher, and passes all understanding in the wake of its victory.

This battlefield of the mind is clear in the Bible. The greatest commandment, Matthew 22:37, calls you to love God with your entire mind. Romans 12:2 states that the Holy Spirit separates you from the world through the renewing of your mind. Second Corinthians 10:5 compels you to take every thought captive. Each and every single thought must be within your control. Instead of taking control of your circumstances, peace assists you to take control of your thoughts.

The Bible identifies the mind as a strategic point. The mind originally elected to trust God. The mind must be supported by thoughts that support this trust in God. Peace stands where contentment upholds complete trust in God. These three variables have a powerful relationship: peace, contentment, and trust. You choose to trust. Your choice to trust enables your choice to be content. Your choice to be content supports God's provision of peace. Isaiah brings them together. Isaiah 26:3 says, "You will keep in perfect peace him whose mind is steadfast, because he trusts in you." The Hebrew word for steadfast is *camak* (saw-mak'). It means to "bear up, establish, hold, lean, and stand fast." It creates stability in commitment and belief. It holds your trust in place.

Being steadfast of mind means to literally hold your ground against the forces attempting to defeat your position. The discipline of your will must follow this conviction.

Take a moment to record the traffic in your mind. Now, ask yourself which message is good and which is bad. How are you to know? What is the best process to screen your messages? In the world of counterfeiting, Secret Service agents are trained to recognize the good from the bad. They become experts in the trade of identifying. How? They are simply trained to become very, very familiar with genuine bills. Sure they are looking for fake bills, but they are asked to recognize genuine bills. Experience has established this technique as the best technique. When they easily recognize genuine bills, they are able to recognize fake bills with ease.

Peace screens through a similar process. Paul provides the means to become familiar with good messages. In Philippians 4:8, he outlines the standard to measure all messages. He says, "Finally, brothers, whatever is true, whatever is noble, whatever is right, whatever is pure, whatever is lovely, whatever is admirable— if anything is excellent or praiseworthy— think about such things." This verse provides a filter through which all messages should flow. Catch each message presently flowing through your situation and examine its content and composition. Only feelings and thoughts affirmed by this list are welcome to proceed. Any feelings and thoughts not affirmed by this list are considered harmful and must be discarded.

Look at your list. Are the items true? Are they noble? Are they right or pure? Are they lovely ... and so forth. When the message is affirmed by the above verse, the message serves to support your trust in God. The message acknowledges and affirms God's activity in the midst of your circumstance. God is true, noble, right, pure, lovely, admirable and praiseworthy. God is.

Peace assists your steadfast resolve to conform your mind to this truth. As every feeling and thought passes through the guarding function of peace, peace holds the standard. When an anti-virus program screens a file, it compares the file to a list of known files. If there is a match, in this case with a bad file, the file is brought to your consideration for discarding. Additionally, if the file is not recognized, it is opened in a safe zone. This zone allows the anti-virus program to view the file and check for harmful agents. The agents are isolated in this safe zone and cannot infect the computer. Once again, when a bad agent is found, the file is brought to your consideration for discarding.

Harmful thoughts produced by your mind must follow a similar process. Some thoughts are immediately recognized as unhealthy thoughts aimed at destroying your trust in God. These thoughts must be discarded. This takes discipline. Other thoughts are not so clear. You may attempt to discover the potency of these thoughts by "opening" them within the context of Scripture and the company of a wise counselor. Do you see the need for discipline here? The guarding work of peace has a security configuration that attempts to keep some things out and keep some things in.

TRAFFIC CORRIDORS

For example, say you have just experienced the death of a spouse. Many feelings and thoughts are sweeping through your consciousness. Consider the message: you are completely alone. Is this a true message? You may feel a real feeling of loneliness, but the fact that people are present to support you makes the message not true. You are not completely alone. The message is infected with a harmful agent intended to corrupt your heart and mind's trust in God. It compromises the work of God underway to meet you at the point of your need. You are blinded to the incredible hand of God providing you with loving people to support your grief. This message must be discarded.

What about when you are laid off from your job? Consider the message: you will never find a job as great as the one you lost. Is this a true message? You may not see any immediate options. The future may be unknown. You may live in a fantasy that paints your previous place of employment as the perfect place. But, the fact remains you cannot know how other jobs may be equally great. The words "never" and "as great" make this message untrue. It is infected with a harmful agent intended to corrupt your heart and mind. It must be discarded.

How about a divorce? Consider the message: you hate your ex-spouse. Grief, tears, and disbelief are certainly evidence of a devastated world. Your feelings of pain generate a powerful hatred. Is this noble? This is absolutely not noble. This message is void of God's sovereignty. With divorce, there is a healing process. The hand of God supports each step in the aftermath of a tragic event like divorce. Others have walked this path. You must also manage these steps to discover God's provision. This message is not noble because God's love transcends all offenses and works through all situations. The message is infected. It must be discarded.

In His wisdom, God has established this process. The process is an excellent exercise of discipline. The process allows peace to execute its profound function of guarding. But Philippians 4:8 gives more than a standard to filter messages. The last phrase in this verse calls you to think on these things. This clear directive compels you to find good messages. If you lack the presence of good messages, you should generate good messages. Place them on the traffic corridors between your heart and mind. This is the intent of Paul's instruction. He aims to foster the presence of good messages that encourage your heart and mind. You must apply effort to evaluate your situation and discover the things of God surrounding your circumstances. This activity is a prescription in the Bible.

Psalms 77:11-12 says, "I will remember the deeds of the LORD; yes, I will remember your miracles of long ago. I will meditate on all your works and consider all your mighty deeds." Psalms 105:1-5 says, "Give thanks to the LORD, call on his name; make known among the nations what he has done. Sing to him, sing praise to him; tell of all his wonderful acts. Glory in his holy name; let the hearts of those who seek the LORD rejoice. Look to the LORD and his strength; seek his face always. Remember the wonders he has done, his miracles, and the judgments he pronounced." Psalms 103:1-5 says, "Praise the LORD, O my soul; all my inmost being, praise his holy name. Praise the LORD, O my soul, and forget not all his benefits— who forgives all your sins and heals all your diseases, who redeems your life from the pit and crowns you with love and compassion, who satisfies your desires with good things so that your youth is renewed like the eagle's."

As you reflect in this manner, you begin to generate a list of good messages. God has indeed done great things. Wow! Do you feel bad that you could only think of negative thoughts previously? Now you are aware of many, many blessings swimming through your turbulent times. You should write them down. You should post them in places you frequent: your bathroom mirror, the dashboard of your car, or the space above your desk. You should chant them as prayers of praise to the Lord.

Paul finally concludes this passage with an incredible promise. He states in Philippians 4:9, "Whatever you have learned or received or heard from me, or seen in me— put it into practice. And the God of peace will be with you." Here, He is called the God of peace. He is the champion of the work underway to protect your trust in Him. As you do what Paul says and does, you will receive not only the peace of God, but you will also receive the God of peace. You know Christians believe God is with them. There is no question in this matter. But this specific promise of presence aims to communicate comfort. During difficult times, you may be quick to question God's presence. The promise of God's company brings an assurance of safe passage.

Throughout the Bible, the presence of God carried great meaning. David assures Solomon of God's presence as Solomon set out to finish the Temple of God (1 Chronicles 28:20). Moses declares God's presence with Joshua (Deuteronomy 31:7-8). Mary finds favor with the Lord and is assured of His presence during her journey to deliver the Savior of the World (Luke 1:28). Psalms 23 reveals the rod and staff of God are with you in the valleys of your life. Many, many more verses record the meaning of God's presence. Paul's declaration of this promise should not be taken lightly. Your personal experience in claiming this promise will not be disappointing. With this promise of God's presence, a prize of grand proportion awaits.

Consider the people of Israel. They journeyed in the land for forty years. Throughout their journey, they were privileged with the presence of God: a cloud by day and a pillar of fire by night. God wanted to assure them they would experience victory. In addition to this tangible presence of God, Moses had the incredible privilege of seeing God Himself. Sure, the burning bush must have been awesome. Mount Sinai must have been spectacular. But Exodus 33 records a most compelling story. Moses sees God Himself. God wanted to give Moses confidence regarding his mission. In addition, God made a promise. Exodus 33:14 says, "The LORD replied, 'My Presence will go with you, and I will give you rest.'" Moses had seen many great difficulties accompanying his trek from Egypt. Much more awaited him. God had not only promised to provide for Moses' physical needs, but He was giving Moses an assurance that the journey would not rob the opportunity for rest. How amazing is the idea of rest in the midst of your difficulties?

A KING'S DISCIPLINE

David provides a compelling picture. In Psalms 131, David says, "Oh LORD, my heart is not proud, nor are my eyes haughty, nor do I involve myself in great matters or things too difficult for me." The first time I read this, I thought I had found an inaccuracy in scripture. King David wrote this. He has all the opportunity in the world to be proud. He has gone from being a shepherd boy to a King. He could be haughty because David is the pinnacle of Israel's social establishment. And, how can he avoid great matters? He is the king of a nation, Commander-in-Chief of an army, and the head of a large family. Did David really write this? He did write this passage and meant every word. In the midst of his complex and busy world, he learned a profound truth.

David understands his relationship with God. When he comes before the Lord, he comes in humility. He knows God will help him. David has lived a life depending on God. Can you see him as a youth in the fields before the wild beasts? Can you see him before Goliath? He hid in caves awaiting God's timing to take Israel's throne. David knows the only success in his life comes directly from God's hand. As a result, David has transferred the great matters of the kingdom to the Lord.

David continues in Psalms 131, "Surely, I have composed and quieted my soul." His soul, like your soul, is often restless. You have a lot on your mind and a lot on your plate. A preacher once said your restless soul is like a cage of monkeys. The monkeys represent the motion of your consciousness. They are bouncing and swinging here and there. They are hyper and looking for something to grab and something to hold. The monkeys grab and hold your worrisome thoughts and difficult feelings. They facilitate a constant pressure against your platform of contentment. David uses discipline to keep back the destructive forces that work against his trust in God. The target of this discipline is his soul. He cannot control what is happening in the world around him. But, he knows

151

his soul is within his reach. He administers an effort to prevent compromise. David applies discipline to guard a steadfast spirit. The circumstances of life aim to undermine God's provision of peace. But, perfect peace supports a discipline to preserve your trust in God.

Psalms 131 continues, "Like a weaned child rests against its mother, so my soul is like a weaned child within me." In applying his discipline, David gives a monumental picture. He identifies rest and masterfully compares it to a weaned child. What is a weaned child? A weaned child is a child that is old enough to communicate its need. Additionally, the child knows the need has been heard. But the child also realizes it is unable to meet its own need. I was my nephew's first babysitter. The responsibility to watch this four-month old ran a full four-hours. Two hours from the start, my brother-in-law came from work to check my success. I assured him the baby was fine. Nevertheless, he checked. He discovered the baby had a very bad diaper. How should I have known I exclaimed? The baby was not crying. I had no idea anything was wrong.

Babies cannot speak. They cry. When they cry, you have no idea why. You have to guess. You just go through a checklist until you discover their need. When they get a little older, they can talk. You know what they need, but they are still too young to know you have heard. They may repeat their request over and over again until the need is met. When they get just a little older, their need is communicated with an awareness that you have understood. No one has to guess if the communication was successful. This marks a weaned child.

David reveals something about himself in this comparison. He is the weaned child before God. Although he is the King and commands the wealth of Israel, he realizes he is completely dependent on God. His circumstances and issues are completely beyond his reach. He must trust God because he cannot do anything else. He equally knows his need is being heard. The image of a weaned child illustrates a powerful truth to all those who call upon God. Why should you stand firm against the forces waging war with your contentment? You stand firm because you trust God for your need. Why do you keep standing firm? You keep standing firm because you have no other option. Like a weaned child, you have absolutely no ability to meet your own need. This revelation should not discomfort you. The picture painted by David is not a weaned child in distress. On the contrary, David paints a picture of a weaned child resting against the mother.

David sees himself in this image. His revelation in this passage should inspire you to be as this weaned child. When you wait on God, He wants to hold you. He wants to give you rest in His arms. A college student was waiting to hear about a summer job. She confessed to me that she was anxious. She begged me to pray for the outcome of her interview. She had no peace. I asked her what day she would hear something. She said Thursday.

Remembering David's image, I asked her to see her time between now and Thursday with new perspective. God intended this time as a special time with her. She knew she would get an answer. She knew God wanted the best for her. She trusted God. I shared Psalms 131 with her. I asked her to imagine God holding her as a weaned child. While you need Him, God may cherish His opportunity to hold you. He may never have an opportunity to hold you again under these same circumstances. If you trust Him, do you really need to be squirming? If you trust Him, do you want to rob Him of the pleasure of this special embrace?

Within the context of your need, God savors His embrace. The image of being held by God should hold you. It is an image that brings purpose to the peace God promises. In the midst of all of your challenges, the God who created the universe makes rest an intimate exchange. The waves that crash your platform of contentment seem distant from His arms. The turbulent waters pull away as a tide. They are no match against the warmth and comfort of God's rest. This rest is the ultimate prize that peace brings.

God is compelling you to rest in the midst of your challenges. Matthew 11:28-30 says, "Come to me, all you who are weary and burdened, and I will give you rest. Take my yoke upon you and learn from me, for I am gentle and humble in heart, and you will find rest for your souls. For my yoke is easy and my burden is light." This invitation is for you. How many impressions does this passage express to support the necessity of its invitation? The image of you carrying burdens is clear. How many burdens do you carry? You may carry them at work, at the mall, and to your bed. The image of you being weary should not be difficult to appreciate. Are you on your last leg? Jesus is receiving you. Simply put, He calls you. Pray. Choose to trust God. Choose to be content. Seek the peace God promises. And with that peace, find rest for your soul. The Psalmist underscores this point. Psalms 62:1 says, "My soul finds rest in God alone; my salvation comes from him." Rest is an important part of God's creation design. He built us to experience rest.

Several images come to mind with the issue of rest. God created for six days and rested on the seventh. God's action became the model for the instruction and observation of the Sabbath, a special day of rest. God instructed the people of Israel to make the Sabbath a deliberate day of separation. The Sabbath was to be considered Holy. In addition to the Sabbath, Jesus provides another picture of rest. Matthew 8:24-25 says, "Without warning, a furious storm came up on the lake, so that the waves swept over the boat. But Jesus was sleeping. The disciples went and woke him, saying, 'Lord, save us! We're going to drown!'" In the midst of a raging storm, Jesus was sleeping. He knew God was in control. He did not let the circumstances surrounding Him alter His state of literal rest. Jesus found rest in the midst of turmoil. The chaos of a ship in stormy waters may make many of your troubles seem small, but you too must receive the rest Jesus experienced and gives.

A BABY'S FACE

This rest became real to me in Wal-Mart. Saturday afternoon in any Wal-Mart around the world is the same. People are frantic and focused. They are pressed for time and overloaded with obligations. In this busy setting, God showed me the face of rest. I arrived at the checkout line behind a lady holding a small child. The head of the child was nestled against the mom's shoulder. A fat little leg protruded from each side just above her waist. A fat little arms dangled from the mom's sides. In the mom's embrace, the child slept. Sleeping children are not unusual. But this sleeping child captured my attention.

How can he sleep through all this chaos? There's so much activity in this store. Outside of Wal-Mart, the city is moving at a mad pace. The city itself is part of a country whose inhabitants are busy. That country is part of a world generating countless expressions of life. And yet, here is this child, totally at rest in his mother's arms. Why is this child sleeping? Does he not see the many concerns that ripple from this point into the far reaches of the globe?

And then God spoke, "the child does not have the capacity to know those complexities." In reality, this is true for you as well. You cannot know the vast sum of miracles making this day possible for you. Like you, the child does not need to know these things. The full breadth and scope of God's activity in supporting life is not a required concern. You, like the child, are only required to know one thing. The child knows his mother will take care of him. That is all that's necessary. He trusts his mother and so finds rest in her arms. The mother knows the pleasure of her embrace. She fondly enjoys every moment. The child knows the comfort from his embrace. He knows rest. In life, the greater your issue, the greater your embrace. The greater your God, the greater His embrace. Peace stands guard to insure that circumstances do not rob you of this intimate embrace in the center of your turbulent world.

Psalms 4:1-8 says, "Answer me when I call to you, O my righteous God. Give me relief from my distress; be merciful to me and hear my prayer. How long, O men, will you turn my glory into shame? How long will you love delusions and seek false gods? Selah. Know that the LORD has set apart the godly for himself; the LORD will hear when I call to him. In your anger do not sin; when you are on your beds, search your hearts and be silent. Selah. Offer right sacrifices and trust in the LORD. Many are asking, 'Who can show us any good?' Let the light of your face shine upon us, O LORD. You have filled my heart with greater joy than when their grain and new wine abound. I will lie down and sleep in peace, for you alone, O LORD, make me dwell in safety."

ENDURING JOY

And, so it begins. Eve is the first mother and the mother of the human race. How does she respond to the alien experience of carrying a child? She probably celebrates each step and sensation with Adam. Together, they watch the wonder of life being formed within her womb. Adam shares many experiences, but one is beyond his reach. He cannot know the pain to which Eve has been destined. Genesis 3:16a says, "To the woman he said, 'I will greatly increase your pains in childbearing; with pain you will give birth to children.'"

Did she know what pain to anticipate? She has no examples to follow or midwives to assist. She is alone in this endeavor. Her pain begins slowly at first. Then, pain mercilessly moves in like a rush-hour locomotive. Her mind is drawn to the day she spoke to the serpent. She remembers his claim, "You will be like God." Yeah, right! She screams and wails to mark her progress through this uncharted world of childbearing. Does pain monopolize her world? No. Pain may dominate childbirth, but pain does not rob her of the joy found within the birth of her child. That joy transcends this experience.

Her joy produces songs and shouts of wonder that compete against the screams of pain. How strange that one instrument can produce two opposite tunes. How astonishing that Eve, like mothers throughout history, has endured childbirth singing this strange melody. The pain is maddening. The joy is amazing. The pain is crazy. The joy is wild. The pain is intense. And, so is the joy. The two coexist. Almost like the act of lovers bringing this child to bear, the two are one in the presence of God's provision.

Do you know this melody? One of these two opposite tunes may be more familiar to you than the other. The other often seems foreign. One is easily experienced in life's situations. The other must be a product of intentional consideration. Many individuals only sing the first. But, life produces opportunities for both. How is your singing? Do you only know pain in your present situation? Is pain the song that lingers in your heart?

THE SCIENCE OF PAIN

What is pain? Pain is the product of the fallen world. It is the consequence of the response Adam and Eve gave Satan in the Garden of Eden. Since then, no individual requires an education to experience pain. You clearly know when pain strikes. You are designed to register and recognize pain.

The unnatural or unpleasant experiences of the body are easily detected. Medical science revels in knowing the human body and the world of physical pain. Medical research provides advances every day to respond to the body's pain. Doctors are revered and expected to bring relief. Pain in the emotional world is different. No cadavers are dissected to map systems that register and recognize this pain. The physiology of emotional pain eludes science. What brings pain to you may not pain your neighbor. And, what pains them may not pain you. The emotional world lacks a predictable scheme.

Even with their differences, emotional and physical pains are allies. They can cripple an individual as independent perpetrators or collaborators. Centuries and millennia have not changed their method of operation. Pain is an invasion that initially encounters little resistance. When it arrives, shock is a common response. When it stays, helplessness greets its occupation. What can you do in the face of pain? Can any defensive counter measure be mounted to extract pain from your domain? Or, does pain automatically claim you as part of its empire?

There is a response. The human body is fascinating in this matter. When an injury occurs or a foreign force invades, the body's immune system scrambles agents to confront the trauma or insurgence. This response is automatic and instantaneous. Medical science knows the effort immediately begins to repair and restore damage to the body. Physical pain cannot survive as an agitation against this effort.

Emotional pain is different. Your body does not seem to have a comparable immune system to confront the efforts of emotional pain. You may feel helpless in the midst of its attack. Understanding this pain seems an insurmountable challenge. Finding a solution may seem a distant fantasy. You ask for something or anything to bring relief. Perhaps you hope for a change in your circumstances or a reversal of fortunes. But, when your circumstances remain the same or worsen, your frustration grows. Ultimately, you believe time will free you from the grip of this menace. But, time betrays your expectation. The longer you wait, the more desperate your pain becomes.

God is mindful of your emotional turmoil. How can you doubt His sovereign watch? You know He designed your body to deal with physical pain. His wisdom mobilizes epic wars on a cellular level to benefit your situation. He orchestrates innumerable miracles to maintain your life. So much evidence supports a conclusion that God cares to meet you at the point of your physical need.

Why do you lose sight of God's provision in the emotional world? Here, God is equally interested in providing for you. His wisdom waits to flood your circumstances with an agent to remove the sting and power of emotional pain. The effort of this agent produces the relief for which you long. The agent creates a feeling similar to being happy, but different. You know God's goal is not to bring you happiness. He knows happiness is dependent upon your circumstances. You are happy when your circumstances are favorable. You feel happy when life is going well. But because you cannot control your circumstances, happiness is rare and not sustainable. Happiness is not immune to the pains of life.

On the contrary, God's agent is remarkably resilient in the fallen world. His effort is an immediate response to your emotional battle. The agent's mission is to nullify the weight of pain and break its chains that enslave you. The agent reinforces the bonds that support your trust in God. It collaborates with peace to maintain hope in the midst of your circumstances. Romans 15:13 says, "May the God of hope fill you with all joy and peace as you trust in him, so that you may overflow with hope by the power of the Holy Spirit."

CLOTHING THAT FITS PERFECTLY

The agent is joy. Joy abides in the presence of the Lord. First Chronicles 16:25-27 says, "For great is the LORD and most worthy of praise; he is to be feared above all gods. For all the gods of the nations are idols, but the LORD made the heavens. Splendor and majesty are before him; strength and joy in his dwelling place." Joy is also a fruit of the Holy Spirit (Galatians 5:22). Joy is an important part of God. The Bible has a large volume of verses that supports the expression of joy. When things are going well, you are easily joyful.

But, joy should not be seen as being absent in the midst of pain. The Bible communicates the opportunity for joy in the presence of your pain.

Joy is immune to pain. It creates a feeling similar to happiness but is not dependent upon circumstances. In fact, joy lives and thrives in the company of pain. Joy has a clear mission during these difficult seasons of life. Nothing hinders joy's ability to accomplish its mission except you.

Do not fail God's design. You must recognize God provides joy for your difficulties. The Psalmist asks God for joy. God responds. Psalms 86:2-4 says, "Guard my life, for I am devoted to you. You are my God; save your servant who trusts in you. Have mercy on me, O LORD, for I call to you all day long. Bring joy to your servant, for to you, O LORD, I lift up my soul." Your prayer for joy, like that of the Psalmist, falls within God's will.

You can be confident God will respond to your request. The Psalmist has a great testimony of God's provision of joy. Psalms 30:11-12 says, "You turned my wailing into dancing; you removed my sackcloth and clothed me with joy, that my heart may sing to you and not be silent. O LORD my God, I will give you thanks for ever." The importance of clothing in this passage should not be overlooked. Sackcloth is worn to symbolize grief or repentance. Wearing sackcloth to demonstrate pain provides a vivid platform on which the change produced by joy is demonstrated. God removes your sackcloth and adorns you with joy. The picture is powerful. The change is evident. It is meant to communicate the successful transformation of your heart. What are you wearing today? Have you allowed God to remove your sackcloth and provide you the clothing of joy?

God's provision of joy is even greater than all your expectations. His joy has a special potency. He will give joy at a measure that exceeds the level of happiness produced by the most favorable circumstances. The Psalmist is aware of this truth. When your life is going well, your happiness is blissful. You feel at the top of your world. A common phrase captures this sentiment: "It doesn't get any better than this." But it does.

Psalms 4:7 says, "You have filled my heart with greater joy than when their grain and new wine abound."

Picture a farmer harvesting his bumper crop of grain. Imagine a vineyard producing more wine than ever before. The owners of both enterprises are experiencing incredible happiness as a result of their great fortune. When you see them, they look happy. They laugh and seem free from any stress or worry. They really rejoice. Say your crop did not go so well. The Psalmist eludes that he is still waiting for God's blessing. In this state of waiting, the joy of other farmers seems more pronounced. They look really happy. The Psalmist clearly states that God's joy measures greater than your perception of another's happiness.

If you find this difficult, try seeing through God's perspective. When you see from your own perspective, you attempt to tie joy to your circumstances. You hope your situation will change. The Psalmist is saying God places joy in your heart without regard to your circumstances. In this passage, the Psalmist does not have what he is waiting for. Yet, he knows God hears his calls and works through his situations. He can see God's hand. Can you see God's hand at work? When you do, the resulting joy tangibly indicates your recognition of God's work underway.

TWO REALITIES

How do you see with God's perspective? Seeing in this way requires a special sight. Your physical eyes provide the great function of sight. They convert images from your world into a form that is digested by your mind. You are able to see colors and shapes with profound clarity. The miraculous process of sight can provide options at times. Have you ever seen one picture that provides two images from which to choose? Look at the following picture illusions. What do you see?

In the first picture, do all the horizontal lines seem parallel to you? They do not? Look at them carefully. When you turn the book to its side

Are the horizontal lines parallel or do they slope?

and stare at the picture from the edge of the page, you realize all the lines are perfectly parallel. The same picture provides two realities. How about the next picture? What do you see? You may see a vase. You may also see two faces staring at each other. Both of these images lie within this one picture. When you see both, you can bounce back and forth at will.

The next picture has two. Do you see a man in one and a woman in the other? Is the woman young or old? The picture contains both. The nose of the old woman is the cheek of the young. Can you see both? How about the picture with the man? Can you see the word "Liar?" Each

picture contains two images. Are you able to see both? The final picture is difficult. A bushy haired man with a beard is easy to see. Look again for a couple kissing. Can you see them? The nose of the bushy man is the face and shoulder of the woman. The space under the bushy man's right eye is the man who is kissing the woman.

In all of these pictures, there are two images. The clear difference is with your perspective. You can see one image immediately. The other usually requires a little bit of effort. When you find the other, you are impressed and excited. Then, you can see both images at will. The two are present simultaneously. But far too often, viewers see one picture and never see the other. This type of failure robs you of your opportunity to experience joy. Without perspective, you only see the pain in your situation: you cannot get a job, your wife left you, your children are experimenting with drugs, and so forth. Without perspective, you fail to see the image of joy embedded in your image of pain.

Perspective is the bridge that spans the world of pain and the world of joy. Perspective adjusts your spiritual eyes to look past the first image and see the other. The joy God placed in your painful situation is not easily seen. Pain dominates. You must willfully make a choice to see the joy by walking across this bridge of perspective. This task to have perspective is not easy, but it is needful. Look past your pain. Do you have perspective? What do you see? In an environment of pain, James, the brother of Jesus, asked the first century church to look.

James sees the church under fire. Persecution is underway. Christians are being beaten, their properties are being seized, and their lives are being destroyed. The picture seems grim. As the storm of persecution rages, the church needs a strong stand. James attempts to lead them to joy through perspective. James 1:2-3 says, "Consider it pure joy, my brothers, whenever you face trials of many kinds, because you know that the testing of your faith develops perseverance." He acknowledges the first image, the pain of various trials. He is not asking them to move away or to run from this pain. He stays with the picture. The perspective James provides is the simple truth of God's hand working with the situation. James says God is forming Christ-like character. This is his bridge. Do not look at the pain only. Look to see what God is doing. When Christians understand this perspective and accept it, they can experience the joy in their trials.

The book of Hebrews records the success of the early church in this matter. Hebrews 10:32-35 says, "Remember those earlier days after you had received the light, when you stood your ground in a great contest in the face of suffering. Sometimes you were publicly exposed to insult and persecution; at other times you stood side by side with those who were so treated. You sympathized with those in prison and joyfully accepted the confiscation of your property, because you knew that you yourselves had better and lasting possessions. So do not throw away your confidence; it will be richly rewarded." Both images of joy and pain are within this picture from Hebrews. The early church made their stand and experienced joy. Their stand has inspired Christians to this day.

HUMAN ATTEMPT

Perspective can come from various sources. Consider asking someone for his or her thoughts. People outside your situation are able to bring perspective with relative ease. They can engage without the weights or limitations that influence your view. They can usually see enough and know enough to bring some encouragement, hope, and/or direction. They may be able to point out the rays of sunshine in your storm filled world. This perspective is needful but not sufficient.

Perspective can also be achieved through comparison. This is the process of comparing your pain with the pain felt from someone else. For example, imagine you are dealing with the great pain of divorce. Try looking at someone who has been paralyzed in a car accident. Or, imagine someone who will be spending twenty years in jail. Or, imagine anyone in any situation that seems worse than yours. This perspective leads you to be thankful for what you conclude as your lighter difficulties. You may conclude your situation is not as bad as it could be.

Both of these perspectives are important. They provide much needed relief. When you employ one or both, they bring some immediate sanity to your insane world. They also bring an anticipation of joy. You may feel you are walking across the bridge that leads to the world of joy. But, this excitement is short-lived. In most cases, the relief is produced from these approaches crumbles under the weight of your situation. As your difficulties persist, they test your perspective's integrity and strength.

This perspective, the product of human effort, cannot hold up because it is laced with limitation and bias. No one really knows what is happening or will happen. When you or someone else looks at your situation, conclusions are relative. They are seen from the lens of personal experience, knowledge, or power. The best intentions of any human perspective cannot escape this limitation. If James used human perspective, he might have told the early church to endure because the disciples have faced similar persecution. Can you see the passage reading, "hang in there and be tough because we have?"

Anyone giving human perspective may say you should do this or that in your situation. Will their advice work for you? Who knows? The prospects of total relief and enduring joy seem unpredictable. The worldliest individual cannot have lived through all of life's experiences. The wisest person cannot know all the variables involved in a situation. The most powerful person is not powerful enough to handle everything that comes his or her way. Therefore, human perspective may provide some relief, but it cannot provide a complete bridge to joy.

Another perspective exists. This perspective is prominent in Scripture. It involves the simple step of seeing God in your situation. James utilizes this heavenly perspective with his charge to the early church in James 1. Joshua employs it to give his report of the Promised Land in Numbers 14. Paul leans on it to draw his conclusion on life and death in Philippians 1. Joseph proclaims it in Genesis 45. Jesus lives by it. They all affirm the sovereignty of God over human situations. They all acknowledge the reality of God at work. The bridge to joy is simply the vital recognition of God's fingerprint on the landscape of your life.

HEAVENLY CLARITY

Look at David's perfect utilization of this perspective. Psalms 23 says, "The LORD is my shepherd, I shall not be in want. He makes me lie down in green pastures, he leads me beside quiet waters, he restores my soul. He guides me in paths of righteousness for his name's sake. Even though I walk through the valley of the shadow of death, I will fear no evil, for you are with me; your rod and your staff, they comfort me. You prepare a table before me in the presence of my enemies. You anoint my head with oil; my cup overflows. Surely goodness and love will follow me all the days of my life, and I will dwell in the house of the LORD forever." Everywhere he turns, he sees the Lord.

This is a very familiar passage. You may have memorized it. You may quote it as a prayer. But, have you every considered Psalms 23 as an eyewitness testimony? David sees God at work in every situation in his life. This passage is the prototype of the perfect bridge to joy. Engineered into the words of this passage, David has masterfully modeled the art of heavenly perspective. Read it. Do you see David's acknowledgement of God's faithfulness? He is not asking God for help. He is reporting what he sees. His perspective shows God moving through his situations.

Heavenly perspective provides David with absolute confidence in his turbulent world. God's fingerprints are all over his present circumstances. Although his future is unknown, heavenly perspective provides some certainty for David's tomorrows. The concluding thoughts of this passage permanently secure the favor of the Lord. David claims God's goodness and love as his company. Everywhere he goes, he finds these two elements following like a shadow. They permeate everything in his life. David does not take a single step without the successive movement of God's provision. Nothing threatens this blessing. Could you imagine God's goodness and love running for cover at the advent of a difficulty? Absolutely not!

As the icing on this cake, David knows his eternal fate is also secure. He has a home in heaven. Although the physical world cannot assure anyone of a permanent residence, God establishes David's eternal home. Have your circumstances removed you from the place you call home? Have you been displaced? Are you one of the millions of people who lose their homes each year? Millions of people live with a knot in their stomach and emptiness in their soul because of this reality. Home is not a certainty in the physical world. However, David feels wherever life's difficulties take him, they cannot derail God's plan. David knows that his present always moves him one step closer to his future eternal home.

Psalms 23 gives every Christian a clear example to follow. Because God is at work in your situations, you too have an opportunity for this heavenly perspective. God has not abandoned you or forsaken you. As you read through Psalms 23, glean a vision for your own perspective. Try rewriting Psalms 23 by listing your difficulties. Then, record ways God is being faithful. Can you see His involvement? Can you see the full breadth and scope of God's provision flooding your difficulties? Cancer, joblessness, or divorce cannot deter God's active engagement. God is at work! He is doing this, and He is doing that. This heavenly perspective is the bridge from the world of pain to the world of enduring joy.

The Psalmist knows this bridge and the joy waiting on the other side. The outcome of his situations is not in question. He rejoices over God's involvement and claims the joy. Psalms 16:7-11 says, "I will praise the LORD, who counsels me; even at night my heart instructs me. I have set the LORD always before me. Because he is at my right hand, I will not be shaken. Therefore my heart is glad and my tongue rejoices; my body also will rest secure, because you will not abandon me to the grave, nor will you let your Holy One see decay. You have made known to me the path of life; you will fill me with joy in your presence, with eternal pleasures at your right hand."

This passage has many intimate exchanges between the Lord and the Psalmist. In the heart of the passage the Psalmist makes a powerful revelation. He discloses the source of his heavenly perspective. He says he has set the Lord before him. This action allows him to see the Lord constantly. In the Old Testament, the people of God struggled with giving God their total focus. One point of battle lay with the "High Places." These were mountain top shrines dedicated to a god. When Israel was not following God, they would erect the "High Places" to honor idols. This action grieved the Lord. The Kings who followed God removed the idols. They put the Lord before them.

As David looks across his empire, he sees the Lord. His situations cannot escape the presence of the Lord. Heavenly perspective requires this action. You too must set the Lord before you. You must see Him as you look into your world. Every detail of your present crises should be bathed with God's presence. Even with complex difficulties, the Psalmist only sees greater opportunity to identify God's fingerprints. This is the spirit and substance of Psalms 23. David covers several challenges and details God's provisions. The passage does not leave one item pending. Not one element of David's life has uncertainty. Heavenly perspective covers the full landscape of life.

JOY AFFECTS

As the Psalmist sees this, he walks across the bridge to the world of joy. Here, the Lord provides the joy. He fills the Psalmist. The Lord is his source and supplier. Joy from the Lord is not a scarce commodity rationed with trepidation. The joy is ample. No matter the level of difficulty, the joy is full. Not a single element of the Psalmist's difficulty can deplete a single ounce of God's joy. The Lord's joy transcends the Psalmist's circumstances. The joy celebrates God's extensive work. Because the joy is not connected to circumstances, it is predictable. Because the joy is from the Lord, it is enduring.

God is the source of this joy. Discovering the measure of this source can be challenging and revealing. Consider rivers as an example. America is a nation with many rivers. Rivers have played a major part in America's history. One river, the Wakala River, in Florida has an unusual source. Eight miles inland on the Florida panhandle, an 800-foot hole in the ground is the river's starting point. From this hole, 14,325 gallons of water flow every second. Every day, 1.2 billon gallons of water bubble to the surface and flow the eight miles to empty into the Gulf of Mexico. The source of the Wakala River is mind-boggling. Geologists speculate that underground channels feeding the Wakala River stretch across North America. Can you imagine this extreme possibility?

God is the source of your joy. Philippians 4:19 says, "And my God will meet all your needs according to his glorious riches in Christ Jesus." Like the Wakala River, the source of this joy stretches across the full expanse of God's goodness and love. As the source of your joy, God's rich supply cannot be fully known. The joy that flows knows no end because God's riches are unlimited. It stretches beyond space, time, and the material world. God's joy will never end.

The effects of God's joy are felt internally. The enduring joy produces a sense of happiness in the midst of your difficulties. This joy is the feeling of seeing a child playing in the rain. It is the feeling of watching your baby fall after his or her first step. This joy is the embrace of a loved one returning from war with a wound. The circumstances cannot drown the feeling of happiness. Enduring joy transcends the pains of life. Have you connected with God's joy? Are your circumstances bathed in the rich supply of His provision? Do you see His hand at work in your life?

As the Wakala River moves eight miles to the gulf, it alters the land adjacent to its banks. The arid conditions typical of that region are transformed into a luscious tropical jungle. Fish, birds, plants, and alligators are some of the many life forms thriving in and around the Wakala River. As the river flows, it blesses the world around it.

Can you imagine your world being a blessing to others during your difficulties? God's enduring joy flows like the Wakala to accomplish this "impossibility." The presence of joy initiates an internal feeling that is manifested externally. As the Psalmist crosses the bridge of perspective and arrives in the world of joy, his joy bubbles over as expressions of shouting and singing. Psalms 71:22-23 says, "I will praise you with the harp for your faithfulness, O my God; I will sing praise to you with the lyre, O Holy One of Israel. My lips will shout for joy when I sing praise to you— I, whom you have redeemed."

When perspective leads an individual to the world of joy, it connects the traveler to the reality of God's fingerprints. Psalms 126:2-3 says, "Our mouths were filled with laughter, our tongues with songs of joy. Then it was said among the nations, 'The LORD has done great things for them.' The LORD has done great things for us, and we are filled with joy." Shouting and singing draws attention to the evidence of God's work. The level of desperation and the level of God's provision mix to produce an uncontainable song. The image of pain begins to fade as the image of joy become more concrete. Joy is not just a feeling of happiness that erases a sad face. It does not just place a smile in response to God's work. Instead, it induces shouting and singing reflecting the magnitude of God's goodness.

Expressions of joy in the midst of your difficulties transform your world. Those who find enduring joy mystify those who do not. Your joy introduces others to a possibility of this inconceivable prize. Your singing and shouting compels the world to take notice. You have something they do not have. They see the light that shines from your heart and will long for the bridge that leads to the world of joy. Psalms 118:14-17 says, "The LORD is my strength and my song; he has become my salvation. Shouts of joy and victory resound in the tents of the righteous: 'The LORD's right hand has done mighty things! The LORD's right hand is lifted high; the LORD's right hand has done mighty things!' I will not die but live, and will proclaim what the LORD has done." As you proclaim, others are able to know the source of your joy. They will be blessed to witness and experience your constant and unending source of joy. They will discover hope. They will see your heart's awareness of God's goodness.

Singing and shouting are expressions rooted deep in your heart. How many people have you seen expressing love, honor, or devotion through these two mediums? Have you seen a soldier sing his national anthem during a war? Have you used a song to communicate love to your spouse or friend? Have you attended a church service where songs moved your heart to a reverent awe? Singing and shouting are powerful tools to express yourself.

Can you remember the last time you shouted? Shouting fans at a football game can be crazy. They shout at the top of their lungs as if they can be heard in a stadium of thousands. Can you imagine the sporting world without shouting? Picture someone winning a new car on a game show. Yes, passion flows in fanatical forms. People shout and sing with such fervor they often lose their voice in the process. Singing and shouting are motivated by an individual's connection with the object of his or her joy.

The Psalmist affirms these expressions. He reminds the reader that God's creation shouts and sings with joy to the Lord. Psalms 65 says the meadows and valleys shout for joy and sing. Psalms 65 adds the dawn calls for a song of joy. Psalms 96 says all the trees of the forest sing for joy. Psalms 98 says the rivers and mountains shout for joy. Psalms 66 says all the earth shouts with joy and sings to God's glory. The question is now posed to you. Can you follow creation's consistent lead? They do not falter in their ability to express joy because they constantly know the goodness of God.

Do you know the goodness of God? Do you see His hand at work in your life? Your body is only a temporary vessel. The troubles that plague your body provide God with an opportunity to flood your life with His joy. Regardless of whatever pains you today, discover God's joy. Sing and shout because God is at work.

RESCUE ME

The waves are fast and furious. Without a doubt, this is the best vacation of your life. The smile on your face and the laughter in your voice are seen and heard for miles. Your euphoria has been supported by at least one toe touching the sand below you. You venture out but never too far because you are a poor swimmer. You always check the depth. Then, without notice, terror strikes. A strong rip tide moves in and pushes you much farther than you can bear.

You begin to swim straight for shore. The motion of swimming does not move you. You dog paddle to get a bearing. The tide has commanded your location and moved you further from shore. You try swimming again. No good. The tide is still too strong. Your breathing becomes frantic. Your heart starts to race, and panic grips you. You gulp water as you begin to scream for help. Your muscles tire. Did any one hear your cry? Your fatigued muscles finally shut down. You begin to sink.

At that moment, you feel a hand grab your arm. A strong pull brings you to the surface. Immediately and instinctively, you resume your effort for shore. You flail. Your arms begin reaching. Your legs kick. A strong voice begins to shout. "Stop struggling. Listen to me. Let me help you." The voice attempts to direct your attention and your body. Are you ready to be rescued?

DESPERATELY SEEKING

Life is similar. You are moving through life and having a great time. The smile on your face and the laughter in your voice are seen and heard for miles. Your euphoria is supported by the stability of life. You have at least one foot on solid ground. Then, without warning, your world turns upside down. Your predictability falls to unpredictability. Your stability moves to instability. You scramble to fix your problems but nothing seems to help. You begin to panic. You look across the expanse of your world and cry out for help. God responds. Immediately and instinctively, you resume your frantic attempt to save your own life. God says, "Let me help you." What will you do? If you could see His rescue plan, you would not struggle on your own. Jeremiah 29:11 says, "For I know the plans I have for you, declares the LORD, plans to prosper you and not to harm you, plans to give you hope and a future."

How desperate do you have to be before you look to God? At what point do you stop struggling? Jehoshaphat finds that point. Second Chronicles 20:1-2 says, "After this, the Moabites and Ammonites with some of the Meunites came to make war on Jehoshaphat. Some men came and told Jehoshaphat, 'A vast army is coming against you from Edom, from the other side of the Sea. It is already in Hazazon Tamar' (that is, En Gedi)." Verse 3 reveals Jehoshaphat's immediate resolve to ask God for help. He moves the people to fast. As the armies are approaching, Jehoshaphat leans on his only option, God.

He says in Verse 12, "O our God, will you not judge them? For we have no power to face this vast army that is attacking us. We do not know what to do, but our eyes are upon you." Jehoshaphat is clueless. He knows how to fight, but not on this occasion. He realizes he has no power. He only looks to God. His eyes are focused. He needs a miracle, and God is in the business of providing miraculous rescues.

Have you ever been in a place where you needed a miraculous rescue? I have. One Saturday, I drove six hours to the beach. Leaving early, I arrived late in the afternoon. My objective was to see an amazing sunset. I intended to drive home that same night. Little sleep seemed a simple sacrifice to facilitate my objective. As my time on the beach slipped away, the sunset was more brilliant than I had hoped.

The picture was perfect. The white powder sand moved to the blue green water. The waves broke into white foam. I sat on this shore to watch the rays of the sun paint each cloud with colors from red to gray. Then the moment was over. The light was gone, and the beach fell into a colorless panorama. I returned to my car with a feeling of serenity, but the reality of my drive pushed serenity from my mind. Exhaustion inspired the thought of an alternate route home.

As I pressed northwest across Alabama, the partly cloudy skies at the beach gave way to thunder clouds. Rain began to fall. Near the Mississippi border, I made a quick decision to leave the state highway for a county road. The county road was very narrow, curvy, and in poor condition. My challenge to find a prescribed turn became impossible. No street signs were on the road. I was lost. The few minutes allotted for this portion of the trip turned into an hour. Where was that turn? After a lot of driving, I surprisingly returned to the spot where I entered the county road. I was astonished. Nevertheless, I felt this road could be navigated. I made another attempt. The turn was found. Relief and frustration fought for my heart. Frustration won, as I began to drive faster in the rain.

In one fateful moment, I came over a small hill to meet a sharp curve leading to a narrow bridge. As I slammed my brakes, my car began to hydroplane. Immediately, the car swung sideways: first to the right and then to the left. Miraculously, the car made the turn but headed for the bridge, completely out of control. The car moved across the bridge sideways. On the other side, my car spun around and dropped into a ditch. The car had gone from sixty to zero in seconds. My heart had gone from frustrated to frantic.

I had not seen another car since the county road scenario started. I could not remember the last time I had seen a house. The time now was twelve-thirty in the morning. As I forced the car door open and staggered out, my mind was racing. What a miracle that I was not injured. What a miracle that I had found the shallowest part of the ditch. Several more miracles were noted before questions began to arrive. What do I do now? My cell phone had no signal. Wow, I had no options. When I turned the car off, total darkness swallowed me. The rain pitter-pattered on my windshield. How long would I sit here? Who was I waiting for? What if I got robbed or killed? God, where are you? After only ten minutes of waiting, I began to panic.

In the distance, I could see the glow of a light. I took a deep breath and begged God for help. "Oh Lord, please help me! Please, please, help me! Oh Lord, help me." This continual prayer and rain accompanied my walk through total darkness. The prayers turned into cries. Every step was marked with desperation. As I approached the light, I found a house. As I stepped on the muddy driveway, a barking dog ran from the porch. Dogs terrify me. Would the owner hear his dog and come outside? After several tense minutes, I realized I would have to make my way to the house. The dog stood in my path. I was desperate. Dropping to my knees, my quivering voice cried, "Here boy, come here boy, it's okay. Come here." The voice of my heart simultaneously cried, "God, please help me!" After some time, the dog nudged closer and closer.

Now I could touch him. The barking stopped. As I stood up, the dog jumped away and resumed barking. Keeping my eyes on the dog, I made a decision to walk slowly to the door. The dog shadowed and barked. Reaching the porch, I began to knock. The whole time I prayed, "Lord, please let somebody answer the door!" I begin to shout, "Hello ... Hello! Can someone please help me?" The knocking persisted, as did the barking, but neither summoned anyone to the door. What could I do?

Leaving the porch proved as difficult as approaching. When I reached the road, I could see another house. Here, three dogs greeted my first step on this property. Once again, I dropped to my knees. After some time, they allowed me to reach the door. My knocking and shouting got a response. A lady answered, and my nightmare was over. From the moment my car started sliding until the moment that lady spoke to me, I was looking to God. God was all that mattered. I did not care about anything else! My car did not matter. My clothes did not matter. My job did not matter. My family did not matter. Nothing mattered but God. He heard me call with every breath I took. He rescued me.

A LOOK UP MOVEMENT

How desperate do you have to be before you look to God? When Jehoshaphat looked to God, how desperate was he? God was his only option. Looking to God should be a natural expression of your relationship with Him, not always just your last resort. Colossians 3:1-2 says, "Since, then, you have been raised with Christ, set your hearts on things above, where Christ is seated at the right hand of God. Set your minds on things above, not on earthly things." The heart and mind were identified as strategic points in a previous chapter. These strategic points in the battle to maintain trust are being directed by this passage. Where is the focus of your life? Look up! That is the simplest way to summarize this verse.

Can Christians literally look up? Although the task would be difficult, the practice would make a very distinctive statement. Imagine hundreds of people walking with their heads raised to the heavens. Practicing a specific distinctive is not foreign to the Christian world. Look at the beard of a Mennonite, the dress of a Catholic nun, or the communal living of the Amish. How about a "Look Up" movement?

When a person in a public place looks up, a passerby will look up to see what is being seen. One person looking up can collect an audience. The scene is compelling. Few will pass by without yielding to the temptation. To be completely successful, you must have an object to hold attention. If no object holds attention, observers drop from the ranks. During the Fourth of July, individuals ignore pain to look up at fireworks. The object is important. What is the object holding your attention today? To what do you look? Do you look to God, as did Jehoshaphat? Psalms 105:4 says, "Look to the LORD and his strength; seek his face always." A complete focus is required.

Imagine the shell game. You have three shells side-by-side. Under one shell, a ball is placed. You are asked to identify which shell has the ball. At this point, the shell is easy to identify. They have not moved. Now, the shells are being moved to the side, across each other, and zigzagging. Are you looking? How intensely? The shells stop. Where is the ball? Are you sure it is under the shell to which you point? Wow! You picked the right shell. How did you know? Yes, you kept looking at the shell that had the ball. You never took your eyes off it, right? Why not? Because you wanted to know where the ball would end up. You looked without blinking. You did not miss a moment. The shell with the ball had your total focus. You are asked to look to God in a similar way.

RIGHT OR LEFT?

When you look to God, what do you see? Psalms 121:1-8 says, "I lift up my eyes to the hills— where does my help come from? My help comes from the LORD, the Maker of heaven and earth. He will not let your foot slip— he who watches over you will not slumber; indeed, he who watches over Israel will neither slumber nor sleep. The LORD watches over you— the LORD is your shade at your right hand; the sun will not harm you by day, nor the moon by night. The LORD will keep you from all harm— he will watch over your life; the LORD will watch over your coming and going both now and forevermore."

How amazing is this description of God? He watches over you. He watches you right now and in every tomorrow you will ever have. This passage is full of God's promise to look at you. When you look up and see God, He is totally focused on you. Why does He look at you like that? Have you ever looked into the face of a person you love? How impossible is it to look away? That's how much God is in love with you. He cannot take His eyes off you.

Do you see Him in this way? Consider a simple exercise. On the right side of a page, generate a list describing God from verses in the Bible. Write down your findings: God is faithful, God is compassionate, and so forth. This is God as the Bible declares Him to be. On the left side of the page, list how God presently meets you at the point of your need. You may see some similarities in the two lists. However, you may produce a left side list that does not mirror the right. Your left side list may be altered by difficulties and unanswered prayers. You may struggle to know if God still cares about you. You may be tempted to think God is absent from your affairs. When you look at God from your left side list, your circumstances shape your view of God.

Viewing God from this perspective is harmful. God is not what He does or does not do in your life. He is who He is. Viewing God from the right side column helps you look at God as He is. Several exercises can help you become totally focused on God through your right column. First, recognize you occasionally make a single glance to God. Your view into the eternal may be only momentary. You jumped from a left column view of God to the right column and back to the left. Now, do it again. Make the effort. Good. Do it one more time. Initially, your efforts may be irregular and sporadic, but the effort should be intentional.

A step toward looking at God with total focus is made when your right column look is more frequent and predictable. Several Christian forefathers provide some clues for success in this effort. One says his look at God swings like a clock's pendulum between two worlds, the material and the eternal. For this reading, see the pendulum between two columns, the right and the left. The moments of the day are deliberately rationed between the two worlds before you. You may look at your circumstances, but you must consistently and constantly push the view into the eternal, right column. Back and forth, back and forth, keep a vigil to swing the pendulum. As you practice this exercise, you are able to see God as God. Then, your circumstances are regularly seen through your right column.

Another Christian leader takes this idea one step further. He literally claims to place one foot in the eternal world and one in the material. He is an active citizen of two worlds. He lives with one eye in the right column and one in the left. When he looks to God, God is the God of everything in his life. When he looks at his circumstances, he sees God's hand actively involved with his affairs.

A final perspective completely accomplishes the spirit of Colossians 3:1-2. This Christian leader has taken his residency with God. He lives in the right column. He elects to see his material world only from the eternal. What God sees of his circumstances is what this leader desires to see; nothing more, nothing less. He does not move from the right column to the left. His discipline maintains a right column upward look. The severity of his situation does not alter his view. Maintaining the eternal, right column, perspective takes faith and discipline.

Peter did not have this discipline. As Jesus called him onto the water, Peter looked from the right column. He saw Jesus. He believed he could walk on the water. He experienced a miracle. But, then he looked at his circumstances. Peter failed to hold his attention on the eternal. He began to sink. Discipline is paramount. God plans to direct your steps through your difficult circumstances. He plans to rescue you. But you must pay attention.

ATTENTIVE

How can you be ready? Psalms 123:1-2 says, "I lift up my eyes to you, to you whose throne is in heaven. As the eyes of slaves look to the hand of their master, as the eyes of a maid look to the hand of her mistress, so our eyes look to the LORD our God, till he shows us his mercy." Look at where their eyes are. A slave or servant in somebody's house is summoned for a task. During dinner, the servant stands at a distance and watches the master. When the master calls, he motions with his hand. The servant rushes forward. The master may point to his glass. The servant responds by providing more drink. He returns to his observation point awaiting the next command. The servant continues to watch the master's hand. When you are looking at God from the right column, you must be attentive to His direction.

His direction may not be easy. But, if you see God from the right column, you will give Him the latitude to direct your steps without question. Imagine adultery as an issue in your marriage. Colossians 3:13 says, "Bear with each other and forgive whatever grievances you may have against one another. Forgive as the LORD forgave you." From the left column view of God, you may not respond to this instruction. You may argue that God cannot ask this of you because He has not responded to your prayers. He has not pronounced judgment on your spouse. From the right column, you are able to see God's sovereign hand on this situation. You are able to see His love for you. You are able to see His hate for your spouse's sin. You are able to see God's love for your spouse despite that sin.

Look at the last part of Colossians 3:13. You are prompted to forgive your spouse as God has forgiven you. The right column identifies your sin as adultery against God's holiness. As He calls for forgiveness, He knows the difficulty. If you see God from only your left column, you may not be able to respond freely to His direction. The pain and damage from your situation may keep you from responding. Responsiveness is the beautiful product of a dynamic right column relationship with God.

Relationship with God is the basis of following Him. One day, I introduced a baby duck to my backyard pond. When I was home, I spent time playing with the duck. As days passed into weeks, I noticed something very peculiar. Anytime I entered the backyard, the duck ran to me. She followed me anywhere I walked and stayed with me as I worked in the yard. This baby duck bonded to me. Baby ducks line up behind their mommy. They have a special bond. They do not follow just any duck. They follow mom, and they follow her anywhere. My baby duck considered me her surrogate dad. She followed me without reservation. She followed me as a natural expression of our bond.

God has adopted you into His family. Do you follow Him as a natural expression of your relationship? On the Mount of Transfiguration, Peter, John, and James witnessed many wonders. Here, they discovered the key to following. Luke 9:35 says, "A voice came from the cloud, saying, 'This is my Son, whom I have chosen; listen to him.'" Much can be debated in this simple phrase. But, no confusion should exist regarding the instruction to listen.

When you wish to follow Jesus, you must listen to His voice. He designed you to follow. God knows there are many voices competing for your attention. He also knows you can only follow one voice. Luke 16:13a, "No servant can serve two masters. Either he will hate the one and love the other, or he will be devoted to the one and despise the other." Try watching the television and listening to the radio. Can you give your attention to both at the same time? No! If you try to listen to both, you mostly miss both.

The thoughts in your head, the things you read, and the people around you have a lot to say. They aim to direct your steps. How do you know which voice is good? How do you know which voice is Jesus? John 10:14-15 says, "I am the good shepherd; I know my sheep and my sheep know me—just as the Father knows me and I know the Father— and I lay down my life for the sheep." This verse affirms a relationship between Jesus and His followers. They have a bond. The sheep also have an ability to recognize Jesus' voice. John 10:25-27 says, "Jesus answered, 'I did tell you, but you do not believe. The miracles I do in my Father's name speak for me, but you do not believe because you are not my sheep. My sheep listen to my voice; I know them, and they follow me.'" If you are one of Jesus' sheep, then you will hear His voice. If you hear His voice, you will follow Him. Following Jesus is considered a no-brainer within the bonds of this relationship.

A VOICE TO FOLLOW

How then is Jesus' voice recognized? Recognizing the content of the voice identifies the voice. For example, Jesus spoke about the issue of lust. Matthew 5:27-28 says, "You have heard that it was said, 'Do not commit adultery.' But I tell you that anyone who looks at a woman lustfully has already committed adultery with her in his heart." When you are tempted to look at a woman, you should hear the voice of Jesus through this verse. Did you hear? Christians should be well versed in the teachings of the Bible. This is God's voice given to humanity. Many people wait for some mysterious, supernatural voice. Why?

Try another situation. Did someone pick a fight with you? Matthew

5:38-39 says, "You have heard that it was said, 'Eye for eye, and tooth for tooth.' But I tell you, do not resist an evil person. If someone strikes you on the right cheek, turn to him the other also." In eighth grade, a boy actually broke his hand by hitting me in the face. I had no warning. Instinctively, I started swinging at him. I failed to turn the other cheek. I ignored the voice of Jesus. Shame filled me. My fellow students knew I loved Jesus, but they did not see any evidence of that love in this situation. If you are Jesus' sheep, you will hear and follow His voice. When you follow Jesus' instruction, your life will be radically transformed.

A trained lifeguard will tell you of the importance of following instruction. The rescuer in the water needs you to be still and relaxed. This instruction seems foolish. But, your cooperation is totally necessary. That's what Jesus needs to make your rescue possible. When God wants to rescue you, He will tell you things that require your participation. What God asks may seem crazy to you. However, they are the necessary elements of God's rescue plan.

With this in view, you should be eager to discover what God instructs. Look at the Bible or get wise counsel. Listen for Jesus' voice and get started on His instructions. Have things come to mind already? The Holy Spirit is always providing steps. Psalms 32:8 says, "I will instruct you and teach you in the way you should go; I will counsel you and watch over you." Once you have discerned a clear step, take it. Or, do you just think about what to do? In high school I wrote this phrase: "Why spend so much time thinking about doing what you think you should be doing ... When you know you should be doing what you know you should be doing!"

Recently, a college student was struggling with his parents' divorce. A lot of anger was building against his dad. The student contemplated and engaged opportunities to argue the issues with his dad, but nothing seemed to change; except more anger was building. The frustration enslaved the student to more contemplation and stress. What should he do? What could he do? The questions involved too much time and energy.

The voice of the Lord spoke to him. James 4:17 says, "Anyone, then, who knows the good he ought to do and doesn't do it, sins." This student needs to survey his life and list those things that are clearly understood as steps from the Lord. He knows he needs to spend time in prayer and in reading the Bible. He knows he needs to spend more time with his mother. He needs to talk to her and help with housework. This is a critical need. Mom cannot make a home without help. He knows his younger brother needs an older brother who models the Lord's strength and confidence in this situation. He needs to demonstrate God's love and support to his younger brother who is looking for someone to look up to. These are clear no-brainer steps. This is the list that needs the student's time and energy. God will take care of the rest. The student needs to act on Jesus' instruction.

Jesus says you will be wise to follow Him. He makes a comparison to help you understand. Matthew 7:24-27 says, "Therefore everyone who hears these words of mine and puts them into practice is like a wise man who built his house on the rock. The rain came down, the streams rose, and the winds blew and beat against that house; yet it did not fall, because it had its foundation on the rock. But everyone who hears these words of mine and does not put them into practice is like a foolish man who built his house on sand. The rain came down, the streams rose, and the winds blew and beat against that house, and it fell with a great crash."

If you follow Jesus, the forces of this world will not prevail. You will stand strong on the foundation of the Rock, Jesus. Jesus uses a house to teach this important truth. Jesus brings what you ultimately lack in your situation: resiliency. Hurricanes produce the elements of nature identified in this passage. They can destroy a house like a matchbox. Most homes seem helpless against this fury. When Jesus makes this comparison, He is being very bold. Following Him will have miraculous results.

Jesus is your rescuer. Cherish the relationship that helps you navigate your troubled journey. You will endure the trials and challenges of this life. You are going to be all right. Do you believe Jesus will rescue you? If you do, sing this song to Him as you follow: "Give me a heart to know and follow hard after you."

SURRENDER

The dusty road stretches for miles. The sun cast no shadows as it beats upon everything within its reach. The air is still as the weary travelers wade through the space between destinations. Home is behind them. Uncertainty is in front. Sound familiar? This is very familiar. How many times has Abraham taken these very steps? Years may separate him from his last journey, but the mind has not forgotten the pain and the agony experienced on the path to a new destination. His heart and mind struggle in different ways. But, Abraham does not need his mind. His heart insures that one foot is placed in front of the other.

His mind is busy wrestling with the destination. He does not like it. He does not walk along this path because the destination is his choice. He walks because he is surrendering. Genesis 22:1-4 says, "Some time later God tested Abraham. He said to him, 'Abraham!' 'Here I am,' he replied. Then God said, 'Take your son, your only son, Isaac, whom you love, and go to the region of Moriah. Sacrifice him there as a burnt offering on one of the mountains I will tell you about.' Early the next morning Abraham got up and saddled his donkey. He took with him two of his servants and his son Isaac. When he had cut enough wood for the burnt offering, he set out for the place God had told him about. On the third day Abraham looked up and saw the place in the distance."

The first day has been long. Their progress has been slow. Abraham's mind must be racing. It reacts to the Lord's instructions. He is well aware of the Lord's voice. He is intimate with every word. The words have echoed in his mind since the moment they were spoken. Did God really intend to ask for Isaac's life? The Bible does not hint if Abraham had trouble accepting his new direction. The Bible only records Abraham's immediate activity to accomplish God's task. As the morning sun pushes the night sky from the horizon, Abraham begins to prepare for the journey. Abraham alone carries the weight of the task required that day. No one can join his nightmare.

That morning, did Abraham move to Isaac's room before the boy awoke? Did he look at Isaac sleeping in his bed for the last time? Before Isaac arrived, Abraham remembers the volume of tears that accompanied his prayers for a son. Did he attempt to remind God about the volume of praises lifted from that room for God's provision? Now the tears move his joy to grief. God knows Abraham loves his son. The issue is not about a love for his son but a love for his God.

THE MARKERS OF LIFE

Walking along the road, Abraham remembers that challenges have always marked the course of his life. At this point in Abraham's story, life has been a grand journey of trusting God's direction. Over thirty years earlier, God speaks to Abraham and asks him to move from his home. At seventy-five years of age, Abraham packs up his family, collects his belongings, and turns his face away from his father's burial site. Behind him lay his home, his predictable world, and his future. Uncertainty and obedience lay in front. Who can grasp the enormity of the Lord's instruction? This move is riddled with ambiguity and extreme difficulties. But, the choice is not hard for Abraham. He surrenders to God and walks along the path God has set.

About twenty-five years later, God speaks to Abraham again. This time, God affirms His promise to give Abraham a child. As the head of a household in that day and time, Abraham considers this a prized promise. In light of his age, this is a promise for which he waits with baited breath. The waiting has been long. The waiting has been extra difficult because God had also promised to make Abraham the father of many nations. Neither has been granted. He has watched one year after another pass without the slightest hint of a single heir. But, Abraham is faithful. Each episode of God's interaction interrupts his life long turmoil.

The turmoil comes from the expectations he and the world place on life. They, like you, may believe certain things should come at certain times in life. Early in childhood, people begin to script their life. They begin to create a picture that is a product of their environment and their dreams. Life is meticulously fabricated within the frame of this picture. Throughout the course of life, the picture may be modified and updated, but it always has a central place. The picture is the standard against which life is judged and evaluated. How is life? Well, just check it against the picture you have now.

Perhaps Abraham has this picture. He is a man who is carving out a successful living. He finds a beautiful wife. The Bible records Sarah's beauty several times. He probably has great family members, neighbors, and friends who talk about Abraham's future. They form a consensus that this beautiful couple will be blessed with the most beautiful children. They all cannot wait for the day Abraham's house is overrun with several little "rug rats." How many will they have? What will be their names? More than one conversation has discussed the expectations for the future.

But, very few things in Abraham's life conform to the expectations that have been generated. The expectations paint markers along the path of life. According to the markers, Abraham has missed the course and lost the path. Markers move people along the path to provide some level of predictability and control. The markers maintain the course to accomplish the ideal picture of life. Abraham's markers reveal he has lost control. Every area of his life has challenged the markers. Nothing seems in compliance with their wishes.

Consider some of the markers in your world. Are you fighting to maintain a life that is being driven by markers? Did someone expect you to go to college after you finished high school? After college, did you feel you should get a good job and save money? Do you have enough money saved? Did your family expect you to get married soon after college? How about your wedding? Were people surprised when you got pregnant on your honeymoon? Do you have too much debt at 40? Do you have the right job? Do you have the right husband? Have you saved enough for your retirement? Is your health sound for your age? These are all markers.

While the markers direct your steps to accomplish your ideal picture of life, they also have a strange relationship with you. They are parasites. They suck life from you as they generate more life for themselves. They are very active. Driving down a highway, road markers are different. They serve a passive purpose. They tell you how far you have been and how far you have to go. They are needful and helpful. You can gauge your journey's progress without error. Markers are nothing more than a point of identification between two points.

But, in the journey of life, markers have a dynamic relationship with the traveler. They are more than indicators in the space between destinations. They can control your life. Without regard to your present blessings, markers focus your attention on the things you fail to have. They play this bizarre role with exceptional results during a tragedy. During this vulnerable time, markers ambush your life. They create pain because they refuse to accept the circumstances that have destroyed your life and sabotaged your future. In a sense, they bite the hands that feed them. You gave markers their life by having expectations.

Generally, having expectations, hopes, and goals are good to press life through its stages. Take the issue of pregnancy. Some people plan when to have a family. They decide the number of children they want and the years separating their arrival. This type of planning can certainly benefit children and parents alike. But, when are pregnancies just right on time? Any failure to maintain timelines reveals the power markers have over you. Think about it.

If the first pregnancy it too soon, you may spend the rest of your life feeling you lost an opportunity to "live a little." If the pregnancy is too late, you feel your opportunity to be a parent is robbed. The markers create a world where absolute conformity is essential for maximum living. If you are unable to have children at all, markers make the weight of this reality unbearable. Markers tend to seethe if you deviate from their path in any way. Abraham carries a heavy burden as he waits decades for a child.

When God promises Abraham a child, Abraham is ready for that blessing. After all, he is a hundred years old and has waited twenty-five years with God's promise in hand. Markers would say Abraham should be holding his grandchildren by this age. He agrees, but he just longs to hold a child that is his. Markers would say he is too old to start having children. He would have started a family many years earlier, but what choice did Abraham have? Markers would say this and that should be in his life by now. Abraham is not even close to these expectations. Has Abraham missed out on life? The markers would lead to this conclusion.

But, Abraham refuses to accept these markers. He could not be walking on today's path with his son if he held to markers. He would not have awakened early in the morning if markers guided his path. He realizes markers attempt to maintain life within a zone of predictability. Abraham has had anything but a predictable life. Today's walk to Moriah is typical. Markers clearly limit God's opportunity to direct life. Abraham understands this truth. Now the truth must be applied. Abraham wants a child, and the markers say he needs an heir. But, God has asked him to kill Isaac. With this instruction, God is outside the frame of predictability.

As he stands to catch his breath under the hot scorching sun, Abraham ponders. He sees Isaac. His eyes fill with tears. Abraham wipes them quickly. Isaac must not see his heart. What is God doing? Abraham realizes God's instruction does not make sense. But, he does not require God to make sense. He realizes other options exist for a sacrifice. But, Abraham does not try to create his own way to those options. He completely trusts God. He knows God does as He pleases. The markers do not apply to God. So, they do not apply to Abraham.

"No more markers!" This has been the cry of Abraham's heart since the first day God spoke to him. He did as God commanded. Can you imagine how many markers Abraham destroys with his move to the land of Canaan? He leaves a complex web of family and friends. He places his wife and possessions at great risk. He has no idea where he is going. People are in shock. They cannot understand his reasoning. They frantically remind him of the markers. But, as Abraham follows God, he dismantles and abandons one marker after another.

Dismantling markers has been the theme of Abraham's life. Day after day, year after year, and marker after marker, Abraham has been faithful to follow God. Abraham's faith prompts his steps of surrender. Today, as he walks to Moriah, he recalls God's provisions through previous difficulties. He revisits each to affirm his resolve to trust God: the death of his brother, moving from Ur and Haran, through famine, through Egypt, separation from Lot, war against the kings, and much more. Abraham has always surrendered to God. This particular call of God for Isaac's life garners the same response.

OPTIONS TO SURRENDER

Surrender has a high price. It requires the complete transfer of control from one to another. In a contest where two sides are in opposition, surrender involves crowning one as victor. The consent to this coronation comes with the resignation of the other's sovereignty. No one surrenders easily because of this extreme price. Surrender requires releasing goals and dreams. Surrender requires abandoning markers. Surrender requires rejecting the picture that embodied your perfect and ideal life. Abraham rejects that picture. As he surrenders, he is moving closer to Moriah.

Surrender runs contrary to the natural motion and inclination of life. As you travel through life, markers seem to chart your course and progress. Notice that you move past markers as you accomplish one goal after another. You may begin to believe life should float in this direction. The markers of life claim to support this motion by masquerading as the sentinels of the future. Surrender contradicts this motion of life. It derails the agenda of markers by jettisoning all expectations, dreams, and goals. It releases the ideal picture of life. In Abraham's case, sacrificing Isaac is the ultimate expression of surrender. Abraham is willing to transfer everything he loves into the loving and sovereign hands of God.

Surrendering is a must. But you may not choose to surrender. There are alternatives. One option is to fight to the death. A heroic slave rebellion in the Roman Empire has immortalized a man named Spartacus. He is credited with starting and leading the most successful and costly campaign against Rome. He was a Roman citizen who deserted the army to become a fugitive. He was captured and enslaved as a gladiator. After escaping, he and 80 other gladiators moved into the countryside. Spartacus longed to leave the Roman Empire. The others wanted to stay and fight. Over the preceding year, 70,000 men, mostly escaped slaves, joined their ranks.

At his peak, Spartacus commanded 120,000 men and routed everything in his path. Eventually, Rome assembled a force that moved decisively against him. In the ensuing battles, Spartacus and his men fought with a "no surrender" mind-set. Only six thousand men were captured in the final battle. The victorious general was so disgusted with Spartacus and the slaves that he gave a bizarre order. One man after another would be crucified along the roadway leading back to Rome. The bodies were never removed from the crosses. They rotted where they hung. Today, the Appian Way is world famous. It is a powerful example of the commitment and cost to a "no surrender" mind-set.

Abraham is aware of this option. He did not surrender when his cousin, Lot, is taken captive. He did not accept this event as his fate. He leads a small army of men into battle. Abraham is willing to fight to the death to free Lot. In the end, Abraham is victorious and celebrates the spoils of war. But with God's call to Moriah, Abraham does not fight. He lays down his weapons of opposition and follows God. His decision seems automatic with no indication of difficulty.

Another option to surrender also exists. This option engages an effort of opposition against anything that impedes a quest for total victory. World War II provides the best example of this mind-set. The Axis powers of Germany, Italy, and Japan are attempting to conquer the world. The Allies stand in opposition. Over the course of the war, over 55 million people die world wide because each side refuses to surrender. The well-trained and well-equipped Germany army is becoming infamous for its rapid strike warfare known as "Blitzkrieg." For them, there is no surrender as they sweep across Europe, Asia, and Africa. The Japanese army begins with a notorious assault on Nanking, China. In one short six-week period, 300,000 humans are systematically murdered and 80,000 women are raped. This invasion is touted as training for the Imperial army and a message of woe to the world.

As the Allies persist and begin to prevail in the various theaters of battle, Axis forces are faced with a decision. They must decide to fight to the death or surrender in defeat. In World War II, Allied nations attempt to compel surrender. Traditional and eventually atomic weapons are employed to bring submission. Finally, the Axis nations surrender in defeat. This is the second option to surrender.

The leaders of the defeated nations sign a document declaring their acceptance of defeat. They agree to the terms of surrender on behalf of their nation. The surrender is unconditional. No special consideration is given to the defeated forces. They are not granted rights or privileges. They may have fought with valor, but unconditional surrender does not appropriate favor for sacrifice. Defeat is defeat. The winning forces are in control. The sovereignty of each defeated nation is lost.

Had Abraham opposed God's instruction for Isaac's sacrifice, he would have declared war against God. The ensuing battles would have left Abraham with two alternatives, fight to the death or to defeat. Abraham could not fight against God. He knows he cannot win. Moreover, he does not want to embrace the markers that would incite the war by placing value for Isaac over God. He loves God. Clearly, the option to fight is foolish. You may agree. But, do you choose to fight?

How do you respond to tragedy? How do you respond to change? How do you respond to challenges? Do you accept God's hand of sovereignty? When tragedy strikes and your markers wield enormous power over you, do you ally yourself with their ideology and engage a fight? Sure, all the things happening in your life may not be what you think God desires. You may be able to argue your case with complete effectiveness. But, as you choose to hold the markers in your life, you insist your ideal picture of life is of greater value than God. You struggle because you do not surrender. You do not discard the picture of what life should be. You want control, and you want your life back.

The picture you have regarding how life "should be" must be completely lost. You cannot know surrender without this vital step of abandonment. Surrendering does not take into account what was lost or what you hope can be recovered. Surrendering does not try to save anything. It submits to God's sovereignty. As you release the ideal picture of life, the war ends. You are under God's authority. He accepts your unconditional surrender.

God requires unconditional surrender. He is not looking to make deals. He does not need to grant favors or privileges. He does not take into consideration the circumstances that brought you to the point of surrender. You may see yourself as the victim. You may cry out to God and ask Him for help. You may be able to produce an incredible argument to support your claims or position. But, in the end, your surrender brings you completely under God's control. He may not plan to fix what you think was broken or destroyed. He may have a totally different picture in mind for you. You must release your ideal picture that you love so much.

AFFECTION AFFECTS

Abraham gives up control. He is determined to carry out the wishes of God. Isaac, the son whom he loves, will be the son whom he kills. For three long days, Abraham walks along the road. He savors every step. They are the last he will take with his son. He takes joy in seeing the boy kick a rock along their path. Isaac runs ahead and runs back attempting to push the old man's slow steps. "Hurry up, father. Hurry!" The boy has no idea what he says. Abraham's steps of surrender cannot be hurried.

He experiences every moment as if they are his last breath. He watches his precious son Isaac. He savors the sweat Isaac wipes from his brow to register the effort of this trip. He gazes with wonder as Isaac sleeps and eats. He holds Isaac in his arms. He recalls every memory from the previous thirteen years in which Isaac brought happiness to Abraham. Abraham feasts at this banquet table of life as if life is serving its last meal. Abraham's drink is a mix of anguish and joy, washing down the blessing of his meal.

Abraham loves his son. He loves Isaac very, very much. Years of anticipating Isaac's arrival have deepened Abraham's love. Abraham remembers holding and playing with Lot's girls. The sum total of all his time spent with other children could not compare with one moment he has had with Isaac. Abraham is blessed. Isaac is his life and his future. Isaac is his joy. The boy is Abraham's laughter. Abraham looks forward to the morning because Isaac gives hugs and kisses with such amazing purity. No one in Abraham's long life has had this affect on him.

"I love you, father!" These words ring in Abraham's heart and melt every cell. He is a proud father. What would Abraham live for after Isaac is gone? Abraham's mind does not have the capacity to begin this deliberation. Strong affection connects Abraham to Isaac. The markers applaud this connection and the presence of Isaac. They consider Isaac vital to Abraham's future. They consider Isaac the validation to Abraham's past. Without Isaac, the future and past lose meaning and hope. The markers of life attempt to tell Abraham that the ideal picture of life is within his grasp. But Abraham knows the price of holding the ideal picture of life is accepting the "no surrender" mind-set. Instead, he reminds himself, "No more markers!"

Markers refuse to release the ideal picture of life. When life falls apart through tragedy or difficult circumstances, you are clearly aware of your present misfortune. But, do you realize how your appreciation of the past and hopes for the future is equally affected? Through hindsight, the ideal picture of life serves as the standard by which you evaluate the past. After a divorce, you look back to cherish the days you had as a couple or family. Or, you look back and see the pain that charted your course through marriage. Markers use hindsight to reinforce their power. They affirm their value by reminding you what life should have been. They force you to wrestle with questions. Where did life go wrong? How could it go so badly? What could have been done differently? The present is not at peace with the past.

You have a strong affection with the past. You may have loved what you had and what you had hoped for. The affection for the ideal past is so strong your present turmoil inflames your reflection. You long for what you lost or hoped for. The past inadvertently serves as an anchor. It will not let you move. You begin to bog down with regret and anger. You wish to go back. But, how can you? You say you cannot move forward. The past hinders you. By failing to let go of the ideal picture of life, you fail to let go of the past.

Abraham relates well to this phenomenon. The more time Abraham spends thinking about what he has with Isaac, the less likely he is to accept God's direction. His affection for Isaac is real, and it is very important. But, it should not prevail. His affections for God must supercede all other affections. Abraham knows this. As he reflects on his past, he remembers many things. He may spend time savoring the past, but he is careful not to provide an opportunity for the past to sever his surrender to God.

Markers also have a strong hold on the future. Through foresight, the ideal picture of life serves as the blueprint for rebuilding the future from the ruins of the present. A broken family, a lost career, a medical crisis, or a financial set back intensify the marker's efforts to get life back on track. Moreover, they wish to direct life in a manner that accomplishes their expectations. Markers pose as sympathetic representatives of your best interest. However, they hijack your faith and trust in God. They enslave you to their design in such a manner that you cannot accept alternate steps. Markers limit God's opportunity to move by attaching your affection to their anticipated results.

It is not wrong to be concerned about how your circumstances may affect your future. You are free to guess and pray. But, are you free to conclude that God cannot use your tragedy or difficult circumstances as agents of change? Too often, markers dictate that your difficulties should be viewed with disdain. After all, your ideal picture of life has been obliterated by your tragedy. But the Bible teaches another truth about life in the context of pain. Look at Paul. He catalogs a long list of difficult circumstances in 2 Corinthians 11. His summary in chapter 12 claims that these events provide God an opportunity to manifest His strength in Paul.

If you can accept your present set of circumstances as being within the scope of God's sovereign hand, then you have taken a major step. You forsake your markers and allow God to move in your future. He will take your ruins and bring about His good. Paul says, "And we know that in all things God works for the good of those who love Him, who have been called according to His purpose." This is biblical truth. God loves you. His future for you has one guarantee: He is in charge. When you surrender your future to Him, you can end all your speculation about where life is headed. You can let go of the future because you no longer need your ideal picture of life. God is painting now.

Surrender involves loving God more than anything in this world. Abraham accepts this term as part of his unconditional surrender. He learns to trust God beyond what he can see. As he arrives in Moriah, he realizes this destination is like all others to which God has directed. He could never see all the way down any road on which he followed God.

He places full confidence in God to see his next step. Hebrews 11:1 says, "Now faith is being sure of what we hope for and certain of what we do not see." In every situation, Abraham surrenders to God because he trusts God. He knows God has a plan that exceeds anything he could have hoped for.

Listen to Abraham's steps of surrender. Genesis 22:5-10 says, "He said to his servants, 'Stay here with the donkey while I and the boy go over there. We will worship and then we will come back to you.' Abraham took the wood for the burnt offering and placed it on his son Isaac, and he himself carried the fire and the knife. As the two of them went on together, Isaac spoke up and said to his father Abraham, 'Father?' 'Yes, my son?' Abraham replied. 'The fire and wood are here,' Isaac said, 'but where is the lamb for the burnt offering?' Abraham answered, 'God himself will provide the lamb for the burnt offering, my son.' And the two of them went on together. When they reached the place God had told him about, Abraham built an altar there and arranged the wood on it. He bound his son Isaac and laid him on the altar, on top of the wood."

He prepares the sacrificial altar in an altered state of mind. He has built so many. The boy's question breaks his trance. "Father, where is the sacrifice?" How does Abraham hold his composure? The past, present and future make one last ditch effort. The past screams, "Isaac is God's fulfillment of a long awaited promise." The present shouts, "This boy is everything you have hoped for." The future warns, "You and your wife are over a hundred. How will you be the father of many nations without Isaac?" The markers press to break Abraham's surrender.

But, the final image of surrender provided by Abraham is amazing. No father can imagine the horror Abraham feels. He is a heart surgeon performing his own bypass. The Bible says Abraham bound his son. So much affection connects Abraham to Isaac. Previously, Abraham held

Isaac for a hug now he holds him for the altar. Abraham records Isaac's soft precious skin and little frame as he picks him up. Abraham kisses the boy and places him on the sacrificial altar.

The next touch will be with a knife. The markers of life exploit Abraham's affection for Isaac to mobilizes the past, present, and future for one final stand at this altar. They cry, "This is your son whom you love." But, there is no battle. On this mountain, Abraham continues to surrender to God. He forsakes the past, present, and future to affirm his love for God. He draws a deep breath. He draws his knife. Tears flood his eyes as he maintains his composure. "Father in heaven, I sacrifice my ideal picture of life to acknowledge my love for you. Although I love Isaac like no father has ever loved a son, my love for you is greater. Accept my unconditional surrender."

NOT MY WILL

Yes, Abraham does not have to kill the boy. An angel of the Lord shouts to interrupt his resolve. Genesis 22:11-13 says, "But the angel of the LORD called out to him from heaven, 'Abraham! Abraham!' 'Here I am,' he replied. 'Do not lay a hand on the boy,' he said. 'Do not do anything to him. Now I know that you fear God, because you have not withheld from me your son, your only son.' Abraham looked up and there in a thicket he saw a ram caught by its horns. He went over and took the ram and sacrificed it as a burnt offering instead of his son."

The angel stops the knife. But, Abraham has already sacrificed Isaac in principle. The sacrifice came with the surrender. The knife is only a formality. God notices Abraham's perfect submission. The Bible states, "Because you have not withheld from me your son, your only son." Abraham's love for God prevails over his love for Isaac. Abraham destroys that ideal picture of life. Abraham rejects the markers of life. This is unconditional surrender. Every step leading to Moriah has been a perfect expression of unconditional surrender. Abraham gives God the latitude to do whatever He wants.

In your life, do you allow God to do as He pleases? Have you experienced unconditional surrender? God did not guarantee you a bed of roses. He did not say you would have a "white picket-fence dream." He did not promise that He would work to accomplish your ideal picture of life. However, He did promise to be faithful. He promises to meet you at the point of your need. He promises to be a blessing to you. He promises to direct your path to destinations that accomplish His good purpose.

You must let go of the markers. You must release all the elements that comprise your ideal picture of life. Do not hinder God's opportunity with your life. Accept the sovereign hand of God. If He says He wants everything, you cannot withhold anything. If He calls you to forgive someone, you cannot say you will not forgive. If he says you must forget the ideal picture of life, you cannot have any affection with it. You must unconditionally surrender.

Jesus is the perfect example of unconditional surrender. He did not hold back in any way as He yields to God's sovereign hand. Look at the life of Jesus. His ministry has had a profound impact. His love has been a great blessing to the masses. Outside of meeting physical needs, Jesus does not forget His mission to die. In one of the most powerful scenes in Scripture, Jesus pronounces His unconditional surrender in the Garden of Gethsemane. Praying here is not an unusual act. The disciples are so familiar with this activity they elect to sleep while Jesus prays. They do not understand the significance of this night. But, Jesus does.

Sin enters the world in the Garden of Eden. But in the Garden of Gethsemane, Jesus accomplishes the unconditional surrender that sets the course. After the prayer in the Garden of Gethsemane, the cross may be considered a formality, but this formality is a needful reality. Jesus must die. The cross would satisfy God's wrath against sin. Jesus accepts the picture God has painted for Him. He will conquer sin and death. There is no other option.

Jesus' prayer in the garden is rich. It depicts a struggle with surrendering. Luke 22:42 says, "Father, if you are willing, take this cup from me; yet not my will, but yours be done." Could there be another option? He makes a plea, "If you are willing, Father." Jesus is within the authority of God's sovereignty. Could these be the words that Isaac cries to his father? Who can know? Isaac is young and probably able to overtake his frail father. Certainly, Isaac could run and hide. Abraham does not record difficulty in binding and placing Isaac. The boy is under authority. Abraham also is under authority. He, too, may have echoed the same words, calling out to God for mercy. He could run and hide, but he does no such thing. For Abraham, there are no other options to unconditional surrender. He must yield to God and follow through.

Jesus has no options. He yields, "Yet not my will, but Your will be done." Jesus' statement in its entirety is important. With it, He implies the presence of a picture that embodies God's will. He may have generated options, but they no longer matter. In His statement, He first rejects His own will. He dismantles His ideal picture of life, destroys His markers, and yields. He gives God complete opportunity to accomplish His good will. Jesus models for you the important steps of unconditional surrender. Follow His example. Take your ideal picture of life, your markers, and hold them in your hands. Hold your hands to God and say, "Yet not my will, but Your will be done."

SECTION 3
Transparent Applications

J A M E S   1 : 2 2
Do not merely listen to the word, and so deceive yourselves. Do what it says.

Look around you. Most likely nothing has changed in your world after reading the previous section. Your difficulties are probably still present. Do not be surprised or disappointed. You are not reading a magical book casting spells to transform your circumstances. This book is just a book. It is like every other book with pages filled by words. If you discover any truths within these pages, they support the potential for change. However, the key to change requires more than just reading.

Let me explain. My graphics designer is named Bill Kersey. As you can see with this book, he knows his stuff. Bill made a great first impression by showing me books he had previously designed. Two of his books deal with cooking. Cookbooks are full of pictures and techniques. Although I would learn a lot from reading, I do not cook. I realized that if I do not try any of these recipes, I could not truly benefit from such books.

The following section is my experience in the kitchen with God's truths. I wrote these short stories during a difficult season in my life. To "change" I got into the habit of reading these stories over and over again. The stories encouraged me. The reading supported the application of truth on a daily basis. I felt like I was in the kitchen with the book open reading a recipe and applying it to my dish in process. Yes, this book is full of truths. As you read, apply them to your circumstances. Watch God transform your world. He promises to do so. John 8:32 says, "Then you will know the truth, and the truth will set you free." Freedom awaits you.

NEVER WOULD HAVE GUESSED

Today is my birthday. On such a day, I should celebrate the occasion of my birth. Perhaps family, friends, and festive activity should surround me. But, none of that is to be had. Have I read the wrong script? Without reservation, this will be considered one of my most memorable birthdays as silence and solitude provide the mood for the script entitled "Never Would Have Guessed."

I am free to guess. Life would not be the same without pretending to be part-time future tellers. We sit and have visions. We talk and create fiction. We sleep to dream the fantasies with never-ending happy endings. If it were possible to count the scenarios I had hoped for on this day, the heart would ache as the mind rehearsed each one after another just outside of my reach. The disappointment is deep.

On the occasion of this celebration for my birth, I declare without care, caution, or strength that I am sad. Sadness changes life. Helplessly, I have watched my seconds transformed into hours, my countless conversations reduced to polite greetings, and my event-jammed calendar to scrap paper. Where has my life gone? The life that demands celebration is being robbed of its rightful consideration as piece by piece a dismantling is taking place.

There are no family or friends in this restaurant in the middle of Austria. I know no face. Today I have spoken only a few words to puzzled individuals failing to understand the only language I speak. My inner voice is my conversation. My shadow is my only company. If I have had joy today, they were moments of sunshine in an otherwise stormy day. The clouds are ominous. The mixture of rain and snow continue to dampen and freeze the soul. Gone is the warmth from the fire of a great hearth. Perhaps I should have said great heart, since this was my intention. In either case, the heart is the well spring of life; the source that feeds the mind and body. Today in my heart, ashes provide the stage for a lone stream of smoke rising in tribute to my life past.

Have I been reading the wrong script? As a boy, God moved in my life changing my heart as I reached out to Him with all I had. He handed me a script. The title was not important to me as I turned the pages to discover the steps for each day. Wow! Unbelievable! Without disappointment I have seen God move. The fire of my life consisted of a great flame. Warmth and light feed not only my body and soul, but others found in my company.

Now, I have closed the script. The events in my life have slowly quenched the fire. Time had only sealed its fate. As both hands clench the closed script, tears stream from the eyes of my soul. What happened to the script? I was sure the title had read "Abundant Life." If not, perhaps the authors name was the "Life-Giver." In either case, I was under the impression that the fire of my heart would always burn.

The tears of the soul and the mourning of the heart are ending. Like those who have buried a loved one, I am finding that tears have their limits as acceptance makes its residence. Have I watched the fire burn for the last time? Will I never feel the warmth that brings life to my body, soul, and surroundings? As my mind begins to generate the countless scenarios of a hopeless life, my eyes see the words printed on the cover of the script: "Never Would Have Guessed."

How true this title! My life has been filled with blessing beyond my wildest dreams: friends, family, jobs, adventures, and the list goes on. Each time something wonderful happened, I entered a private conversation with the scriptwriter to see if He had made a mistake. Are you kidding? Are you sure you meant this for me? "Never Would Have Guessed" has been the theme of a life filled with faith. Now, faith is the theme of a life filled with "Never Would Have Guessed." I ask the scriptwriter if a mistake has been made. "No," He responds. He placed His hand on my back and encouraged me to "read on."

The warmth of His divine touch provided strength to read once. When will the pain end? My fingers are eager to turn the pages to discover the answer. When will I start living again? My eyes are poised not to miss one word as the pages turn. What will be the impact of my life? My heart is racing to fan a new flame. I brush the tears from my soul. My birthday has occasioned not a celebration for my birth, but a celebration for my faith. My hands tremble as pages begin to turn. The last page read recorded the death of the fire. Faith eager to experience life drives the eyes to read on from the script entitled, "Never Would Have Guessed."

THE BOX IS ON THE MANTLE

That's obvious – what's obvious is not always what's obvious until it becomes obvious. Is that obvious? Maybe not, let me explain. Have you ever sat with a two-year-old to find Waldo? The room was hers. The Waldo book I held was hers, but the leg she leaned on as we sat on the floor was mine. Although older and much smarter, I quickly realized my gross disadvantage. The more time we spent on the floor, the more painful became my introduction to her mastery of Waldo.

The pain came from her elbow as it dug into my leg during her pointing performance. "There," she said as quickly as my fingers left the turned page. I was amazed and humiliated. I was looking for Waldo. He was obviously placed on every page. My frantic gaze from one side to the other failed to produce him before she cried out. Am I that slow? Her mom laughed and said, "My baby has all the pages memorized." Waldo was obvious to her because she knew where to look. With relief, I continued to play, reinforcing her expertise of the obvious. God wanted to help me develop my expertise of the obvious, and my lesson was just beginning.

My responsibility was to deliver my brother to a friend's house for a visit. "Are you kidding," I responded to his invitation? My quick refusal to visit Hans was motivated by my awareness of his personal pain. With so much pain in my own life, my soul wanted no part of hearing or seeing anyone else's pain. I decided to walk the streets in an attempt to relieve the pressure in my soul. At that point, grief had processed one death, denied another, and projected a third. Too much fear, pain, and anguish propelled my fast walk away from "Hans' House of Tragedy."

The levels of despair began accelerating. As I returned to Hans' house, my pain collapsed my body to the curb. I was trapped between the hell in my life and the hell waiting in Hans' house. The wonderful expressions of life around me failed to alter the heart's perception of death. My frantic eyes scanned from side to side, but nothing communicated comfort to me. The stench of three deaths lingered in the air as my mind wished I would be the fourth. Finally out of desperation, I walked to Hans' door.

The frail 63-year-old man struggled to push the screen door, assuring an irresistible invitation. My brother had alerted Hans to my pain. Why did that motivate this man to ignore my agenda? "Come in. Come in, sit down," he said. Moving past Hans, I gave my brother a glare, demanding his assistance to exit this house of tragedy. I did not want to talk with Hans. Even if misery loves company, I only wanted the sympathetic company of my inner voice. My brother thought differently. Irritated with me, his eyes moved to Hans and mine followed.

Hans spoke slowly. A stroke left his right side paralyzed. Intense therapy yielded remarkable results evidenced by his walk and speech. Sitting next to my brother, I stared into Hans' eyes. Why were they so inviting? The stroke had not wielded its fury on them. I returned his incredible gaze, my soul accepting my sequestration. Every word from his mouth was an injection of hope within the deep roots of my soul. Few could understand my pain. But he knew. When pain and despair attach their talons, the penetration enters the deepest crevices of the soul. At this depth, every drop of hope is drained, inducing a cry for mercy through death. Hans' eyes made this accurate prognosis.

As he spoke, my heart pondered if God orchestrated this meeting to identify the obvious in my life. As we sat, I turned the pages only to hear Hans shout "There," a pointer's performance. In this case, the room was his. The furniture was his, but the book was mine. He was an expert. Not because he memorized my pages, but because he knew what to look for. With sixty-three years of practice, he was good. To me, the obvious seemed as child's play to him. I was amazed, but not humiliated.

His words were an injection of hope to stabilize my soul. "You are going to be all right. You are going to be all right. Look at me, it's only been one month and I can already walk, use my right arm, and bathe my self." A well-deserved flavor of pride coated his words. Yes, he was a miracle. As a result of his stroke, Hans lost his job and his freedom. With his hands, he had programmed computers, led companies, and built a home. He cared for a garden with 160 rose bushes. He raised birds, maintained a fishpond, and held his wife. Now his great victories were measured by the same physical stages of an infant moving to childhood. How humiliating, yet he was not humiliated.

His testimony continued. Within the same month of his stroke, Hans lost his wife of forty years to a car accident. Theirs was an incredible marriage. In the beginning, so obvious was its future that she alerted him of her plans for a wedding. How can these few lines do justice to forty years? What war rages in his heart as the memories of the past battle with the dreams of the future? The losses are unimaginable. Most men cower and surrender after a stroke or the loss of a spouse. Hans was dealing with both. What was Hans? He did not seem human. He was living in the midst of so much sorrow. He did not just live. He did not awake in the morning only to watch the sun walk across the sky. There was more.

As my eyes transcended our brief encounter, I saw a man who wanted more from life than just to smell the roses. He wanted to grow them and nurture them so others could be blessed by their appearance and smell. As we concluded our time together, he pointed to a small black box on his mantle. "That's the ashes of my wife," he said. I wish now I had moved closer to see her pictures that surrounded the box. We stood to leave. His stroke ridden right arm wrapped around me to meet his left. A tight squeeze was the final period to his lessons on the obvious.

The next 24 hours proved to be the most critical of my life. During this time, the events were moving so fast I felt God was playing a cruel game. Frustration was building. Where was Hans? My mind and heart savored his hug, a trace of hope in a desert of despair. Once again, I found my senses sober to all the details, yet no signs of God. Was God there? Did He care?

In the battle for the heart and soul, the enemy is tenacious. With limited weapons, he unleashes a relentless barrage. My shield of faith is tailor-made to extinguish these fiery missiles. The shield is effective when faith acknowledges the obvious within my life. The obvious are the "Waldos" of our pages. They are the distinctive fingerprints of God in a very busy canvas called life. Seeing the obvious injects hope because the fingerprints remind the soul that God is at work. In the midst of any situation, God is the same yesterday, today, and forever.

My final observation of the obvious yields the greatest lesson from Hans. Who can imagine the questions that plague Hans' mind? They are prompted by many senses: a smell, a picture, a song, or a touch. How many times did he rethink the events preceding the car accident? If only we had left sooner. What if we had not stopped here? What if we turned right instead of left? If only something different had been done to miss the train called fate that rammed his car.

God had graciously given and now He has taken. Hans' memories are the lingering aroma of blessing. The same God that brought Hans' wife into his life is the same God that now sustains him. When questions attempt to resurrect her, Hans points to the most powerful obvious of all. He walks into the living room, sits in his favorite chair, and stares without reservation at the mantle. There, the power of his pain, the fury of all his fears, and the paralysis of all his anguish cannot alter the reality he sees. She is gone. The box is on the mantle.

When I find myself in these trenches of pain, no weapon is more powerful than to embrace reality and accept the unchangeable past. Like the phrase, "Remember the Alamo," I cry out with all of my might, "The box is on the mantle" to combat the relentless barrage of fear, pain, and anguish. During some of my worst moments, I imagine sitting in Hans' living room. My lips are chanting, "The box is on the mantle." At other more difficult times, I imagine holding my own box, containing the ashes of my three loves. With tears in my eyes, my mind watches as my fingers stir the ashes. This is my reality. No "what ifs" can resurrect these losses. With time, I begin to see the sovereign fingerprint of God on the box. He placed that fingerprint there to remind me of His love.

Sit on the floor beside God and place your elbow on His leg. He holds your book steady and turns the pages. "There, There, There," you point. The obvious contained on each page causes your eyes to flood with tears. Yes, God is at work. "There, there, there … you're going to be alright," He responds. God's right hand wraps around you to meet His left. A tight squeeze is the comma He places in this lesson on the obvious.

213

SPACE BETWEEN DESTINATIONS

Many walk by as I sit at a table hosting a cold lunch. From a distance I watch closely the movement of a world potentially more complex than our galaxy. The galaxy moves within laws, patterns, and boundaries. Although fast and complex, a night sky assures all is well. People move past. Yet, they have no predictable pattern. They are not as the wind whose directions wave the flags in unison. Nor of the rivers whose water yields not to obstacles yet stay within the bounds of the banks. The masses see the distance between destinations as mere space. Each step taken counts one less to take.

I see a girl running. Watching as she escapes my sight, my mind wonders what drives her pace. Others walk very slowly. Questions arise. Do they have an abundance of time or abundance of thought? Some walk alone; hands in pockets and eyes recklessly moving about. Others walk and pause, a solitary motionless body. Perhaps I see them as a stalled car in a Grand prix race; helpless and hopeless. Some walk in groups side by side or hand in hand. Their steps equal each other's in pace and direction. The larger groups make motion as fish schooling in the deep. What a wonder that one or two serve to guide the rest in this harmony of motion. Yes people move past; today, yesterday, and tomorrow. Soon, I shall join the masses. My heart desperately ponders the walker I would be, disappearing into the appearance of chaos.

Although life is fast, running would rob the fruit of my pilgrimage. Sights and sounds that make space meaningful would blur and give way as standing in a train speeding through a tunnel. Walking with a group would be nice. They would fill my time and heart with meaning and energy. Thoughts of conversation, laughter, touch, and presence are as inviting for me as standing on the bow of the Titanic pulling into New York harbor. Today, I have no opportunity to create my company: neither one nor more may walk by my side.

What then of walking alone? When one has no choice, this becomes a meaningless question. I am alone. The masses only reinforce the signs of my solitude. The heart begins to weep as fear brings paralysis to the soul. Please, please, no more envy and jealousy produced within my heart as the eyes identify those who possess my longings. I have nothing and nowhere to go. Please, more steps in the space without destinations. Nevertheless, a step is the next step because I cannot stay where I am.

I remember steps. Everyone said I was one of the toughest people to catch; my steps almost as well known as my work. Fast steps hailed a demanding schedule, while slow steps savored the company in my presence. In those days, no thought was required for steps. They came as automatic as breathing and as effortless as a heartbeat. But now, the steps are gone. I must learn to walk again. An education is required because my previous expertise came naturally. No thought was made to record the elements of this motion. Having always walked well, an assumption was embraced that this art would never be lost. Standing at this threshold in life, I ask, "How do I take the next step?"

Creator of life, hear my cry. Teach me the art of walking. "My child," responds the Creator, "learning to walk requires that you yield to me. A mother teaching her child to walk grasps both arms of the child lifting the child until she stands. This movement is not natural or comfortable but necessary. If the child fights, progress is limited. If the child yields, growth is assumed. Give me your arms and yield your body as I first teach you to stand." Father hold my arms, for now I stand. Do not let go. "My child, letting go is the most impossible thought to a teacher in love with the pupil. A mother's grip on a child cannot be equaled."

As the legs grow strong, the mother relaxes her lift, allowing the child to develop confidence. Finally, a solo stand is made. The mother's celebration equals the cheer given at a tickertape parade. How great is her joy? The commotion brings a smile to the small delicate face that does not quite comprehend her accomplishment. Quickly, the mother resumes her hold to save the child from crashing to the floor. More than likely, the fall would have blown away the child's smile.

Father, as I briefly stood, fear waged war against my trust in You. You teach me to walk again because my life was blown away. I thought Your hands held me tight. Were You absent during my crisis? As my pain diminished, I felt Your hands holding me. Too bad the pain blocked the evidence of Your presence. I know I have come a long way. This brief stand is indeed a major milestone. Although the sound of your cheer escapes my ears, my heart realizes You are my only prospect for walking. Nothing but trust remains. It is all I have.

A mother now prods her child to make her first step. The words from her mouth are encouraging, but the motion of the mother's hands produce the result. Gently, the mother lifts with her right hand. Her grip on the child's arm lifts the right side of the child's body. As skillfully as a crane operator moves a large metal beam, the mother pushes the elevated right side slightly forward causing the child's right leg to spring. Her excitement builds. She repeats the procedure for the left side, introducing the child to an exercise that soon dominates her little world. Practice builds skill. More practice brings confidence and strength.

Then the most anticipated day of the mother's life blows in like a thunderstorm on a warm spring afternoon. Suddenly, the child stands on her own, shifts her right side, and pulls her right leg forward; one small step. The moment ends as the child collapses to the floor. Her fall is not the picture of failure. The mother erupts, "Very good, Yea!" She will forget man's first step on the moon long before this moment is erased from her mind. Family and friends are called to report the greatest news since the birth of Christ. A ripple of excitement moves across the surface of her life. The mother takes pictures to mark the progress of each step. The walk to dad and the stroll across the room are also captured. More steps move the child into the unlimited world of walking for one lifetime.

Father, I wish to walk the world. To experience the limitless expressions of Your creation would be a joy beyond my wildest imagination. But, I do not know how to start. Neither do I understand where to go. Destinations seem extinct like the dinosaurs of worlds past. Command me to step from this threshold as Peter was called from his boat in the middle of the waves. Peter was well acquainted with the waves of a storm. Although I have not been on a boat far from shore, sitting on a beach at night brings personal appreciation for this power. The thunder and ripple of crashing waves make their mark on my heart, leaving me thankful for the shore.

What would be the experience riding out a storm? My body shudders at the horror faced by the countless individuals who have braved such an adventure. The Psalmist records waves towering to the heavens and dropping to the depths. The men in storm driven ships desperately cry out to You to spare their lives. Life becomes the only commodity of value as the ship's contents are tossed to improve their chances for survival. Ironically, the ship that brought them into the belly of the storm is the safest place for the sailors during its duration. How desperate is their plight? Only You who created the waves can calm them. No other hope exists.

Father, the storm clouds rule the skies of my tomorrows. My gaze fixed in the distance fails to discover the end to the waves crashing the threshold at my feet. Peter, was this what you saw when faith inspired you to take a step? Father, what inspired Peter's faith? "My child, Peter saw Jesus. When Jesus walked on the water, He did not first calm the water to ease His journey. Neither did He calm the sea to beckon Peter onto the water. Peter did as he saw Jesus doing. Peter's faith powered his steps, and the sight of Jesus provided inspiration to put faith into action."

As I stand at this threshold, faith compels me to resign my demands for an end to the crashing waves in my world. If they remained for Peter, what reason can I give to remove them for me? Like Peter, I am asking to walk. He did not first request the calming of the sea. His faith overcame all fears. With his faith inspiring mine, I withdraw my demand to calm my raging storm. Circumstances may have generated the waves, but now faith sees that fear sustains their power over me. I must take my first step.

Father, although one request has been withdrawn, may others be made? Peter stepped out into the waves as shall I, but Peter had Jesus just in front. Not only did this inspire Peter, but also, Jesus lifted Peter from the water when his faith yielded to sight. My first request is for Your presence to journey with me in these troubled waters. Please, help my eyes of faith see You walking beside me. I want the assurance of Your sustaining grace. I want to place my life in Your righteous right hand.

Father, my second is that I journey as a child with you. In the city center, many people passed with children. Watching them taught the beautiful lessons to be applied to life in the space between destinations.

What purpose do little children serve on trips taken by parents? They did not have a choice with any aspect of the trip including the clothes on their body. Their parents dress and bundle; a masterpiece of art displayed on a moving canvas. How proud the hearts of the parents as children hover close.

Some parents held one hand, a steady walk guiding with a pull to the right or a push to the left. How precious is the sight of little bodies reaching out with little hands? How tireless are little feet working extra hard to prevent a tug from above? Some children held a parent with each hand. Father on the right and mother on the left provided a moving swing. The child in the middle purposely jumped up, retracted legs, and counted on the parents to sustain a fun ride suspended inches from the ground.

For various reasons, other children were carried on the parent's waist; this blessing was definitely felt as the arms of the parent wrapped tightly around the child. My heart was blessed to see the child's head resting on the parent's shoulder. More animated than this were the children who sat on parent's shoulders. Theirs' was a world of adventure in the clouds. Some had their arms extended to simulate a plane. Others had arms grasping the parent's neck to mimic the gallant ride of a brave knight. Other children rode in strollers. Content faces marked their leisurely progress in the space between destinations. Yet, the children have no destinations. Without destinations, what compels them to journey?

What are my destinations? I do not know. I am like the children in the space between destinations. Will You move with me as the children's parents moved with them? Hold my hand. My journey is bound to provide plenty of moments to rescue my weary soul with a touch of Your grace. Today, my body is weak. My arms and legs are limp and unable to produce the motion required to journey in the space between destinations. My heart is faint from the terror produced by the waves crashing before me. My soul in agony screams for You, Father.

With all my strength, I reach my arms to You. My tear-filled eyes pronounce my desperate request without a word. My first step must be in the embrace of Your strong arms. My feet will not touch the water. My legs will not feel the crash of the waves as You begin my journey. I am a child being carried on your waist. Your right arm is snug around me. Your left hand wipes the tears on my eyes. My head upon your shoulder continues to mutter the sounds of agony. Father, Your first step is my first step in the space between destinations. Today, it seems our progress is measured more by my diminishing groans than by Your sovereign steps.

THE STILL NIGHT SKY

How many stars dot the night sky? How many have watched their lazy progress, slow and quiet, as if not to disturb the masses in slumber below? God the Creator of the universe watches and guides their path, maintaining a picture that compels man to marvel. Now we know the truth: the stars are millions of light years away, all moving millions of miles per hour. How my feelings become mixed at this contrast with the still night sky! Do I feel more awe or more confused? Is peace coasting across the sky amid a solar sail, or does chaos post a stormy mount, thundering within silence?

A shooting star commands a glance, compels a whisper of wonder, and prompts a wishful sigh. This streak of light disturbed the motionless canvas, producing a sign of life. No painting by any artist could yield this portrait possessing its own life. With energy, strength, and direction, our heart cannot refuse its invitation for attention; predictable, yet without predictability. We seldom stand, sit, or lie to measure the progress of a scrolling canvas. This requires hours of patient observation. Instead, we proudly and sometimes with fanatical enthusiasm compete to report the most shooting star sightings in a single night.

The speed of a single shooting star cannot be fully appreciated by most observers. Sister stars remain still as if to make way for a sibling anxious to answer the phone. Our perception of speed is measured against a calibration that assigns a value of zero to the bright citizens of the solar nation. Stars stand motionless on the canvas. When one breaks free from this conformity, we are delighted to witness its rebellion. This infraction in the laws of order is as forgivable as driving a single golf ball to the ocean floor from the bow of a cruise ship. Not a threat, not a danger. As the streak of light vanishes, so do the faint voices of fear that wonder if the sky is falling.

What of these fears? One night of gazing may yield a handful of sightings. What if one moment of gazing produced a shower of twenty to a hundred shooting stars? Would our mind produce questions that would lead our heart to fear? Is the sky falling? Would not our heart cling to this fear until scientists reported the reasons for this phenomenon? Life is so fragile. What brings joy and marvel can also bring anxiety and fear. The space that divides these extreme differences is not great. In reality, only the measure equal to the length of perception holds the delicate balance between a calm night sky and a sky that is falling.

For example, a shooting star is unique for its motion. Motion alone is what we seek to score a sighting. Duration, direction, brightness, and length of a tail are scoreless bonuses. Perception plays the critical role. We see motion against motionlessness. Change your perception. Remind your mind that all the stars in the sky speed through space faster than our capacity to conceptualize. The true picture is motion against motion. The heart begins to beat faster. Our scrolling canvas no longer seems lifeless interrupted by moments of life. In reality, the stars swim in deep oceans.

With one perception, we see their slow progression moving from the eastern horizon to the west. Yet, in reality, every star celebrates its unique direction governed by pulls and pushes within the property of its present home. If the stars could be watched in this motion, would they fly similar to a swarm of bees hovering over a hive, or locusts migrating to their next field of prey? The true picture brings to light the constant motion in the still night sky. Perception brings appreciation. One reality allows the children to count the dots on the canvas; the other reality compels us to praise the Creator for His goodness and wisdom. Which reality yields the best fruit for life?

The writers of the Old Testament praised God for the stars in the sky. In that day, humanity's gaze into the night lacked the insight of our modern science. They only saw the canvas similar to children counting dots. Even with their limited understanding of the stars, the people sailed the seas, kept their calendars, and anticipated the seasons. The scrolling motion of the canvas provided many facts for their earnest minds. Could Columbus have sailed across the ocean or the wise men journeyed to Bethlehem under a cloudy night sky? Clearly, the stars of the heaven have played an important role in people's journeys on earth.

Now, how much more important are the stars above the dark valley through which I presently walk. A gaze heavenward yields no fruit of direction. I am not trained as a navigator, for my eyes cannot distinguish meaning in the placement of the dots on the canvas. Weary from my journey, my body drops to the ground, rolls over, and casts a heavenward stare. A shooting star screams across the sky. The soul makes a desperate wish to end the misery of the valley. As quickly as the streak appeared, it disappeared carrying away my hopes of freedom.

Hours of observation chart the slow progress of the canvas and log several streaks of light. Life seems unchanged; still and hopeless. What do I seek from the night sky? Do I hope for a star to guide my path without error? Do I long for a sign of wonder to interrupt the quiet anguish of my fearful soul? Throughout history, many have praised the Creator as a result of the dots on the canvas; stars held in wonder and employed with purpose. My lips in willful resignation join their chorus of praise. Accepting that no miracle will break the order of space, my eyes prayerfully acknowledge a sense of awe with new perspective.

My gaze into the calm night sky now clings to the later reality; stars screaming in motion. As motionless takes on motion, my heart reflects on the issues of my life. Each individual issue is a star on the canvas of my life. One star breaking from the order of predictability invites love. A feeling of being compelled and wishing for more because as soon as it appeared it disappeared returning a sense of peace. The sovereignty of God is affirmed with each episode of momentary rebellion. The thought of thousands of stars streaking at one time ignites fear. The heart shrinks and hides assuming the Creator is derelict in duty. Life is falling apart.

How delicate is our perception of life? Most of us choose to see life as a canvas of dots. We strive to maintain predictability, order, and thus experience peace. When the sky falls, we are overwhelmed and question the very foundations on which life found meaning and hope. The questions are many. The answers are scarce. Our mind reminds our heart that the stars have always been in motion. This motion is the wonderful harmony of God's wisdom. The Master Creator has and will continue to conduct order in the midst of chaos. Change in our life has only occurred with our perspective. We have been given a better seat; one that allows the observer to see life in its true reality of motion. No longer are we children counting stationary dots; now we are aware of the countless miracles that yield a still night sky. Now, we realize life is placed in the context of innumerable miracles. Our new peace calms the anxious soul. The sky is not falling. God has privileged us with a view that will forever change our gaze into the still night sky.

JOYFUL PRIVILEGE

Are you engaged and awaiting marriage? During the engagement, do you wait with God in mind? Or, do you struggle with strong temptations? The issues are deeper then your temptation with the body. It is with the heart. Can you see that all temptation is the same because it is rooted in the battlefield of the heart? In the heart, the stage is set to demonstrate your bonds of relationship. The Bible says from the heart the mouth speaks. Indeed, the mouth has the final say, "No or Yes" in the face of temptations. What will you say when God asks you to wait?

With one couple, the issue may not be completely physical. The girl runs from her sin but fails to run to God. She has not yet yielded her life to Him completely. Before she became a Christian, she lived in the midst of sin despite a life bathed in spiritual moorings. She knew God wanted a relationship. When she became a Christian, her motive was to escape. She ran in the direction of moral living; she ran to the church. Here, she dedicated herself to being free from the sin that plagued her youth. But, she missed the critical point.

Moving to a new town, she arrived with a fresh image and played the drama of being a Christian. This was only an act. The moment came when what she fled returned to tempt again. As this temptation returned to test her resolve, she did not wait but yielded. She said confusion obstructed her sight. When she repented, she turned from her sin again to establish a safe zone: no more dating for a year. Here again, she ran from sin but not to God.

When asked what her relationship with God meant to her, she said it meant a lot. If so, then she should run to Him. She should hide in His arms and let Him hold her. She was confused. Did she see that God was waiting for her? You need not run from sin as much as you need to run to God. You need to trust Him. He will provide for your needs and love you as no one can. You need to wait with Him in mind. Find the love of God and let it be the ultimate fulfillment in your life. I suspect as a youth she searched for love, but did not find the fulfillment she longed.

Now although engaged, she does not see the love from God as being the ultimate goal. She finds affection and comfort in the arms of a man. She believes the search may be at its end. The wedding is just months away. Maybe she fails to realize the search will continue even after the wedding because only God can bring this fulfillment.

The other is on an opposite path. He is failing to stop his actions. He cannot be still. Fretting is leading to many actions. He easily yields to sin. He says he does not see it coming. But, this is a lie. Anyone can see temptation coming. You know when it is at your door. You smell its stench and feel its breath. Then, I ask him what part of "don't" does he not understand? He is quiet. I ask another question. What is more important, to love God or to hate sin? I state that both are most important.

Does he love God? Love for God must be backed up by obedience. Each time he is tempted, God is asking him if he loves. Each time he fails, he is saying he does not love God as he claims. During this time, he says he loves his fiancé. Yet, my question is how can he truly love her when he cannot truly love God? He does not know how to love. Each infraction provides more proof of his poor grasp of love. In fact, the very gift God gave, this girl, is the object with which he demonstrates his disobedience. He must love God first before he can love others, especially his future wife.

During this engagement, the time of waiting is a special time in which God has an agenda. There will never be a time like this again. This is a window in which God places His hands on these two to refine their ability to give and receive love. They must see this as a special season. They must embrace this as a valuable time. God must have full opportunity. In a few months, the wedding will take place. At that time, I hope they did not see their engagement as a burden borne with great effort. The wedding is not a finish line marking the end of waiting and the release of a great difficulty. Instead, they must see this as a finish line that takes away a precious and purposeful time with their Lord. This time should be the sad parting of a teachable season. Never again will God have this peculiar time with them. For Him, this is the loss of a joyful privilege. What issue presently affords you a joyful privilege with God? Don't wish this season away.

Two Generals, Two Fronts, One War

How many images of war can you see? Documentaries on television tell stories with reenactments and testimonies creating a sensation that you are there. The cesspool of war becomes more and more a hellish nightmare as reality unveils the gruesome truth. You can smell the stench. You can hear the cries. The pain is so real the heart begins to beat faster to provide the reflexive actions for survival. Despite his cries for home, the soldier is bound by duty to demonstrate courage and maintain the lines of battle.

War makes the body coil. How many wives, fathers, mothers, brothers, sisters, and children have kissed the cheeks of their soldier, masking a terror-filled attempt at a joy-filled good-bye. Fear, pain, and anguish provide company to the cherished sensation of these kisses. In their heart, there is a desperate wish for a brief parting; a bearable season of hell prescribed by the generals whose cheeks they did not kiss. Life had been peaceful. Until that moment, the rising sun promised predictable blessings. Yes, uncertainty existed, but they were like the brief transitions between the scores of a finely conducted symphony. That silence was always welcome, allowing a time to digest and anticipate.

With the advent of war, the world turns upside down. When leaders declare war, they assess their ability to sustain and conclude victory on two or three battlefronts. Do they deliberately fail to perceive how their declaration of war immediately ignites millions of battlefronts along the shores of prayer? The soldier's picture on the mantel had hardly been noticed, but now it is the focal centerpiece of a shrine erected to host countless prayers for his safe return. Soldiers are given uniforms, guns, and orders. What do generals give family and friends to assist in their combat? These soldiers on the battlefields of prayer are most diligent and faithful. They have no choice. They fight for their sanity and their loved one. How unfortunate no medals are given to recognize their valor.

For everyone, life will never be the same. Hope erodes with the constant flow of time. In far too many battlefields, hope gives way to grief. One afternoon, uniformed individuals arrive to make a solemn announcement. They pronounce what had been feared. The soldier will not return. Mothers weep and wives enter the doorway of shock, beckoning them to a long life of torment. Because the prayers failed to return this soldier, the shrine becomes a memorial, and the war on this front ends in defeat. Perhaps the nations are still active on the battlefields of death and destruction, but this home front is silent. How can one accept defeat in a war they did not declare? Who will receive their rage? How can justice be administered when reality is the enemy?

In the frame of your life, reality declares war without notice. Almost instantaneously predictably falls to the guns of uncertainty. When reality attacks, your empire is its target. In the aftermath, fear, pain, and anguish line the devastated streets. Sensing an innate need to defend the fallen empire, troops are scrambled to respond to the onslaught. These troops are from two powerful regiments known as "time" and "energy." They are the empire's elite. Without reservation, they are sent to the two most formidable fronts in the battle with reality.

One battlefront is labeled the "past." In the painful light of hot scorching sun, this battle line graphically displays all the losses and wounds of reality's fury. The soldier's objective on this front is to constantly wade through the carnage hoping to undo what has been done. Soldiers attempt to survey and resurrect. They are vigilant hoping to restore the losses of the empire. However, they are master craftsmen with no arms. Their eyes can see what the hands need to fix, but they have no hands.

The other battlefront is labeled the "future." Here no light exists. The darkness shrouds in mystery the best of reality's armament. Sight is impossible. The soldier's motion through this space is desperate to discover any sign of the enemy. Capturing one soldier of reality may provide the necessary intelligence to defeat the approaching armies. Everyone knows such a find would provide incredible hope for the empire. With no sight, hearing becomes the weapon of choice. A keen focus on this sniper's rifle produces only silence in its scope. Desperation heightens fear. Fear ushers in the legion of reality's best soldiers: hopelessness.

Two generals command the troops on both battlefronts. Each general serves the empire with heroic resolve. One general is called "General Heart." This general is incensed with the tragedy of the attack. His love of the empire and his pride as its citizen are greatly pained by reality's strike. Feeling the depth of injury, he orders troops to the two fronts. His orders are conveyed through an inspiring speech.

"Friends, citizens, and countrymen, we have been attacked. This sudden invasion has greatly infiltrated our sanctity as an empire. We have been dealt an unfair blow, and the losses are horrific. I could not have imagined the ambition of this barbaric enemy. Without consideration, their forces pressed through our boundaries lacking any regard for innocence. Our empire was not prepared. But, we will not be silent. We are just beginning to return this challenge. Move with anguish, press forward with fear, and carry the pain.

Despair will shape your anger. Let anger motivate and build your resolve until this enemy is vanquished. Return the empire to its former glory. One piece at a time, rebuild until every sign of realities' madness is removed. Each front to which you march is urgently awaiting your arrival. The campaign has begun. The combat is critical. Success requires your courage and fortitude. Do not fail. You cannot fail. You are the empire's only hope. My pain is desperately anticipating your success. Move out. May the Emperor bless your mission."

In a reprieve, the other general commits more troops to the battlefronts. This general is called "General Mind." He is thoughtful, meticulous, and a master strategist. He has analyzed and evaluated reality's advances and victories. Over and over again, he has labored with details until he is convinced that victory to his design is within his grasp. The more time he spends considering this war, the more convinced he becomes that victory is just ahead. Driven by plans and scenarios, General Mind begins to believe complete victory would erase any evidence or memory of reality's wounds.

The empire has two wonderful generals managing the war on two fronts. Troops fight without reservation. Passion, enthusiasm, and hope build as more and more troops arrive. They arrive because of the constant attention given by the generals to the battlefields. When General Mind thinks about the war, he calls more troops. When he notices something new or makes an unexpected discovery with regard to reality's intention, he calls more troops. The more time he spends thinking, the more troops he calls.

When General Mind is too tired to think, General Heart takes over;

he feels the pain of the empire. He cannot disengage from her losses and her future. The more he feels, the more troops he sends. The longer the battle rages, the more pain General Heart records. With the passing of time, General Heart believes victory will be had with greater effort. More and more troops are sent. Both the generals are soon lost in the activity of sending troops. They exchange command back and forth, back and forth. Each cycle only seems to produce more desperation. And, more troops.

These troops, time and energy, expire on the battlefields. Reports seldom pronounce signs of victory. Day by day, morale withers in the repetitious application of battle objectives that produce no results. The empire is in trouble. Her resources are drained. Complete defeat seems imminent. Something must be done. The generals have commanded many battles but none against any foe this fierce. Their lack of progress does not make them failures. With humility, they approach the Emperor whose wisdom stretches beyond the barriers of time. They seek His counsel because they know He created all things.

"Withdraw the troops," says the Emperor. "Let them return to their homes and loved ones." The generals respond with shock. The Emperor continues, "The present battle is in vain. Not because of the desired result, but because you fail to understand the enemy. Reality has power to defeat you on the battlefronts of the past and the future. Every ounce of its power is gleaned by your lack of power in these realms. The minute you engage reality on these battlefields, victory belongs to him. You cannot defeat reality. However, this same reality is not a foe but a friend in the present. On this line, reality is not engaged in battle but provides the means for life. Do not be foolish and fight a war you will never win. Do not be overwhelmed by fear, pain, and anguish because you do not understand what has happened or will happen. Abandon the battlefronts and recall the troops. Celebrate life and embrace reality as a friend. This one war should be no war." The generals heed the Emperor's advice and bring an end to hostilities.

What about your life? Wars are raging all over the world. They are also raging in your life. In the battles of your life, you are the general. When your mind thinks about your problems in the past or the future, you expend valuable time and energy on a war you can never win. When your heart rehearses each loss or hopes for future justice, you spend time and energy on a losing battle. Stop the fighting. Your war should be no war.

A SUFFICIENT GRACE

Until recently, I had not known true pain. Now, pain is all I know. From the moment I awake until I am lost in sleep, my heart hurts. Often, sleep is not a freedom, as dreams rehearsed the issues of my life. I do not like any part of this process, but I am fast discovering and slowly accepting that pain is a part of life here on earth. In my own pain, I try to look at the lives of others. When I see happy people, I refuse to look because happiness is lost in my past. When I see successful people, I refuse to look because my uncertain future could not guarantee success. When I see hurting people, my heart is tempted to curse God because my pain becomes ignited by the futility of this life. What hope did humanity have? No one seems immune to pain.

To me, hurting people seem to live hollowed lives, their eyes communicating a dual message of children anticipating ice cream and the elderly awaiting death. I am awaiting death. Life seems a long road of hardship and grief, and I want no part. Malls, churches, and news stories provide an ample supply of hurting people to watch. From the back of a church service, I notice several individuals sitting alone. What did this

Thursday night Bible study offer them? Perhaps some come to escape loneliness. Others may come hoping to find comfort.

Out of frustration, I walk to the churches' bookstore. The room is comfortable for thought as a few faceless people stir. I begin to think. What is God doing? What did He have in mind for me? How and where would I find any comfort? I want the pain removed. I am desperate for God to hold me. Although I did not feel His embrace, books nearby hold my attention. One book causes me to reflect on Paul's request for the removal of a thorn from his flesh. Finding some solidarity with Paul, I draw comfort in his request for relief.

How many times have I prayed a similar prayer? I connect and read on to discover the author's thought. The author concludes that God's grace is sufficient for Paul's situation. He said this grace would also be sufficient for all of life's issues. God's grace meets life's needs. God's ultimate expression of grace is found in His provision of salvation for humanity. The author pushed this point. He adds that we should be content with life in light of this one expression of grace, salvation. I was not content. Neither was I very excited given the level of pain in my life.

I start to think. Why did God's grace not free me from my present problems? Should God's grace be the big ticket to a happy life? With salvation, grace meant free and unmerited favor. Yes, we do not deserve heaven. But thankfully, God's grace freed us from an eternal Hell. With life issues, God's grace seems to be different. This grace is unmerited favor with a twist. Grace that freed me from eternal Hell does not seem to automatically free me from my "earthly hell."

Second Corinthians 2:9 says, "My grace is sufficient for my strength is perfected in weakness." Careful consideration of this passage leads to the conclusion that grace is active and involved in the context of pain. Grace means God works with my pain to display Christ's strength. Paul continues in the same passage, "Therefore I will boast all the more gladly about my weaknesses, so that Christ's power may rest on me." God's wisdom manifests Christ's power in life. Can you see how this power works?

Imagine life as a train. The full length of the track would be the course of life's journey. When a train encounters a large hill, it does not decide the hill is too great for passage. The engineer increases the power to propel the train forward over the grade of incline in its path. At this hill, the true power of the train is harnessed. Powerful engines push and pull against the forces of gravity. The rumble of the engines makes a clear case for the level of power presently employed. The engineer did not wish the hill away because he had full confidence in the train's engines. The power was there. The engine's power was not really known until the hill was encountered.

Paul recognizes this truth in the above passage. For many people, life seems an easy course within the parameters of their own strength. People normally go from day to day hardly noticing the effort required to make that day successful. Occasionally, life makes a turn into a big "hill." The challenge is easily seen. When Paul faces challenges, he realizes the power of Christ responds within him. The issues of our life provide a clear platform for Christ to shine. Paul continues in 2 Corinthians 12:10, "That is why, for Christ's sake, I delight in weaknesses, in insults, in hardships, in persecutions, in difficulties. For when I am weak, then I am strong."

Paul understands pain and difficulty invite opportunity for the expression of God's strength. If life had no "hills," who would discover the power of God's hands? Buddha wanted to eliminate pain, the "hills." He felt human desire led to pain. His master plan involved meditations and disciplines designed to eliminate human desire. Had he been successful in eliminating pain, we would not have the opportunity to see Christ's sufficient power at work.

From another perspective, the train engineer also had confidence in the design of the track. He calls the engines to power because he knows the track is designed with the engines in mind. The grade of the incline ascending the hill is determined to enable each train safe passage. No train is intended to fail in its ascent. Each and every train approaches this point with confidence not only because of its engines, but also because of the thoughtful construction of the track. In the children's story of the little train that thought it could, the little train should have known it could. The track is built with the little train in mind. In our life issues, we may be saying, "I think I can. I think I can." Should we not be saying, "I know I can."

My mind begins to think about Christ's power. Yes, life is tough, but God promises to support each step. My life is in His hands. The Bible proclaims that God knows the plans He has for us. He promises to instruct and teach us in the way we should go. He watches us with His eye on us. The Bible makes many such promises. Paul boasts in this reality. He knows God has an agenda with his pain. The pain serves God's pleasure.

I have helped several people pressing through difficulties. Until now I had no clue to the level of their pain. The hurting people from my past now speak with a whole new meaning. Sitting here I start to think of all their conversations. Resurrecting their stories, my mind desperately moves past their words. I stare into their eyes providing new access to their heart. The wonder of their pain expressed and experienced, as rejection, humiliation, grief, fear, anger, betrayal, frustration, panic, and hopelessness are now very clear. The solutions they need or hope for no longer matter to me.

Isabel, your pain is so great with the loss of your 10-year old daughter. Emily, how great the pain of your teenage heart with your boyfriend breakup. I know it doesn't help when he says he just wants to be friends. James, I am sorry your dad left your mom for another woman. Mary, I am sorry for the trials of single parenting. Kim, your husband lost his job after twenty years. I am sorry he lives like that loss is his death. Bill, no one can know the difficulty of a wheel chair. The drunk driver who caused your injury is running liberally through life. Charlie, your wife's battle with cancer was heroic. I am sorry she has passed. Pain this great is crippling.

This sinful world always has and always will create pain. What matters now is seeing God in the midst of the pain. Buddha wanted to eliminate pain. In truth, the fallen nature of man, and not the presence of desire, will forever make Buddha's vision impossible. But is coping with pain and finding life after crisis equally impossible?

"My grace is sufficient." I have searched these words hoping that they possess God's promise of making me feel as I did before my crisis. Jesus healed the sick and raised the dead. The Bible promises if we believe and pray anything can be done. The faith of a mustard seed can move mountains. We can apply that faith here. Let's fix this problem and move on with life. Life? What life? The life I knew? Before my crisis, effort was needed to make and keep God number one in my daily affairs. Now, God is all I seek.

The phrase that follows this promise of grace convinces me that God's design may be distant from my plans: "My strength is perfected in weakness." Strength excites me. I am so desperate for strength. Each morning, I wake to a sudden sense of pain that immediately consumes me with despair. I need strength to get out of bed. Yet, strength is absent to keep my mind in check when I remain in bed. The promise of strength compels me to God like a child responding to the music of an ice cream truck as it slowly passes by. I want some of that. I jump, scream, wave my arms and run in circles knowing any delay may forfeit my opportunity for ice cream. "How much," I gasp short of breath from my frantic dash to the truck? My parents gave me money for ice cream. Each time I ordered, I was confident I had enough change.

How much for strength I ask God? He answers by asking me to embrace my weakness. What? Are you kidding? I am asking for strength to get away from my weakness. God tells us to embrace our weakness because life will produce troubles. You cannot spend all of your life running from pain. You quickly realize you cannot control life. Let God be your sufficiency. Strength is perfected in weakness when you engage a dependent relationship with God. He is teaching you to trust.

As a kid, ice cream on a hot Texas summer afternoon is just the right thing. Mom and Dad did not make hot summer days disappear, but they were always there to provide the change for ice cream. Because of God's sovereignty, He chooses to allow those "hot trying summer days in life." His grace will sustain us day to day. Not just to survive but to thrive in joy. Like my parents, God wants to be there for us; to provide ice cream in a sense; His goodness to meet you at the point of your need.

In my child like faith, I now understand Paul's enthusiasm as he says, "Most gladly I embrace my weakness." For Paul, it forges the conduit to God's grace. A rich ample supply of grace just enough to sustain faith one day at a time. He may be saying if I have to have hot days then I love hot days because I love ice cream. The forecast in your life may be more hot days but be content. And, trust God.

I am a child with God when it comes to this issue of trust. I remember those Texas summers. But, I do not remember the heat: All I remember is the music of the ice cream truck and the excitement that followed. The excitement could not be contained. I would run in every direction attempting to find my parents. The anticipation of the ice cream erased all sensations. Today, hot summer days or the occasional music of an ice cream truck remind me of the pleasures of ice cream. I believe with all my heart, when this season of drought and high temperatures are over in my life, I will fondly recall His provision of sufficient grace, ice cream from His hands.

As I stand in this bookstore, my heart fills with hope. God is able to meet all of us at the point of our need. The needs I saw in people earlier had triggered my fear of pain. Now in faith, I see the same people as loved and blessed by God. He has not abandoned them. In the midst of their crisis, He holds out His loving arms. He is desperate to provide grace. Regardless of the issues, His grace is sufficient. Can you hear the music playing under the hot sun? The ice cream is here.

Praise from Joyful Lips

A verse in Psalms 63 says, "My soul is satisfied as with marrow and fatness and my heart offers praise with joyful lips." My soul is restless. The roller coaster of my emotions continues to swing up and down, but progress is being made. How can I be satisfied? My head responds by grasping at God's sovereignty in my life. As I look all around, I can see God is working. Today, I taste the reality of God preparing my future. Quickly I looked back at myself. If God was working, what was I doing: being anxious, deaf to the voice that said wait, and confused by God's allowance of pain in my life? What exactly is God looking for? Is He asking me to acknowledge the splendor of His grace? When I do, I believe my soul will be satisfied as with marrow and fatness.

My life has been blessed to experience an incredible variety of foods. From many different places around the world, my mouth has facilitated the consumption of a large variety of exotic foods. Without a doubt, the world of food is elaborate with endless possibilities. Many great memories preserve my encounters with food. One memory dear to my heart is that of my mom's cooking. My mom is a great cook. She is very loving and giving in every way to her children. She freely gives through the medium of food. Traditional Indian food done correctly is made from scratch. An average meal could take several hours to prepare. New to America, my parents had not learned many of the tricks of the parenting trade. One trick, the after school snack, may have saved my mom a lot of heartache. She never realized a simple snack could curb my hunger attacks.

In grade school, many distractions kept us away from home until our parents arrived from work. Our pre-dinner ritual consisted of watching television and doing homework. Soon after arriving from work, my mom started preparing the evening meal. How many times did I leave my activity to remind my mom I was hungry? I remember times when my hunger pangs fueled my statement with anger. "Mom, I am hungry!" I was impatient with the long process of Indian cooking. My selfish thoughts blocked all other perceptions as my lips burst out with anger. "I am hungry! How much longer?"

As I look back on those days, my heart fills with tears. All I can think about is how a young mother of three loved her children enough to excuse their selfishness while selflessly working to meet their needs. I think today about how she labored long, physically challenging hours at her blue collar job and then came home to labor two more to feed her children. With my tone and attitude, I was more demanding than her bosses at work. My words intended to inflict my pain on her. Why not give us a T.V. dinner that would only take a few minutes or order pizza with one phone call?

Her love for me overcame my insensitivity. She worked quickly to meet my needs but was bound by the laws of time. With all her love, she was preparing the best meals she knew how to prepare: a meal that would nourish our bodies, a meal that our friends would beg to share, and today, a meal that we desperately miss from her hands. When the call finally came, we ate without gratitude. The food erased the feeling of hunger, and we felt completely satisfied. My lips were now inhaling food. How is it that earlier these same lips were spouting words of anger? Out of politeness and a subtle attempt at seeking forgiveness, I would say "Thanks, mom." I never truly expressed my amazement with the excellence of each meal she prepared.

Hunger has a purpose. We must know hunger to know satisfaction. The Psalmist says, "My soul is satisfied as with marrow and fatness." He has tested God's goodness and grace. He continues, "My mouth offers praise with joyful lips." In the midst of my struggles, I wonder how I can participate with the Psalmist to praise God with joyful lips. In hindsight with my mom, understanding her attention and diligence to meet my need would have eliminated the pain my anger inflicted on her. The pain of hunger was real, but it should have been met with the reality of her love for me. She was cooking and soon my need would be met. If I could go back, I would have spent the two hours of waiting praising her. My lips of anger would be transformed into joyful lips of praise.

How true with God. My pain causes the hunger of my life. God is busy preparing to meet me at the point of my need. It may take a little time because it's the best He can give. What He gives will become a living testimony to compel others to partake. In my anxiety, I want tangible results now. I want my restless soul satisfied. With faith, I must believe God is laboring with love. My understanding of this reality causes me to burst forth with joyful lips. Praise God! He is so good! So loving! Soon my soul will be satisfied, but now the call from God is to wait. At this point, I wish the Psalmist had reversed the order of the phrases in this verse. Sure, I will praise God when my soul is satisfied. But faith calls me to praise Him while I patiently wait!

THE LANGUAGE OF OUR LOVE

There is no one to call. No conversation to be had. I am alone in France. My eyes search the room for anyone who will bring relief to my wearied soul. But each face speaks a different language with ears trained to listen to sounds my mouth cannot form. Nevertheless, some things are easy to understand: a boisterous laugh, gestures with the hands, and heads nodding in agreement. Here, individuals sit face-to-face, eyes locked to insure dialogue; meaningful communication.

Father in heaven ... Speak to me. You have my attention, yet silence is all I hear. The silence creates anticipation. As if sitting in the best seat at Carnegie Hall, yet no orchestra graces the stage and no audience shares my unnecessary excitement. As if standing in the kitchen anticipating the timer of an oven, yet no dish fills the room with its exquisite aroma. As if drifting on the high seas anticipating the embrace of a maiden, yet there is no maiden. Father, what is silence from You but torture to the soul? Will You speak to me and free me from the chains that bind my heart? My attention is presently focused on You, Father. I hear the voices of the market. They are temptations calling me to wander away from

You. They call night and day. They speak to me with shouts that compel my attention. When I call out for help, Your silence responds with words written on my heart, spoken by You to generations long ago.

Certainly the words keep my feet from slipping, but the heart slips slightly deeper into despair. I love You and You love me, but what is the language of our love? I search Your words desperate to discover the language of Your love. Sacrifices, offerings, oaths, and the like seem to fail. Sometimes these acts lack heart. Without the heart, any act is as flattering to You as a wife moved by a jeweled necklace presented by an unfaithful husband. Love for You is born in the depths of the heart and transforms the body and soul. When true love is communicated in Your language, no failure can occur as our hearts unite. What are the words of Your language, the sounds that communicate?

"If you love me, keep my commandments." From this passage, generations of humanity have translated Your language into terms of simple obedience. Love to You is not sounds produced from the mouth, but actions driven by the heart. Father, You receive love through intentional decisions of unconditional surrender to Your will. This is the dance that moves me closer to the source of love itself. If this is my portion of our language, allow me the privilege of becoming a master of its grammar and diction. Let me possess a vocabulary reserved for the elite minds of Your kingdom. With every act, thought and breath compel me to speak only Your language presenting myself as a jeweled necklace adorning Your neck. "The Law of his God is in his heart and his feet do not slip."

With obedience, my feet will not slip but what of my heart? If now I understand how to love You, how do You return my love? I sit in silence, my heart broken in despair as solitude fills my space creating an atmosphere appreciated by the ships that grace the ocean's floor. Silence is grueling. With squirming in my body, gasping in my lungs, and focusing a blind stare, my body responds to the silence of Your voice.

Nevertheless, I love You with all that I have. For years, my heart has strived to be pleasing in Your sight, yet silence, only silence, is the return of my voice hurled from the mountaintop.

A thousand ideas of my love returned pass through the mind, but the heart sighs knowing that You are the author of love. Only You possess the knowledge of the language of my love received. The desperate mind substitutes antidotes for answers hoping to hold the heart within the bounds of sanity. Yet at the risk of insanity, the heart proceeds in its quest to know the love of its Creator. Until I hear, I will love You with obedience. When You are ready, grant me the knowledge of Your love returned to me. I am alone. No conversation to be had. There is no one to call.

"But, God demonstrates His love towards us, that while we were yet sinners, Christ died for us." Finally, humanity hears a faint whisper presented as a momentous gift. Not mere words to be heard by human ears, but an act to speak to the heart. My soul is relieved. Love from God has been communicated to me. The expression of His love is clear. This love is communicated as the cross of Christ. This cross is the primary and initial act of the Creator meeting humanity at the point of their need. This is the first and the best.

How can words heard by my ears compare with the actions of the cross? From this incredible expression of Love, I have relationship with God. I have hope. True love is spoken. True love in Your language, Father, is that which makes noise heard only by the heart. The language of our Love is clear. A Love so profound words are unnecessary. A language so deep, the mouth and ears are bypassed to involve only the heart. And what of the silence, it ushers in an opportunity to savor our love. I am not alone. Conversation is abundant. Call on God, my soul. Your quest for love will find a perfect language that communicates.

HANDS OF GRACE

Her eyes posed a challenge. The longer she waited, the bigger her beautiful eyes got. Her feet danced to pronounce her excitement as if her eyes could not have accomplished the task alone. Her eyes were riveted on my hands. My stare was equally engaged not on my hands, but on her eyes. My hands had made hundreds of balloon sculptures. They did not need the assistance of my eyes. I was free to stare at her. I was overwhelmed by the excitement of this child. Could it be that this was the first balloon sculpture she had ever received? The long red balloon was being molded into the form of a graceful swan. She anticipated the completion of my masterpiece. Her dancing feet and beautiful eyes were now joined by a priceless smile. Amazing! The face of this child reflected the glory of God's creation.

I held the balloon to prolong my opportunity to see this wonder. Her face created an awe for God in me. The ocean, the sky, nor the vastness of the universe could compete at that moment with the harmony of her big, beautiful eyes and priceless smile. Her hands reached for the balloon. For a moment, her face changed to reflect uncertainty and fear. How brief that moment. Yet, the moment captured a daily face for many who approach their world with apprehension. Tragic to think that soon this child may wear that momentary face far too often.

I quickly moved the balloon to her hand. As her finger gripped the swan's neck, her face returned to its former precious state. With hardly a gester of thanks, she turned and ran from me on feet powered by happiness. Each step seemed effortless; the motion through space as elegant as a cloud racing past a snow covered mountain. She stopped in front of a shop where a man with a mustache held two bags. I could see her face again. Her lips began to move. For the first time, her heart was speaking, a volcano of joy-filled emotion, "Padre, meria, padre, meria, meria, padre!"

The man's glance, nod, and pat on the child's head seemed to communicate he was happy and pleased for her. The child turned and created an imaginary world of water, flowers, and blue skies. Here, her swan would reign supreme and live happily ever after. Wow! The child was so happy about the balloon that she first ran to her father. Before she could truly enjoy the balloon, she sought his affirmation.

Father in heaven; make me as this child when good things come into my life. Drive me to run straight to You. Compel my heart to seek Your audience. I want You to see my face of excitement first. Before anyone else is happy for me, I want to feel Your hand patting my head and Your voice saying You are pleased for me. In some ways, I also want to be different from her. Your word says every good thing bestowed and every perfect gift is from above. If that is the case, I was You to this little girl as the balloon was sculpted. Yet, as I sculpted the balloon, she watched my hands. I would rather have had the joy of her returning my gaze into her eyes. She needed to watch my hands because she didn't know me or even trust me.

I know You, and I trust You. As You make good things in my life,

Father, let me return Your gaze. You, like me, are not watching Your hands. Your gaze is fixed on the big eyes and dancing feet of a small boy eagerly anticipating a blessing in his life. I want to look up to Your eyes to see the love that powers the hand of grace.

CONCLUDING THOUGHTS

MARK 5:20

"So the man went away and began to tell in the Decapolis how much Jesus had done for him. And all the people were amazed."

As you have read through these pages, my prayer is that you will see your circumstance and your God in a new way. Life in the material world is just the beginning of the eternal. Count on God being faithful to meet you at the point of your need in this material world. He is in the business of producing miracles. When Jesus healed, the blind received sight, the lame walked, and the dead were raised. When He met a need, the one who received that miracle had a very predictable response. They would celebrate. They jumped up, ran around, and celebrated. As I have read the healing miracles of Jesus, I do not find anyone who begins to complain about his or her losses.

Mark 5:25-26 says, "And a woman was there who had been subject to bleeding for twelve years. She had suffered a great deal under the care of many doctors and had spent all she had, yet instead of getting better she grew worse." At the point Jesus healed her, she had two choices: she could think about the twelve years of misery or celebrate her future. Which did she choose? This may be the easiest choice in her journey. The woman's determination fueled her goal for healing. When she reached her goal, it launched her into a life of freedom. In fact, Mark 5:34 says, "He said to her, 'Daughter, your faith has healed you. Go in peace and be freed from your suffering.'" She is thrilled about her future. Which will you choose? Will you choose to celebrate or sulk?

As God moves to supply His provisions, you are witnessing a miracle in your life. You should celebrate your future because at present you lean on the eternal God, the Great I AM. Define your dependent relationship, and then watch. Keep your eyes locked with His. The world will be amazed. Go in peace and be free.

Notes, Reflections, Exercises, Meditations, and Prayers

NOTES, REFLECTIONS, EXERCISES, MEDITATIONS, AND PRAYERS

NOTES, REFLECTIONS, EXERCISES, MEDITATIONS, AND PRAYERS

Notes, Reflections, Exercises, Meditations, and Prayers

Notes, Reflections, Exercises, Meditations, and Prayers

Notes, Reflections, Exercises, Meditations, and Prayers

NOTES, REFLECTIONS, EXERCISES, MEDITATIONS, AND PRAYERS

NOTES, REFLECTIONS, EXERCISES, MEDITATIONS, AND PRAYERS

Notes, Reflections, Exercises, Meditations, and Prayers